D1736627

Disability and Mothering

Critical Perspectives on Disability
Steven J. Taylor, *Series Editor*

Disability
a n d
Mothering

Liminal Spaces of Embodied Knowledge

Edited by **Cynthia Lewiecki-Wilson**
and **Jen Cellio**

Syracuse University Press

First Edition 2011

11 12 13 14 15 16   6 5 4 3 2 1

∞ The paper used in this publication meets the minimum requirements
of the American National Standard for Information Sciences—Permanence
of Paper for Printed Library Materials, ANSI Z39.48-1992.

For a listing of books published and distributed by Syracuse University Press,
visit our Web site at SyracuseUniversityPress.syr.edu.

ISBN: 978-0-8156-3284-9

Library of Congress Cataloging-in-Publication Data

Lewiecki-Wilson, Cynthia.
   Disability and mothering : liminal spaces of embodied knowledge /
Cynthia Lewiecki-Wilson and Jen Cellio.
      p. cm. — (Critical perspectives on disability)
   Includes bibliographical references and index.
   ISBN 978-0-8156-3284-9 (cloth : alk. paper)
 1. Mothers of children with disabilities.   2. Children with disabilities.
3. Women with disabilities.   4. Mothers—Psychology.   5. Motherhood.
I. Cellio, Jen.   II. Title.
   HQ759.913.L49 2011
   306.874'3087—dc23   2011021857

Manufactured in the United States of America

Contents

Illustrations

Acknowledgments

This volume is truly a collaborative effort whose roots extend back many years to a graduate seminar on the body and the rhetoric of science where we, the editors, first explored and shared ideas about disability and women. As we took on the project of editing and shaping this volume, we had invaluable help and guidance from many people. First, we would like to thank Andrea O'Reilly from the Association for Research on Mothering, as well as Brenda Jo Brueggemann, Rebecca Dingo, and an anonymous reviewer for their thoughtful suggestions for revision and for support of this project in its early stages. At Syracuse University Press, we owe special thanks to Annelise Finegan, acquisitions editor, who saw the merits of this book and moved the project along quickly. We are delighted that this book will be a part of the Critical Perspective on Disabilities series at Syracuse, and we thank series editor Steven Taylor and an anonymous reviewer for their enthusiasm and helpful comments. We are grateful to all for such generous readings and suggestions, which reaffirmed the value of this work and guided us through many revisions. We hope our efforts to reach the broad and diverse audience we imagine for this volume have been successful. Where the book succeeds, it does so because of this sound advice. Finally, we would like to thank all those who contributed essays, distributed our call, and otherwise expressed interest in the importance of this topic. Knowing that others were equally passionate about the need for such a book sustained us through each step of this process.

Contributors

FELICITY BOARDMAN is a disabled research fellow based at the Health Sciences Research Institute, Warwick Medical School, UK. She recently completed her doctoral thesis exploring reproductive decision making, the conceptualization of responsibility, and the valuation of disability within families affected by an inheritable condition.

SUZANNE BOST is associate professor of English at Loyola University Chicago. She is the author of *Mulattas and Mestizas: Representing Mixed Identities in the Americas, 1850–2000* and *Encarnación: Illness and Body Politics in Chicana Feminist Literature.*

SHAWN A. CASSIMAN, assistant professor of social work at the University of Dayton, completed her dissertation in social welfare at the University of Wisconsin–Madison. Her research focuses on the impact of poverty and disability on women and their children and the potential of social welfare policy to contribute to well-being. She is developing a new project among sex workers in Calcutta examining the intersection of health and disability.

JEN CELLIO is assistant professor of English and director of the Writing Program at Northern Kentucky University. She studies composition theory, rhetorical theory, and rhetorics of science, especially connections between eugenics and reproduction.

MARILYN DOLMAGE, advocate, community organizer, trainer, policy analyst, researcher, consultant, mother, and grandmother, works across

Ontario, Canada, to stop the segregation of people with disabilities, support families, and promote effective inclusion, particularly in schools.

ABBY M. DUBISAR, assistant professor of English at Iowa State University, works in the areas of activist and feminist rhetorics, disability studies, writing in the disciplines, composition pedagogy, and multimodal writing.

LINNÉA E. FRANITS is associate professor of occupational therapy at Utica College in Utica, New York, and lives in Syracuse, New York, with her husband and fourteen-year-old son. She is also a doctoral student in disability studies at Syracuse University.

DENISE CORDELLA HUGHES-TAFEN is from the Caribbean island of Antigua and has taught at West Virginia University and Ohio University. Her interests include postcolonial studies, disability studies, performance arts, and emancipatory forms of education.

WHITNEY JONES-GARCIA is the pseudonym of an associate professor in the humanities at a university in the northeast United States. She has previously published essays on mental illness in film and literature.

HEATHER KUTTAI is a researcher, writer, public speaker, three-time Paralympic medalist, coach, and university administrator, in addition to her most treasured roles of wife to Darrell Seib and mother to Patrick and Chelsea.

CYNTHIA LEWIECKI-WILSON, mother of a son with disability, is professor of English and affiliate in women, gender, and sexuality, and disability studies at Miami University, where she is director of graduate studies in English. Among other publications, she is co-editor of *Disability and the Teaching of Writing: A Critical Sourcebook* and *Embodied Rhetorics: Disability in Language and Culture.*

KRISTIN LINDGREN directs the Writing Center and teaches courses in literature, writing, and disability studies at Haverford College. She has published numerous essays about illness and disability and is co-editor of

Signs and Voices and *Access*, two books about Deaf culture. She lives near Philadelphia with her husband and two sons.

CORINNE MANNING, a research associate at La Trobe University (Australia), specializes in oral and digital histories. Her previous publications explore issues of human rights, identity, colonialism, and diversity in Australia.

JULIE E. MAYBEE is associate professor of philosophy at Lehman College, City University of New York. Her specialties include nineteenth-century continental philosophy (especially Hegel), African philosophy, philosophy and race, and disability studies.

ELIZABETH METCALF is a doctoral student in women's studies and disability studies at Syracuse University. Her work considers intersectionality in theory/method/praxis with a focus in feminist disability studies. Prior to doctoral study, she earned her MSW at Smith College, School for Social Work, and practiced as a clinical social worker with children and adults with psychiatric disabilities.

TERRI BETH MILLER is a PhD candidate in English at the University of Tennessee, Knoxville. Her dissertation analyzes cultural, scientific, and political constructions of "monstrosity" in the early twentieth century. Other research interests include modernism, postcolonial studies, and rhetoric.

JULIE AVRIL MINICH is assistant professor of English at Miami University, where she teaches Latina/o cultural studies. She is currently working on a book about the intersection of race, disability, and sexuality in Chicana/o literature.

RACHEL ROBERTSON is a lecturer at Curtin University, Western Australia. She won the 2008 Calibre Award for Outstanding Australian Essay and has published in *Life Writing, Best Australian Essays,* and *Griffith Review.* A memoir about parenting her autistic son will be published in 2012.

JULIA MIELE RODAS, assistant professor of English at the City University of New York (CUNY), teaches writing at CUNY's Bronx Community College and is on the faculty of the master's program in disability studies at the CUNY School of Professional Studies. Her writing has appeared in *Victorian Literature & Culture, Dickens Studies Annual,* the *Victorian Review,* the *Journal of Literary & Cultural Disability Studies, Disability Studies Quarterly,* the *Explicator,* and other venues. She is currently working on a book that theorizes the place of autistic rhetoric and aesthetics in familiar texts.

SAMANTHA WALSH is a third-year PhD student in sociology and equity studies at the University of Toronto. The focus of her research is the lived experience of disabled people and social policy; much of her work is rooted in narrative. She received her MA in critical disability studies from York University, and her BA in sociology from University of Guelph.

ABBY WILKERSON is a philosopher whose work focuses on embodied agency and social movements, particularly in the contexts of food, disability, health, and sexuality. Her publications include *The Thin Contract: Social Justice and the Political Rhetoric of Obesity* (forthcoming); *Diagnosis: Difference: The Moral Authority of Medicine;* a Forum article in *Food, Culture, and Society* assessing the current conversation between disability studies and food studies; and other articles in anthologies and journals. She co-edited the award-winning "Desiring Disability: Queer Theory Meets Disability Studies," a special issue of *GLQ: A Journal of Lesbian and Gay Studies,* with Robert McRuer. She teaches in the University Writing Program at George Washington University in Washington, DC.

Disability and Mothering

Introduction

On Liminality and Cultural Embodiment

CYNTHIA LEWIECKI-WILSON
and JEN CELLIO

This book has both personal and academic roots in the lives of its editors and contributors. We are academics and activists interested in feminism and disability studies: mothers; mothers with disability; mothers of disabled children; disabled academics; community activists; activists who have mothered a child with disability; women with and without disability, considering or refusing motherhood; literary and language scholars, philosophers, social scientists, and historians studying disability and mothering. As this list suggests, we have many overlapping and multiple identities, and this fact underscores one of the central features of this collection. First, this study explores the multiple relations and intersectional contexts of subject positions, such as those shaped by race, class, gender, sexuality, and national and postcolonial forces of identity formation and oppression. Chapters in this volume examine the ways that these multiple identities and forces overlap or exist in tension with disability and mothering.

But subject positions are not the whole story. We propose that the liminal spaces where borders flow into one another, particularly the borders between the social and the personal, outside and inside, others and self, are important as well. Deriving from the Latin word for threshold or doorway, liminality indicates an in-between, transitional state of potential (in what directions will tensions be resolved?). However elusive, ineffable,

1

unstable, or hybrid, this fluid boundary space is not a "no place," nor an abstract space, but particular, embodied, situated.

We argue that in liminal spaces, cultural constructions of the subject and situated, embodied experiences intermix, and from/in this fluid boundary state, resistance to cultural scripts and emergent knowledge can potentially arise. We say "potentially arise" because liminality is unstable, and while a liminal space may be generative it is also fraught with risks.

Liminality is not always experienced in positive ways, not always considered positive by others. In anthropology, liminality is understood as a between state, potentially a place for a symbolic rite of passage, which if sustained can result in a failure to incorporate into a new social role (Willett and Deegan 2001). In psychiatry, the term indicates shifting states of mind. Used as a label, *liminal* may function as a "symptom" for a diagnosis—a diagnosis that may or may not be helpful for the person to whom it is attached and for their family members. For social workers, the term may describe an in-between place that is hard to place, an uncertainty about the subject breeding doubt. Several contributors to this volume describe their experiences negotiating threshold mental states. Sometimes uncertainty—or the ability to remain in a liminal position—seems advantageous. At other times, diagnosis brings needed support, and in other cases the refusal of diagnosis is important to survival.

Women have been associated with doorways, historically positioned at the boundary, verge, or margin demarcating the public from the private sphere. A pregnant woman's body itself can be thought of as a threshold, a doorway between self and other, providing a metaphor—not a biological argument—for understanding the self in relation to others and self *as* relation to others, thereby leading us to think of subjectivity as relational, interdependent, and again, unstable.

Our approach of emphasizing both situated embodiment and movement across conceptual and experiential borders may seem paradoxical, but this paradox is characteristic of both disability and mothering. While some disabilities are fixed and unchanging through much of the lifespan, the cultural ways they are experienced and treated change across time. Many more disabilities are experienced as waxing and waning; others arrive unpredictably and with a jolt, or gradually and almost imperceptibly with aging. In short, disability is not a thing, an essence, a fixed identity, or a single kind of experience, even though language often leads us to talk about it that way. It is an embodied, situated, and social experience in culture, constituted out of an ever-changing flow of relations among bodies, practices, institutions, experienced personally *and* socially constructed. Motherhood, likewise, is not a single or life-long condition: mothering does not require giving birth, and for those who do give birth, the experience is not the same for every mother or even for every child one mothers. Mothering is a relation to another and an experience in flux, and like disability, an experience that is both personal and social, bodily and socially shaped by local as well as broader cultures. As a nurturing relation to another, mothering need not even be gendered female. Men can and today do perform primary parenting, and, interestingly, the voices of fathers on parenting a child with disability (e.g., Bérubé 1996, Savarese 2007, Wilson 2008) have been better represented in recent disability studies scholarship than voices of mothers, a gap this book seeks to fill.

A focus on disability and mothering together provides a frame—to return to the liminal, like looking through the space of a doorway or window—through which we can see tensions and shadows, overlaps and gaps in dynamic interaction. A specific embodiment in culture comes into view when comparing the two: for example, vulnerable conditions of being, and destabilized binaries such as independence/dependence, choice/contingency, and self/other. Similar problems become discernable. The figure of the mother is overdetermined and vexed for both feminism and disability studies. Liberal feminists have run from the maternal body, perhaps because of its dependency needs and the blurring of the individual's boundaries in pregnancy. In the United States, liberal feminists have not fought as vigorously for social supports for mothers and children as they have for women's individual rights, perhaps in fear that such support programs reinforce patriarchal ideas of women's roles and that the bodily difference of childbearing might seem to disqualify women from full civil rights. Said another way, they worry that a woman's body, seen as vulnerable, will be considered *disabled*.

The mother is also a vexed figure in the disability community. Mothers of disabled children are often castigated for infantilizing their children, or treating their children's disabilities as tragedy, or for increasing disability stigma through the negative rhetoric of their political advocacy (e.g., as in "Cure Autism Now" campaigns). Disability activists and advocates may also shun dependency. As is true for the large and varied group labeled *women*, the disability community does not speak with one voice: some emphasize individual rights, fearing that the disabled body will be seen as feminized, that is, dependent, and therefore disqualified from claiming equal rights with the nondisabled. Others argue that the disabled are no different from all people, in that we all face lifelong bodily vicissitudes and vulnerability.

THEORIES OF DEPENDENCY AND RELATIONALITY

Because subjectivity based on abstract and autonomous individualism does not serve women or disabled people well, a number of feminist philosophers have been investigating and theorizing dependency. Nancy Fraser and Linda Gordon (1994) trace the shift in the term *dependency* historically from an earlier usage, when both women and certain classes of men were deemed dependent, to the twentieth-century concept of housewife dependency as a specifically female position, to a "postindustrial" usage of the term with increased stigma where working women and men claim independence while deviant groups are defined as dependent based on supposed deficiencies of character—people in poverty, on welfare, drug addicts, the homeless, the disabled. Dependency, they argue, has always been ideologically defined.

Eva Feder Kittay (1999) seeks a positive, complex concept of dependency, pointing to the nested relations involved in dependency care, which encompasses not only caring for dependents themselves, but also for those who provide their care. Dependency care, she notes, was traditionally done by women, and it continues to be considered women's work, although today dependency workers are likely to be poor women and women of color—unpaid family members, low-paid aides, attendants, immigrants. At the core of her argument is the fact that those who provide dependency care themselves also need adequate care and support, but that the current socioeconomic order does not provide it because dependency needs are considered an aberration from the "normal" state of abstract and autonomous individualism. Kittay argues that this "normal" state ignores the fact that at the beginning, middle, and end of life, all humans experience dependency, and so dependency is not an exception, but a common condition. She concludes that dependency needs are, in reality, central to the social order and that when dependency is understood as central, a different model of relationality can be seen as fundamental to human needs. This relationality is not one of reciprocity, as in classic contract theory, but a nested set of relations fostered by social cooperation based on the need for care. Kittay looks to childbirth for a term to express this relationality, which she calls *doulia*. The *doula* is a caregiver who helps a new mother as she begins caring for her own new infant. "Just as the *doula* gives care to the one who cares for the dependent infant," Kittay writes, "the direction of the obligation in connection-based reciprocity goes from those in position to discharge the obligations to those to whom they are relevantly connected" (68). Several of the contributors to this volume revise and complicate received notions of dependency—from showing how the direction of its energy in reverse affirms the value of the caregiver, to demonstrating the importance of supportive postpartum caregiving for a mother with disability.

THE OTHER SIDE OF MOTHERING, OR DISABILITY TALKS BACK

As a figure for rethinking dependency relations, the image of the new mother is nice and presentable, nonthreatening, and middle-class, but it has problems. It grows out of, but also clashes with, the mother's historical role, at least since the early nineteenth century, as the child's first educator (Kittler 1990). Her duty was to inculcate in her children a sense of society's norms, and these included a belief in individualism and independence and a fear of disability as deviant and unpresentable. Even as she instructed her children in reading, writing, and correct speech, the mother herself was supposed to remain dependent and quietly mute. Cal Montgomery (2001), a disability activist, writer, and survivor of institutionalization, challenges romantic constructions of presentable disability because they continue to exclude the unpresentable and cast dependency as only a minority condition. Montgomery creates two figures of her own, uncle Bruce and sister Mary. They are her shadow selves and convey the unstable subjectivity and differential needs of the disabled. Montgomery describes her uncle Bruce as "a descendant of Carrie Buck, of the Jukes and the Kallikaks, a cousin to the Rain Man and the wild children of the forests. You've seen him rocking in the corner, headbanging. He cannot speak and, people assume, has nothing to say." By contrast, Mary is "more comfortable for other people . . . she represents disability. So often, when people talk about barrier removal and leveling the playing field, they imagine freeing Mary to live my life" (sec. 2). Montgomery reminds us of the dangers of assuming that care is wholly benevolent and "that disabled people are dependent on others for the development of their talents in a way that nondisabled people are not" (sec. 1b). Montgomery's point is that although all humans need and receive care, the nondisabled misperceive their own periods of dependency (which has nurtured their talents) as autonomy: they imagine they are quite different from a person with a severe disability. Montgomery reminds us that this difference is one of degree, not of kind, and further that we need to embrace not just the acceptable Marys, but the "other"—headbanging Bruces—as fundamentally like us.

In rethinking dependency, some disability studies and feminist scholars have moved to the concept of interdependency (Lewiecki-Wilson, 2011; M. Price 2011). Several pieces included here make a start in this direction, invoking new models of interdependency. It could be argued that we are already always interdependent, but current theories and models of interdependent relationality have not yet been fully articulated, and a politics of interdependency has not yet been realized.

The mother that might stand as a figure for rethinking interdependent relations is suggested by the psychoanalytic term frequently used in the 1980s: the (m) in parentheses o-t-h-e-r, introduced to convey the complex metaphorical relations of self (*moi*) and other. This "(m)other" can be understood as a metaphor that multiply signifies women's historical social roles as caretakers of others, the biological processes of being born and sustained by others—which are also historical and culturally variable—and the conflicted tensions in the mutual constitution of self and other. This is not on an idealized mother, which Julia Kristeva (1986, 161) calls a "misconception," a "fantasy" of the adult for a "lost territory," an "idealization of primary narcissism" that "circumvents the real." The (m)other in this metaphorical construct is neither ideal nor whole but a divided and multiple subject, conveying the liminal state of between-ness, of one becoming two, or two conjoined but also separating to oneness.

Disabled cultural anthropologist Robert Murphy (1987) turned to the concept of liminality to explain the sense of between-ness and stigma he felt when he became disabled late in life. As Castelnuovo and Guthrie (1998, 120) note when discussing Murphy's theory, disability stigma is not an add-on identity but multiplies other social stigmas like race, class, and gender. Like the case of the "(m)other," the disabled person's liminality is a result of inhabiting a transitional state between categories. As Castelnuovo and Guthrie describe it, "a body has been identified as not fitting" in, but also "on the brink of 'a new birth'" (119). This liminal state, however, is dangerous, dirty, threatening to all categories. In a society that values the whole body, the stable identity, the independent subject, the liminal state represents the erratic, the variable, the unstable. In sum, the liminal processes of interdependent and shifting self and other are threatening, stigmatized, and associated with the fear of disability, but they also allow the possibility of transformation and growth. The unstable and shifting identities of mothering and disability can thus both induce a kind of panic because of the blurring of categories, but can also be productive, revealing the impurities and instabilities of categories and concepts themselves.

The move to abject certain "others" has a long psychical and material history relevant to both mothering and disability. While disability theory over the course of the last thirty years has developed several predominant models of analysis, it is in the broadest sense a theoretical lens that centers disability itself and then studies the many ways in which normalcy constitutes and shores itself up by casting disability as its other. A disability studies lens thus brings into view the mechanisms of othering and the construction of the "normate" (Garland-Thomson 1997), and traces how these moves bolster the power of particular groups while abjecting others by labeling them as deviant, abnormal, disabled.

Just as new work on mothering must move beyond the "fantasy" of the good mother or her binary opposite, the evil mother, to embrace multiple, diverse, and impure realities of mothering, productive theories and studies of disability need to embrace the hard cases, not just the easily acceptable "poster children," but the abject and excluded others—the Uncle Bruces, the Carrie Bucks, the Jukes, and the Kallikaks.[1] We think it noteworthy that this collection includes pieces on disabilities that have been often underrepresented and undertheorized in the literature of disability studies—the metaphorical Jukes and Kallikaks—such as intellectual disability and schizophrenia. We include here a history of an Australian institution for children labeled mentally retarded; narratives of mothering autistic children and with the added complexity of such mothering under a racist and colonial legacy; and accounts of mental illness from the perspective of a daughter caring for her ill mother, a daughter being cared for by her mother, and a mother helping her daughter to refuse diagnosis as psychiatrically disabled.

In calling to mind the Jukes and the Kallikaks, Montgomery identifies another connection between mothering and disability—the relative ease with which the dominant social order has been able to deprive women with disability of the basic right to reproduce. As the nineteenth century assigned to the mother in the home the job of insuring the health and normality of her children—their cleanliness, godliness, and literacy—the possibility of disabled women mothering began to be called into question. If the mother was herself not deemed "normal," how could she fulfill the role of teaching normality? Disability historian Catherine Kudlick (2008) has shown how prohibitions against disabled women marrying and bearing children fit with this normative social role demanded of the mother and notes that "marriage prohibitions grew in number and severity, particularly in the second half of the nineteenth century" (203). She states

---

1. The Jukes and the Kallikaks refer to cases in the early twentieth century in which psychologists, under the sway of eugenics and the belief in hereditary disability and criminality, labeled certain people, often poor women, as defective and argued for the advisability of their sterilization. See Goddard [1912] 1925; Estabrook 1916; and Buck v. Bell, 274 US 200 (1927).

that laws "included physical and mental disabilities among the reasons for prohibiting a marriage, although the nature of the disabilities and the reasons would change over time" (203). As the idea of inherited disability gained ground in the nineteenth century, marriage prohibitions took a eugenic turn, aided by the growing power of eugenic discourses. Indeed, the American eugenics movement provides countless examples of injustices—unauthorized birth control research on poor women and women of color, compulsory sterilizations of women labeled "unfit" and people with disability, questionable institutionalization and segregation of people labeled mentally ill. In many ways, the eugenics movement exemplifies society's obsession with clearly delineated categories, norms, and identities.

Although the more overtly cruel practices of the eugenics movement have been brought to a halt, eugenic discourse and rhetorics have not disappeared from discussions about disability and mothering, but appear in new sites for debate on reproductive rights. For example, with the discovery of a fetus with genetic markers for a disability, what role does the medical community play in a mother's decision to bear and raise her child? And how do individual choices to abort fetuses marked by (possible) disabilities contribute to wider social attitudes about living with disability? Several pieces gathered here address the eugenic undercurrents in twenty-first-century reproductive technologies, in political rhetorics of reproduction, and in current welfare policies. Other studies interrogate the cultural norms and attitudes that mothers with disability still face in making reproductive decisions.

Some contemporary thinkers, especially those connected to bioethics and the sociology of bioscience, disagree that contemporary technologies and genetic knowledge constitute a new eugenics. For example, Nikolas Rose (2007, 69) specifically takes issue with feminist Rayna Rapp (1998, 1999) for her argument that the demand inherent in new reproductive testing promotes a kind of neoeugenics. Unlike maternal feminists, and many of the authors in this collection, who wish to replace an emphasis on the individual subject with an understanding of interdependent relationality, Rose lauds individualism, the new possibilities of perfecting bodies made available by technoscience, and "the obligation" to "self-government" (69).

In describing the responsibility for human improvement, he uses a language that has been thoroughly critiqued by disability studies scholars like Simi Linton (1998) and Rosemarie Garland-Thomson (1997), when he says, for example, "those . . . born *afflicted* by any of these conditions" or "children [who] may live lives *blighted* by pain" (69, emphasis added). Such language seals a tragic and hopeless fate upon imagined disabled persons yet unborn. Ironically, it does nothing really to relieve "affliction" and "pain" while contributing to general beliefs that the disabled are miserable and a burden, and relocates the responsibility for mitigation to individual women's choices rather than to medical treatments and discoveries and social supports.

QUEER THEORY, FEMINISM, DISABILITY STUDIES

It is not surprising that work in disability studies overlaps with queer studies and feminism, as these critical-studies approaches also seek to analyze how stigmas and norms function to privilege or delimit certain bodies and sexualities (Brownworth and Raffo 1999; Clare 1999; McRuer 2006). As Robert McRuer has argued, all studies areas—critical race studies, queer studies, feminism, and disability studies—should be allies. However, while the work of opposing oppression can make allies of marginalized groups, it does not necessarily happen; the processes of othering can sadly persist. Victoria A. Brownworth (1999), for example, writes in her introduction to *Restricted Access: Lesbians on Disability* that the more mainstream lesbian and gays agitate for inclusion, the more disabled queers "have become virtually invisible . . . and more marginalized than ever" (xii–xiii). We might ask how practices of mothering still contribute to the reification of norms, especially of bodily norms.

Feminist theory is essential to disability studies because it has worked, albeit through a range of methodologies and theoretical phases, through disagreements and tensions, to denaturalize the body—or put another way, feminists have elucidated the ways that culture shapes expectations about bodies and bodily experience, and they have analyzed how and why it values certain bodies and not others. Further, the two interdisciplinary fields of feminism and disability studies have developed historically along similar trajectories. Both fields have much in common; they are multidimensional, not unitary, employing a variety of methods and theories. Both have followed similar paths of development from political liberation movement to academic study areas. Both have been accused of similar failings (e.g., of being dominated by white, middle-class perspectives), and both have experienced some conflict between those who work inside and outside the academy.

In editing this volume, we set out to engage these various enclaves. We strove to include pieces by and about activist women, personal narratives, theoretical pieces, and research articles. We hope these voices and genres form a contrapuntal dialogue, a talking back to and alongside one another, creating an interweaving of perspectives and methods that enrich and deepen each other. Plural methods can be seen as clashing, but we believe their fault lines can engender productive dissonance, opening up opportunities for reconsiderations, for instance, how we believe we know. For example, a qualitative social study presumes knowledge-making to be grounded in a valid methodology, whereas a personal narrative gains its power from literary and rhetorical traditions of representation and shared language and values. Each genre persuades possibly different audiences and instantiates experiential knowledge and even subjectivity differently: in the social study, subjectivity is understood as externally formed by a set of social roles and determinants shaping the individual, in the personal narrative as an interiority expressed through storytelling and self-reflection. And these different forms of writing and ways of marshaling evidence themselves participate in composing beliefs about who we are, what shapes us, how we know, how we should act.

Like feminist theory, across the last several decades disability-studies theory has developed competing models of analysis, too. The populist model of disability sees it as an unfortunate defect of an individual, leading to disqualification from mainstream life, and justifies this exclusion by seeing the disability as just one person's problem. The individual is expected to "just get over it" by not mentioning her impairment or by "overcoming" his "limits." In other words, mainstream society doesn't have to do anything to accommodate the disabled; the disabled are expected to adjust, or make do, or hide out at home.

The social model of disability, articulated first by British theorists, counters this assumption that it is the disability that causes exclusion. They argue that exclusion is a result of social arrangements that favor some kinds of people and not others. The social model separates the impairment from the socially disabling barriers and attitudes that exclude, and then works to remake the social world to be more accepting and accommodating for those with disability. Analyses using the social model examine how medical discourses, for example, objectify and pathologize the disabled, how language about disability carries negative connotations, how buildings and workplaces are inaccessible. Activists working with the social model were instrumental in gaining passage of the 1990 Americans with Disabilities Act, in changing attitudes and fighting for accommodations, and it is still an important element of disability theory and activism.

However, it became apparent that separating the impaired body from the socially disenabling environment ignored lived experiences of different kinds of embodiment, and even worse, that the body was in danger of being seen again as a "natural," precultural reality (throwing us back to the populist notion of disability). Some disability theorists, influenced by phenomenology, gave renewed attention to considering the body-in-the world, especially of bodies in their relations with environments and cultures. Some theorists take a more "realist" and civic stance, arguing for disability as a minority-rights theory.[2] Still other disability theorists take a more poststructuralist approach, arguing that the impaired body and disenabling social attitudes are not separate: both are historically constituted by institutional and medical discourses, technologies, and practices and everyday texts, which performatively address and call into being the disabled body. Feminist theory, especially that of Judith Butler (1999a), has been useful in this project. Disability scholars also turn to theories of Agamben (1998), Deleuze (2005), Foucault ([1975] 1999, 2003), Haraway ([1990] 1999, 1997), or Hayles (1999), to name just a few examples. *Posthuman* indicates a move away from the view of the human in terms

---

2. Adrienne Asch (2004) argues, "the minority group model is inadequate to the task of affording people with disabilities the conditions to turn legal rights into realities" (13).

of Enlightenment individualism. It signals not the humanist model of action as self-caused or isolated, but instead sees human action as always enmeshed in discourse networks, feedback loops of technologies, and other complex systems. The posthuman subject is considered not so much an individually bounded and stable person, but as one who continually is emerging from breaks and connections with others, other things, and flows in the environment. Under the older model of a stable and bounded individual, a disabled person with a missing limb might be seen as losing part of her "authentic" and whole self, and a prosthetic might be considered an unnatural addition. A posthuman model, in contrast, thinks of the human as always already supplemented by tools and prostheses, which are part of feedback loops linking humans to one another and environments; agency arises through the relations of humans, not from within the bounded individual alone.

In response to these more theoretical and constructivist approaches has come the concern once again that they downplay or ignore lived bodily reality (Siebers 2001). This book examines that liminal space between embodiment-in-the-world and the forces that socially construct bodies. Put another way, embodiment-in-the-world means cultural embodiment, the thoroughly socialized condition of the body that is the only one we can know. We thus contest the claim that bodily knowledge or experience can be accessed or understood outside of, or before, culture bestows meaning. As many feminist theorists have argued (e.g., Butler 1999a; Shildrik 2002; Tremain 2001, 2005, 2006b), we know our bodies only *in* and *through* culture. And, as feminist scientist Ann Fausto-Sterling (2005) argues, culture is embedded *in* bodies; the two are not separable. In "The Bare Bones of Sex: Part 1—Sex and Gender," she explains how cultures shape the very bones of bodies, and argues that we must move beyond the dichotomies of earlier feminist thinking: "[F]eminists must accept the body as simultaneously composed of genes, hormones, cells, and organs . . . *and* of culture and history" (1495, emphasis added).

Undergirding all the pieces in this volume is the assumption that social and cultural expectations, practices, representations, and institutions shape received attitudes toward and treatment of women and the disabled, but also—importantly—that our interactions can remake this world. As Barbara Herrnstein Smith (2006, 51) writes, "the specific features of what we interact with *as* reality are not prior to and independent of those interactions but emerge and acquire their specificity *through* them."

In rehearsing these disability theory models, we do not mean to imply a progressive evolution, one model replacing the other in ascending perfection. As Chela Sandoval (2000) argues in the case of feminist analysis in *Methodology of the Oppressed,* all models have strategic uses, and that has been a principle of inclusion for us as editors of this volume. While most of the authors collected here include a social analysis of disability, many articulate the embodied and personal experience of disability; noteworthy among these are essays about underrepresented and undertheorized conditions, such as pain and mental illness. We have organized the sections, then, not around particular disabilities or research approaches (not in terms of objects and methods), but according to the direction of cultural forces flowing into bodies and shaping personal experience, and the reverse, flowing from personal engagement and resistance outward to remake culture.

In part 1, Reproductive Technologies in the Disciplining of Bodies, contributors examine the ways that technologies and discourses penetrate and reshape practices and expectations related to the body. In part 2, Refusals: Contesting Diagnoses and Cultural Scripts, the authors address the power of stock stories to enforce cultural attitudes, identities, and practices, but they also demonstrate that it is possible to develop agency in resistance to such formations. The essays of part 3, Narrativity and Meaning-Making: Rewriting Stories of Mothering and Disability, seek to recast stories of mothering and disability. These authors encourage readers to consider how narrative itself constitutes values and ways of understanding and living in the world, and they suggest that rewriting familiar narratives can have material consequences. In part 4, Reimagining Activism: A Politics of Disability and Mothering, the contributors illuminate the complexities of social activism. These accounts detail the mixed nature of activist practices and the coming to awareness of a situated politics, as mothers learn how to advocate for social change, get better care for loved ones, or increase awareness of the lives of those with disability. The essays of part 5, Multiple Identities, Overlapping Borders, highlight the problematic concept of identity. In both disability studies and feminist theory, identity is a contested concept, and these authors explore the tensions of identity always already present at the intersections of disability and mothering.

Above all, we think the pieces collected here show that living with disability, like mothering, can be understood as a *techne,* that is, a creative and productive way of seeing and being in the world. New forms of knowledge and values emerge from the constraints and tensions of actual embodied situationality. Disabled bodies can be emergent forces of important values and actions. Bodies that shake, spasm, drool, use a wheelchair, contort and twist during speech, or use sign to communicate can devise new ways of living and convey lessons about purpose, dignity, commitment, humor, and ingenuity. They can also engender movement and change in the relational responses of others: for example, to build a ramp or remake an institution. By trying to aid people or to reimagine ways of living with a different set of constraints, knowledge advances. Complex embodied reality means that what one has learned through disabled embodiment becomes part of one. Even when disability brings pain (and not all disabilities do), pain is part of the fabric of human relations of living in the world.

Near the end of *Love's Labor,* Eva Feder Kittay (1999, 154) writes that a fundamental aspect of a just society is related to the conditions and limits of mothering. In a just society, women with disabilities can mother because there is adequate emotional and material support for them to do so, and given a context of support and approval to reproduce, they can also choose not to bear children. In a just society, mothers of children with disability can mother, and they, their children, and other needed caregivers will be adequately supported. In order to bring about such a just society, we need to start having conversations about disability and mothering. "My own courses on motherhood," disability scholar Adrienne Asch wrote in 2004, "include discussions of women with disabilities as mothers—something I have seen in none of the large number of recent books on the experiences of motherhood" (28). We hope this book will begin and spur many productive discussions about disability and mothering.

PART ONE

Reproductive Technologies in the Disciplining of Bodies

The four essays of part 1 examine how social and cultural discourses—for example, "beauty," "fitness," or "choice"—work together with advanced technologies, such as in vitro fertilization, genetic testing, or selective abortion, to prescribe a specific, limiting, and powerful version of genetic health and fitness for parents and children alike. The authors use a range of theoretical approaches to analyze the material, psychological, social, and cultural consequences of such technologies, not only for women as mothers, but also for the female subject, the disabled body, and the fetus. Taken together, this work shows the ways that technologies and discourses penetrate and reshape bodies.

In "'Healthy, Accomplished, and Attractive': Visual Representations of 'Fitness' in Egg Donors," Jen Cellio uses visual and rhetorical analysis to detail how egg donor websites construct specific versions of fitness through their images and metaphors. Such representations, in turn, lead women to understand themselves in a way that continues the tradition of eugenics, with its notion of hereditary "fitness" associated with certain race, class, sexuality, and body types, but now in the form of neoliberal subjectivity in terms of "choice" and the limiting of risks.

In "Negotiating Discourses of Maternal Responsibility, Disability, and Reprogenetics: The Role of Experiential Knowledge," Felicity Boardman presents three case studies drawn from fifty-five interviews she conducted with women who have spinal muscular atrophy (SMA). After identifying emergent themes and issues, Boardman concludes that women with genetic disability use their experiential knowledge to contest and negotiate the powerful social, cultural, and medical discourses that discourage disabled women from becoming pregnant or bringing a fetus with a potentially disabling genetic condition to term.

Terri Beth Miller takes a Foucauldian approach, examining cultural, legal, and medical examples for their role in the production of normativity. In "Stalking Grendel's Mother: Biomedicine and the Disciplining of the Deviant Body," she reads the practices of prenatal screening and diagnosis as communal efforts to institute boundaries of "humanness." She argues that the ascendance of these procedures can be understood as clinical discursive practices that regulate bodies and reify an image of "normal."

In "Uneasy Subjects: Feminism, Disability, and Abortion," Cynthia Lewiecki-Wilson uses cultural and rhetorical analysis to examine the tensions and fissures created when the politics of abortion intersect with disability and mothering. Lewiecki-Wilson identifies the role of abortion in securing the autonomous female subject in the latter part of the twentieth century. Proabortion's rhetoric of choice, however, not only further solidifies competitive individualism and contributes to the dominance of normative discourses and the stigma of disability, but also forecloses the possibility of giving voice to other models of interdependent relationality.

1

"Healthy, Accomplished, and Attractive"

Visual Representations of "Fitness" in Egg Donors

JEN CELLIO

Eugenic discourses and rhetorics popular during the "race betterment" movement in the early twentieth century have not disappeared but instead have found purchase in new sites for discussion: in debates about current and emerging reproductive technologies and forums on bioethics, and in social and medical discussions about disability and reproduction, especially of healthy and/or "viable" fetuses.[1] In fact, discussions of reproductive technologies, such as in vitro fertilization and surrogacy using donor eggs, donor sperm, or both, and prenatal/genetic screening often contain language that recalls the American eugenics movement and its obsession with "fitness."

As noted in the introduction to this volume, some scholars, especially those connected to bioethics and the sociology of bioscience, dispute the idea that particular reproductive technologies and genetic screening should be considered a new or modern version of eugenics. However, while Nikolas Rose and others emphasize the possibilities for human improvement that such technologies make available, they downplay the power of the attendant rhetoric of "betterment" that accompanies these technologies (Rose 2007). Rhetorics of the eugenics movement of the late nineteenth and early twentieth centuries fostered a belief that more

---

1. The title quote can be found under donor "qualifications" at Egg Donation, Inc., http://www.eggdonation.com/Flash/EggDonation.swf.

children from the "fittest" individuals and fewer from the "unfit" would result in the overall improvement of the nation. These public discourses shaped peoples' attitudes about disability, certainly contributing to its stigma and to the removal of children with disabilities from homes to institutions. But at that time, short of barring certain groups from reproducing, there was little to be done in the way of selecting "fit" offspring. Today's neo-eugenic discourses of "improvement" are founded on what Rose calls "technologies of optimization" (16), and they construct a reality wherein individuals are pressured by doctors and health-care providers to carry only selected fetuses to term. Rose calls such pressure variously "choice, prudence, and responsibility" (39–40), an "opportunity" (51) for "responsible self-management" (94). Thus, in an era when a stated goal of the Human Genome Project is to impose preimplantation genetic diagnosis (PGD) on all embryos in order to locate "flaws" and "abnormalities" before use for in vitro fertilization (as part of an effort to "dramatically improve lives"), it seems essential to ask yet again, who or what is being constructed as "flawed" or "abnormal," as well as to determine what, exactly, defines "improvement" ("Gene Testing" 2008).

The role of analogy and metaphor operate, often unrecognized, in current constructions of so-called hereditary "fitness" in rhetorics of reproduction, especially in images and text on websites and in advertisements dedicated to egg donation for assisted reproductive technologies (ART). In particular, analogy and metaphor construct a reality in which women who seek the services of an egg donor become contemporary iterations of the so-called eugenically "unfit."[2] The growing popularity of ART technologies translates to more frequent and visible representations of egg

2. Few texts address analogy and analogical reasoning in the sciences. Instead, most focus on metaphor. Notable exceptions include work by Dedre Gentner and Michael Jeziorski (1979), Heather Brodie Graves (1998), Alan Gross (1990), and Nancy Stepan (1986). Two patterns emerge in discussions of analogy: one brings metaphor and analogy together as a particular type of thought process—a transfer of meaning from one object (or set of objects) to another; the other uses metaphor to explain analogy in lieu of differentiating between the two. I use the terms together when describing tropes in general and distinguish between them when assessing one or the other.

donation. Information about obtaining donor eggs, or serving as a donor, is widely available using a basic web search, and advertisements appear in a variety of locations: magazines dedicated to women's health, fashion, parenting, and professionalism; websites and weblogs (blogs) dedicated to the same; public news sources such as the *New York Times Sunday Magazine, USA Today,* and MSNBC.com; even the doors of women's restroom stalls in bars and coffee shops. As a result, these texts not only inform the public about the science and availability of egg donation; they also generate the illusion of an "ideal" donor. This ideal, in turn, constructs women seeking donor eggs as "unfit," or *not* ideal for reproduction through analogical reasoning: that is, images and textual descriptions of donors become embodied representations of "the fit" (with regard to fertility and viable ova) while women seeking the donor eggs become embodied representations of "the unfit." These representations continue the tradition of eugenically charged, ossified representations of "fitness" through associations of class, race, sexuality, body type and physical health, intelligence, mental health, and family heritage.

As Dedre Gentner and Michael Jeziorski note, analogy can be understood as "a kind of highly selective similarity," a thought process wherein "people implicitly focus on certain kinds of commonalities and ignore others" (1979, 448). This practice of selecting or ignoring similarities recalls Kenneth Burke's discussion of "terministic screens," or frames produced by language and the reader's and writer's motives, that either select or deflect reality (1966, 45). The process of selection and deflection occurs in analogies and metaphors in egg donor representations and discourses of "fitness." Furthermore, because analogy operates through relationality—by "aligning and focusing on relational commonalities independent of the objects in which those relationships are embedded"—the dissimilarities between the elements of the analogy do not affect its power or effectiveness in making meaning (Gentner and Jeziorski 1979, 448). Gentner and Jeziorski's example of the analogy between the solar system and the hydrogen atom (as originally presented by physicist Ernest Rutherford) reveals as much. Our understanding of the solar system and the relationships between the sun and the planets (sun attracts planets, is more massive, planets revolve around sun) inform the analogy while obvious dissimilarities (sun is yellow, very hot, very large) do not inhibit its meaning: the sun is to the nucleus as the planets are to electrons (449).

Analogies thus have meaning-making power, power that in this case informs the way women living with the possibility of infertility understand their place in society and "nature." Analogous relationships created between visual representations of "ideal" donors and their purported reproductive "fitness" encourage viewers to select a version of reality that suggests controllable, perfectible, and idealized reproductive outcomes—in short, of controllable and perfectible humanity.

ANALOGY AND METAPHOR IN SCIENCE

Inquiries into the work of analogy and metaphor in the "doing" of science and in the writing and reporting of scientific practices often take up the question of legitimacy. Many philosophers of science and scientists themselves view figurative language as stylistic or decorative, identifying its use in scientific texts as embellishment or pandering to an audience. Others allow that tropes, especially analogy, play a heuristic role in scientific discourse by helping readers grasp a connection between the familiar and the novel, but insist that tropes do not themselves create knowledge. Figurative language may help us "see" science, but it does not change science or scientific knowledge itself. It does not perform an epistemological function.

Alan Gross challenges this perspective by arguing for the primary role of rhetoric and rhetorical analysis in science: he views knowledge construction as "a task beginning with self persuasion and ending with the persuasion of others," which places science squarely within the purview of rhetorical analysis (1990, 4). Although others have offered a version of this premise (Bazerman 1988; Fahnestock 2002; Miller 1992; Prelli 1989), Gross's assessment of analogy is novel because he insists that rhetorics of science (and analogy in particular) are rhetorical *and* epistemological. For Gross, the persuasive power of analogy resides in its requirement of agreement: the speaker and the audience must agree on or "commit" to a particular version of reality in order to permit a transfer of meaning

(1990, 22–24). However, new meaning emerges in science's ability to move beyond connecting two ideas or persuading; he suggests that "commitment in science reaches beyond argument and rests ultimately on agreed-upon procedures," or particular ways of doing science (32). Thus, analogical reasoning not only affects the way science is presented but also affects the way science creates knowledge in the world.

In "Marbles, Dimples, Rubber Sheets, and Quantum Wells: The Role of Analogy in the Rhetoric of Science," Heather Brodie Graves offers a more focused assessment, proposing a mechanism for analogical reasoning as epistemic and providing a clear example of its power to impose a particular reality on those who commit to its framework. She demonstrates how physicists use analogy in three distinct and recursive ways in their research: heuristically, to assist their process of grasping and visualizing the data; epistemologically, when they arrive at new insight about the data through the analogy (which in this case produces a new analogy as well); and rhetorically, as they attempt to persuade others in their published article (1998, 34). Applying Graves's methodology to egg donor sites and texts reveals the process by which a reality about "fitness" is constructed and the ways women seeking donor eggs understand, identify, construct, and shape their perceptions of themselves and others. The tropes operate through the interaction of these uses of analogy—understanding a concept, creating new insight, and encouraging the adoption of a knowledge framework.

Finally, it is important to recognize the lasting power of such analogical constructions. In "Race and Gender: The Role of Analogy in Science," Nancy Stepan illustrates the work of analogy and metaphor in descriptions of human difference in the nineteenth century, focusing specifically on constructions of the "lower races" as "feminine" and the female as the "lower race" of gender (1986, 264). Like Graves, Stepan cites the interaction between constructions of gender and race as the source of the analogy's persuasive and epistemological power. During the nineteenth and early twentieth centuries, this system of analogy and metaphor "provided the 'lenses' through which people experienced and 'saw' the differences between classes, races, and sexes, between civilized man and the savage, between rich and poor, between the child and the adult" (265), which in turn produced "new knowledge" about women and the "lower races" and justified their continued oppression. She suggests that, in the case of human difference in the nineteenth century, these metaphors and analogies "functioned as the science itself—that without them the science did not exist" (267). Stepan continues: "because a metaphor or analogy does not directly present a preexisting nature but instead helps 'construct' that nature, the metaphor generates data that conform to it, and accommodates data that are in apparent contradiction to it, so that nature is seen via the metaphor and the metaphor becomes a part of the logic of science itself (274)." Furthermore, these tropes supported (and continue to support) a binary of "other" or "inferior" in contrast to the privileged, wealthy, white male. Stepan notes that their position as "root metaphors" reveals a set of deeply embedded values in Western culture, values that continue to circulate in our perceptions of "other" (265).

The interactive work of both metaphor and analogy demonstrates how these tropes construct a reality about "fitness," one that presents fertile egg donors as "fit" and the (presumably) infertile recipient as "unfit." I also make visible a "terministic screen," highlighting particular similarities these metaphors and analogies create while ignoring others, and resulting in what Stepan refers to as the "normative consequences" of analogy and metaphor.

THE ROLE OF METAPHOR AND ANALOGY IN EGG DONATION

So what might a woman searching for information on egg donation discover when she performs a search via Google.com or another popular Internet search engine? Search results suggest that women are represented as the primary seekers of information on egg donation as a possible solution to infertility. Of course, men may also have an interest or a stake in locating an egg donor; however, my own interests lie in the way that women in particular are encouraged to read themselves as "fit" or "unfit" as a result of viewing the sociocultural representations of fertility and fitness on these sites.

I acted as a woman searching for general information about egg donation might by using Google.com, arguably the most popular and far-reaching search engine. Typing in the search terms "egg donation" brings forth over 680,000 hits, a number that does not include advertisements for specific companies or "sponsored" links, of which there are over 2,000 available. I scanned a few pages before returning to the first page of results to begin my search—in doing so, I made mental notes about the addresses and "titles" of the pages available to discern pertinent and reliable links. Using that first page, I opened five links: the first, entitled "Becoming an Egg Donor," offered advice to donors. I used the second and third pages, "www.eggdonor.com" and "www.eggdonation.com" respectively, as well as the fifth, "www.fertilityneeds.com." The fourth link, a March 2006 headline from USAToday.com, read "Egg-donor business booms on campuses."

Clicking on the website Egg Donation, Inc. at "www.eggdonor.com" opens to a series of images and text presented on a deep blue rectangle, itself atop a background image of blue skies with wispy white clouds. The corporate logo, three wooden "alphabet blocks" reminiscent of a child's nursery, reveals the letters "E" and "D" and the abbreviation "Inc." To the right of these blocks is an image of sunlight piercing through clouds. The words "Where Dreams Come True . . ." in an italicized script are superimposed on this sun-through-clouds image. Directly beneath the clouds is an invitation—"Welcome"—in the same script.

At the top of the page is a series of virtual file tabs that reveal an additional series of tabs below the first when the cursor is placed above the tab. From left to right, the tabs read "About Us," "Recipient Information," "Donor Information," and "Resources"; to the far right are two additional tabs labeled "Donor Database" and "Contact Us." Highlighting the tab for recipient information, as a woman seeking a donor might, yields a list: "The Process: Step by Step," "Medical," "Legal," "Financial," "Sample Donor Profile," and "FAQ." Clicking on any of these links navigates the user away from the front page and into other pages within the site.

More striking, however, and certainly more visually informative to a woman searching for a donor, is the bottom three-quarters of the first page, where a series of five "bubbles" on a blue background contain snapshots of a donor profile. These bubbles resemble the view a magnifying glass might offer; using shading to give the appearance of a convex lens, the bubbles seem to push out at the center and the edges of each bubble are slightly more difficult to read, like the view through a magnifying glass. In addition, each bubble gives the impression of looking more closely or seeing more clearly the information under the glass. Viewers are invited to scrutinize these bubbles as they would biological specimens or words on a page.

The leftmost bubble, the largest of the five, contains an image of a young blond woman with long straight hair and hazel eyes. Like most visual representations of egg donors and babies born via in vitro fertilization, this donor is white. Accompanying the photograph, read from the top of the bubble to the bottom, is a part of her profile: "Status, Available; Age, 25; Height, 5'3"; Weight, 110; Eye color, Hazel; Hair color, Blond; Body type, Petite; and Complexion, Medium" ("Egg Donation for Recipient Parents" 2008). A series of five additional photos occupies the bottom right quarter of the bubble, though they are difficult to see clearly on this page (ibid.). The next two bubbles reveal more of this donor's "profile," here offering more personal information. Asked to indicate whether or not she smokes, the donor has entered "no"; asked her sexual orientation, she has entered "heterosexual"; asked about a history of "psychiatric counseling," the donor has again entered "no" (ibid.). And in a section for "pregnancy complications," the donor has entered "N/A." The next bubble indicates her grade point average (a 3.0) and her employment record is visible showing three jobs, two of which she holds at the time her profile was posted (ibid.).

The final two bubbles are both small and quite crowded with text. However, the curvature of the bubble "magnifies" some of the text. The fourth bubble from the left provides a series of short, two- or three-word questions about the donor's favorite things and her response. Many are innocuous: favorite color, favorite food, favorite season. However, others seem more invasive and revealing. This donor's favorite holiday is Christmas; her favorite sports are "dance" and "tennis." The fifth and rightmost bubble shows a snapshot of the sample profile questionnaire, revealing a series of "drop-down" boxes donors can use to describe their traits.

A woman viewing this page as an introduction to egg donation can glean a lot of data about this particular donor. However, she can also take away a host of impressions about what, exactly, makes this donor "fit" or "worthy" to reproduce or donate. Only the first bubble contains medically pertinent information identifying this woman as suitable for egg donation: she is under thirty years of age, a typical cutoff point for egg donation. In addition, this first bubble contains the only information that qualifies as genetically pertinent: eye color can be inherited, as can hair color and height. However, the presentation of these genetic traits in proximity to social and behavioral traits conflates the two and supports a biologically deterministic view of character. Insofar as these snippets of information "show" the viewer who this donor is as a person, they also mark her with regard to class, physical fitness (in the sense that she appears slim), and religious beliefs. That is, being a Christian and having the time and money for "dance" and "tennis" provide sociocultural clues about this donor. Even her favorite food, "salad," offers embedded "truths" about what a reproductively "fit" woman should be: a light eater, healthy and/or concerned about calories, self-disciplined.[3]

Sample donor profiles available on the other websites match this representation. Again, most sample donors are white, as are the majority of donor images available to viewers who visit the sites. The near-exclusive use of images of white donors bears notice, both for its historical roots in the eugenics movement (with regard to sentiment about who should be having children) and for its current implications (with regard to beliefs about rising minority populations and "welfare queens"). Arguably, the preponderance of white donor profiles and images of white babies not only evokes a particular audience for egg donation but also suggests that white babies alone are the desired "end product" of in vitro fertilization.

Like other depictions of the "ideal donor," the woman on the first page has a clear, flawless complexion, straight, white teeth, and shiny hair worn down around her shoulders. She appears slim and physically fit, and though she appears to use a small amount of makeup, she is what

---

3. Of course, donors take part in this construct, too. In most cases, a donor is compensated only if her eggs are chosen for in vitro fertilization. Savvy donors understand the benefits of portraying themselves in a manner keeping with feminine and/or maternal ideals.

many would describe as "naturally" beautiful. The text accompanying the photo claims that she is one of 5 percent of applicants accepted as a donor, which means she is between twenty and twenty-nine years of age, weighs a maximum of 160 pounds (no mention of height-to-weight ratio), has a "good family/personal health history" and "live[s] a healthy, drug-free lifestyle" ("Egg Donation for Recipient Parents" 2008).

Another donor profile at the National Exchange for Egg Donation and Surrogacy at www.fertilityneeds.com in 2007 offered photographs and provided six pages of personal information, the donor's health and repro- ductive history, an overview of her family and their genetic background, and an assessment of her family's general and psychological health. This profile also provided a comprehensive assessment of the donor's ancestry in the form of detailed medical history. Some of the questions were quite specific and required information about the donor's parents and grand- parents on both sides. For example, inquiries about respiratory health focused on emphysema, asthma, and lung cancer; those about reproduc- tive health asked about fibroids, uterine cancers, and cysts; questions about blood requested information about a history of hemophilia, sickle- cell anemia, immune deficiencies, and leukemia. All had places to input data about each family member. Other questions were decidedly ambigu- ous: "Have you ever had an abnormal baby? If yes (abnormal baby), please explain." Finally, this profile offered not only a close up photograph of the donor's head and neck and a full-length photograph of her body, but it also provided images of the donor as a child and the donor's children, if she had started a family of her own. Metaphorically speaking, the visual and textual descriptions of these sample donor profiles stand in for the idea of fertility and reproductive "fitness" in a social Darwinian context. That is, these women represent the epitome of "survival of the fittest" when an ability to reproduce is held up as a measure of evolutionary fit- ness. Visitors to these websites can infer that these women are "super" fertile, so fertile, in fact, that they have eggs to spare to women in need. In addition, these versions of the "ideal donor" imply a series of socially constructed truths about what it means to be "fit" for reproduction, many of which are entailed in purely physical and sociocultural representations of femininity, race, class, ability, and sexuality.

Consider first, for example, the physical representations of beauty. Regardless of ethnicity and age, all but one of the women has long, straight, shiny hair, and in the vast majority of the headshots the hair is worn down to reveal its full length. There is no sign of cornrows, naturally curly hair, or an afro; there is no very short hair, thinning hair, or hair that has been dyed in a nontraditional color. All of the women have straight, clean, white teeth. All of the women have clear, scar- and acne-free skin on their faces, necks, and shoulders. There is no sign, either, of unfeminine facial hair; eyebrows are thin, tamed, and symmetrical, sideburns are minimal. Donors do wear makeup, but none seems to use it to conceal flaws or to a degree typically considered "too much" or "too loud"— there is nary a trace of red lipstick, and even though many of the women have submitted photos of themselves in formalwear, none has the look of a woman "out on the town." Within these associations is the unifying theme of "natural beauty" as "feminine beauty," and the corresponding notion that this beauty is worthy of reproduction. Arguably, it can be read as raced, classed, and in some cases heteronormative.

Other associations prove more insidious and damaging. Because all of the donors appear to be slim and/or petite, with slender necks and pronounced collarbones, the sense that these women represent an ideal body type emerges. Not surprisingly, not a single donor wears eyeglasses. Not only do these photos reify physical fitness in a traditional sense, they also exclude images of larger bodies, most bodies of color, and bodies with visible disability. In addition, the "backdrops" for these photos contribute to a broader representation of "fitness." Many include a "formal pose," wherein the donor's headshot includes her shoulders and upper torso— often in a strapless dress with a suited arm peeking out from around her waist—offering overlapping associations with traditional femininity and "appropriate" heterosexual dating or marriage. Others incorporate an outdoor scene—a beach, the side of a mountain, a lakeshore or pier— and representations of physical activity, suggesting a level of wealth that allows for vacation while simultaneously devaluing an urban or inner-city lifestyle. These scenes also place a premium on able-bodiedness, physical activity, and ease of movement and travel. A third backdrop places the donor in her home, often with other family members, reifying the nuclear family and suggesting a "traditional" home life. As a group, the photos present a "wholesome," Eurocentric representation of femininity, beauty, class, sexuality, and family life, one that gives the perception of health, able-bodiedness, and physical fitness combined with the "good genes" that bring wealth, happiness, and strong "family values."

As a result of these entailed meanings and associated implications, the potential recipient can be positioned on one side of an analogical relationship: her status as "unfit" is not only informed by her inability to produce or conceive a child with her own ova, but it is also conferred onto her through any number of ways she might exist outside the norms presented by the images and descriptions of these donors. Furthermore, the initial analogical connection can continue beyond the first paired relationship ad infinitum. For example, if reproductive "fitness" is to the donor's fertility as "unfitness" is to the recipient's infertility, the additional pairings produce a "have/lack" series: youth/old age; beauty/homeliness; whiteness/other; wealth/poverty; ability/disability; straight/"homosexual." For example, a woman who identifies as lesbian who visits the site can be constructed as "unfit" not only because of her presumed infertility, but also because the donor database norms heterosexual relationships and heteronormative versions of physical beauty and sexuality. The woman of color sees whiteness as the rule, creating a cascade of perceptions about infertility: that other women of her ethnicity do not experience infertility, that the science of ART does not value children of color, that "fitness" for reproduction does not include women of color. In addition, the working-class woman might interpret these images as classed, that in vitro fertilization is an expensive business, that only middle-class women possess the financial resources necessary to pursue this option. Prominent disavowals of a need for psychological counseling or medication leave women living with depression, schizophrenia, or a neurological disorder without representation. Women with physical disabilities, chronic pain or illness, or potentially debilitating disease— or with a family history of genetic disease or psychiatric care—can infer their "unfitness" for reproduction and, by proxy, parenting, when placed in an analogical relationship with the "fit" donors. And underlying all of these associations is an assumption about the mechanisms of heredity and reproduction: these representations of "fitness" no more guarantee an "ideal" child than the converse assumption that women who have disabilities should not reproduce. Thus, in much the same way individuals labeled "the Unfit" emerged as "other" in opposition to the constructed norm of the white (Anglo) heterosexual male during the American eugenics movement, women who desire these fertility technologies can be constructed as "unfit" when placed in an analogous relationship with the donors.

SUPPRESSING KNOWLEDGE, CREATING KNOWLEDGE, AND THE PRESTIGE OF SCIENCE

Both Graves and Stepan identify the consequences of analogical reasoning as the result of meanings selected and deflected by the "screens" of metaphor and analogy, consequences that involve not merely the discovery of an alternative view or "reality," but that instead limit and/or create new knowledge about both subjects in the interacting pair. For Graves and the physicists, the presence of one (terministic) screen enabled them to "see" particular qualities and conclusions in their data at the same time the screen obscured other qualities and "truths." Stepan, on the other hand, notes the specious "scientific" knowledge created as a result of the analogy connecting gender and race in the nineteenth century. These tropes are especially effective, she contends, because they appear to be neither arbitrary nor personal (1986, 265); as products of scientific research, theory, observation, and data collection, these analogies and metaphors seem objective and "natural." Thus, like the "proof" derived from measurements of skull size and brain weight (a connection itself established by the race and gender analogy), the "proofs" of reproductive "fitness" seem both objective and impersonal.

What knowledge, then, is illuminated and ignored, selected and deflected, as the result of an analogy connecting "fitness" and fertility to a host of other sociocultural representations of "fitness?" And how do discourses of egg donation, in vitro fertilization, and assisted reproductive technologies function within existing scientific discourses of genetics, evolutionary theory, and disability to confer the power, prestige, and presumed objectivity of science onto the decidedly unscientific representations of "fitness"?

The analogical reasoning that creates associations between "fit" and "unfit" as "fertile donors" and "infertile recipients" (complete with all of the corresponding implications and entailments described above) highlights and selects several "truths" about reproductive "fitness." First, the connection constitutes a view of "fitness" that identifies a woman who uses an egg donor as not "fit" for motherhood, parenting, and even for "survival" in an evolutionary sense. The faulty interpretation of "survival of the fittest" that infers an essential role for reproduction treats women who cannot conceive as "unfit." In addition, the analogy suggests a version of reality wherein a "fit" donor will necessarily produce a "fit" child. For example, in one advertisement for "The Genetics & IVF Institute" in Washington, DC, a white baby with bright blue eyes and blond hair represents the "end product" of a successful egg donation. This view also conflates genetic traits with other characteristics; particular traits that may emerge in the child (such as eye color, hair color, right-handedness, etc.) are presented together with characteristics that are not transferred genetically, such as intelligence, behaviors, and moral beliefs.

Connected to these realities is the idea that a "perfect woman" exists and, by proxy, that perfect humans exist. The expression of "ideal" qualities in donor profiles implies a set of desirable qualities in a woman and in her eggs—qualities that reify a norm based on race, class, sexuality, and ability. Finally, this view of reality reestablishes a faith in Progressive-Era science and its positivist ideals; in short, it nurtures a belief that science is all-powerful and that we can control reproduction to create the perfect human while eliminating the "imperfect."

The analogy also deflects certain realities, among them the financial cost of egg donation, making it seem more accessible than perhaps it is. It also deflects the dangers to the donor—as the New York State Department of Health notes, the egg donor may experience "ovarian hyperstimulation syndrome," a condition that may cause symptoms ranging from mild abdominal pain or swelling to more "serious medical complications, including blood clots, kidney failure, fluid build-up in the lungs, and shock" ("Becoming an Egg Donor" 2008). In a few rare cases, the process of harvesting eggs can be life threatening; in other serious cases, one or both of the donor's ovaries may have to be removed (ibid.). Finally, the belief that not bearing children and/or not being able to bear children is an acceptable choice is deflected in this version of reality. For women who do not choose to have children, or who are at peace with their presumed infertility, the construction of an egg donor as "fit" because she is fertile sets up a comparison wherein those who do not bear children are automatically labeled "unfit."

Early-twentieth-century rhetorics of eugenics were largely focused on eliminating "the unfit," on purging from the gene pool any number of individuals and groups of people perceived to be outside the "norm." In current neo-eugenic rhetorics, visible above in the construction of "fit" donors, the opposite is true—these rhetorics insist on the ability to select for an ideal type. And because these rhetorics overlap with powerful rhetorics of choice and consumerism, we tend to approach assisted reproductive technologies and egg donation as a process in which we are compelled to seek an elusive "best," "perfect," "fittest." Rather than reify a "perfectible," "controllable" body, we should instead be wary of these subtle and dangerous neo-eugenic ideals, for the actual robustness of the human species depends upon a richly varied gene pool, not a narrow norm of perfection.

2

Negotiating Discourses of Maternal Responsibility, Disability, and Reprogenetics

The Role of Experiential Knowledge

FELICITY BOARDMAN

Women with disabilities have long experienced constraints on their reproductive choices and rights. For women with genetic disabilities, new technologies have increased these constraints. They, and their relatives, are compelled to consider explicitly the prospect of giving birth to, or terminating, a fetus identified as having the trait associated with their impairment, and they must negotiate powerful discourses of maternal responsibility and assumptions about life with disability to validate their reproductive choices. This chapter presents research on the way in which women with a specific heritable disability, spinal muscular atrophy (SMA), draw on their embodied knowledge of their disability to resist negative assumptions and to rewrite the discourses of maternal responsibility in reproductive decision making. I argue that experiential knowledge can be both empowering and transformative but can also introduce new forms of conflicting obligation to reproductive decisions for women with genetic disabilities.

Historically, pregnant women were discouraged from having any contact with disabled people during the course of their pregnancies and even from thinking about disability lest their child be born impaired (Huet 1993, 457). In contrast, the availability of ultrasound and maternal serum alpha fetoprotein (MSAFP) screening as standard components of most forms of prenatal care, as well as testing for an ever-expanding number of genetic conditions, suggest that nearly all pregnant women are now encouraged to consider the prospect of disability in their unborn child (Press et al. 1998, 48).

These developments have been heralded as offering new forms of choice and control over reproduction, and even as making forms of reassurance available to pregnant women (Lippman, 1991, 22); however, they have also brought with them new forms of genetic responsibility (Kenan 1994, 57). The expectations, boundaries, and definitions of motherhood itself have shifted alongside the development of these technologies. The very availability of previously inaccessible knowledge concerning parents' genetic status and/or that of an unborn fetus may imbue a sense of responsibility not only to obtain this information in the first instance, but also to terminate those pregnancies genetically identified with a trait, which is assumed to be inherently negative and burdensome (Saxton, 1999, 26). Some writers have even suggested that these developments point to the prospect of women eventually being held accountable for their children's disabilities, as they come to be considered "preventable" on account of the very availability of such information (L. Rogers 1999, 28).

While the development of these technologies introduces ethical, social, and moral considerations for *all* prospective mothers, for women with genetic disabilities considering reproduction these concerns take on particular forms and involve very specific tensions. Not only do women with genetic disabilities find themselves being labeled "irresponsible" for reproducing (on the basis of assumptions about their bodies and capabilities), but the very availability and offer of genetic testing technologies also forces them to consider their own "genetic responsibility" (Kenan 1994, 57) toward any prospective child. Discourses of responsibility, therefore, may have particular consequences for women with genetic disabilities.

I will examine how three women with the genetic disability SMA consider reproduction in the context of prenatal testing and preimplantation genetic diagnosis (PGD) and negotiate these discourses of responsibility. I argue that the women's *lived experiences* of their impairments is an important discursive tool enabling them not only to deflect the perceived (and actual) judgments others make about their reproductive choices, but also to transform the boundaries and definitions of responsible motherhood itself.

WOMEN WITH GENETIC DISABILITIES AND REPRODUCTION

The systematic denial of reproductive rights to women with disabilities has a long history, including the widespread practice of coercive abortion, sterilization, and a generalized social resistance to their right to bear children (Kallianes and Rubenfeld 1997, 207). Women with disabilities are often perceived as asexual, as incapable of caring for a child, and are assumed to transmit their disability to their offspring automatically, regardless of its etiology, thus rendering them unsuitable mothers in the eyes of the general public. While there also exists resistance to disabled men taking on parenting roles, the implications of discourses of parental responsibility operate differently for men and women. Indeed, historically, women have been held solely responsible for pregnancy outcomes, as evidenced in theological and medical representations (Dragonas 2001, 138). The works of Lippman (1991, 27–28), as well as that of Hallowell (1999, 599) and Steinberg (1996, 267), have pointed to the survival of such discourses, and to the way in which—in line with the development of genetic technologies—this maternal responsibility has expanded to include the accountability of women for children's genetic health. Responsibility for reproduction is therefore profoundly gendered (Charo and Rothenberg 1994, 108); women are not only physically, but also morally and socially, more heavily implicated in reproduction than men.

As well as being held responsible for producing a healthy child, mothers are also conceptualized as being primarily responsible for the continued nurturance of a child following birth. The perception that a woman with a disability would not be able to fulfil such expectations of motherhood because of her own need for assistance (real or imagined) is evidenced in the number of children of disabled women deemed to be "at risk" or in "danger" (Saxton 1984, 304). Another example of this attitude is the number of children of disabled women assumed to be unrelated to them or adopted when seen with their mothers in public (Morris 1991, 20).

For women with *genetic* disabilities, negative attitudes around reproduction are particularly pronounced; indeed the very possibility of a child inheriting the disability is seen to confirm commonly held assumptions that disabled people *automatically* transmit their disabilities to their offspring.

Women with genetic disabilities may find themselves particularly vulnerable to these assumptions, and the public condemnation of such women—for example, Bree Walker (Holmes 1991) or Sharon Duchesneau ("Couple 'Choose' to Have Deaf Baby" 2002) who were said to knowingly "inflict" (or who took the chance of "inflicting") their own condition onto their offspring—highlights public concerns about the quality and nature of life with disability as well as the capacity of disabled women to be responsible mothers. Some writers have indeed emphasized the moral duty of people affected by inheritable conditions *not* to reproduce when they risk passing on their disability to future generations (Purdy 1996, 49). The availability of genetic technologies exacerbates these concerns. As information about the potential child's genetic status can now be obtained prior to birth, the consideration of selective termination in cases of the transmission of disability may be experienced as an obligation for women with genetic disabilities, rather than as a choice.

While such pressures exerted upon women with genetic disabilities can be understood as contributing to a denial of reproductive choices, it has also been argued that these women may, paradoxically, be in the best position to make informed decisions about the use of genetic technologies and selective termination, given their direct experience of the condition in question (Charo and Rothenberg 1994, 113; Asch 1999, 1652; Russell 1998, 49; Saxton 1999, 27). Indeed, accounts written by women with inheritable disabilities about their reproductive choices have emphasised the relevance and importance of their experience to their decision making but have also referenced the range of dilemmas and considerations that accompany such decisions (R. Atkinson 2008; Bowler 2006; Kent 2000, 61–62; Saxton 1984, 301).

I draw upon a study of sixty-one people with SMA in their family whom I interviewed as part of a larger research project in order to consider the role of experiential knowledge in reproductive decision making.[1] Out

---

1. Participants of the larger study were recruited through the main support group for SMA in the UK today, the Jennifer Trust, and the interviews were conducted either over the telephone, via email, or face-to-face depending on preferences of those who took part.

of the total number of interviews, twenty-one interviews were conducted with women with SMA themselves, who were between twenty-one and sixty-three years of age. I have selected three interviews for discussion here as they represent different standpoints and experiences in relation both to SMA and to reproduction. I focus on how women with genetic disabilities negotiate discourses of responsible motherhood and examine how these women experience discourses of maternal responsibility as both "felt" and "anticipated." I then move on to the ways in which they manage these discourses through the use of their experiential knowledge and claims to a privileged perspective on SMA.

INTERVIEWEES: ANNABELLA, LENA, RACHEL

To better understand the complexities of SMA and reproduction, one needs to know that SMA is a neuromuscular condition generally understood to have three different clinical subtypes, categorized by severity. Infants affected by type I SMA generally do not survive infancy because of impaired respiratory function, whereas individuals affected by types II, III, and IV can survive to adulthood and experience varying degrees of muscle weakness. The majority of people affected by type II SMA are never able to walk and have limited upper-body strength, whereas individuals affected by type III and IV may be able to walk up until adulthood but nevertheless experience generalized muscle weakness (Dubowitz 1995, 325).

This contextual information is of crucial importance when analyzing the nature and function of the women's experiences of SMA in relation to their reproductive decision making, as the level of their impairment as well as their standpoint in relation to reproduction formed the basis of their experiential knowledge as well as their perceptions of maternal responsibility. The three participants I selected for analysis experience

---

The interviews lasted between forty-five minutes and two hours (or between four weeks and five months for mail interviews). Interviews were transcribed verbatim and analyzed using a grounded-theory approach, which involved identifying emergent themes and issues (Glaser and Strauss 1967) with the aid of Nvivo qualitative data analysis software.

their impairment and disability in different ways and represent two of
the four types of SMA described above.

Annabella

Annabella is forty-two years old and has SMA Type III. She is able to
walk with assistance and lives with her husband and two adolescent children in the southwest of England. Annabella used to work full time, but
a health complaint unrelated to SMA has forced her to give up work. She
has a younger brother with Type II SMA.

Lena

Lena is twenty-six years old and has SMA Type III. She lives with her
husband in the north of England, works full time for a disability charity
and has been a full-time wheelchair user since her late teens. Lena has an
older sister who does not have SMA. Lena intends to become pregnant
within the next year.

Rachel

Rachel is thirty-two years old and has SMA Type II. She has never been
able to walk and has had periods of requiring night time ventilation. She
works full time as a teacher and lives with her full-time personal assistant
in the middle of England. Rachel's younger brother has Type III SMA.

SMA has had an impact on the lives of Annabella, Rachel, and Lena in
contrasting ways, and each has a different perspective on reproduction.
Annabella already has two children; Lena and her husband have made the
decision to try to become pregnant in the coming year, and Rachel would
like to have children at some unspecified time in the future. Extracts from
their three interviews demonstrate the ways in which these three women
negotiated discourses of responsibility alongside their experiences of
SMA. I argue that the women's experiences of SMA were crucial to the

way in which they thought through reproductive decisions and ultimately to the ways they both deflected and experienced accusations of parental irresponsibility. While the reality of living alongside a genetic disability was the primary reason these women felt that their ability to be mothers was called into question, these experiences also, paradoxically, formed the basis of their resistance to these discourses. Experiential knowledge provided the women with the means through which to negotiate and redefine the boundaries of maternal responsibility, suggesting that life with SMA can be understood as a positive experience and a positive resource for the challenge of parenting.

DISCOURSES OF MATERNAL RESPONSIBILITY AND REPRODUCTIVE DECISION MAKING

Throughout the women's interviews, there was evidence that they were acutely aware of discourses of maternal responsibility and applied them to their own circumstances. In their accounts, women divided reproductive decisions into those they considered "selfish" and those considered "unselfish," revealing that they negotiated these discourses when considering their own reproductive choices. They emphasized the moral value attached to placing a (potential) child's needs over and above their own. The women interviewed made frequent reference to the ways that their own (real or anticipated) reproductive decisions met the requirements of responsible motherhood, and they were keen to emphasize the morality of their own reproductive choices. For example, Annabella, who has SMA Type III and two adolescent children, made frequent reference to making reproductive choices for the "right" reasons:

> If you're making decisions about having children, you've got to make sure it's for the right reasons, you know, it's got to be in the best interests of the child. Every mother wants to see their child happy and healthy, and I suppose you've got to do everything to make sure that happens.

In the same way that Goffman ([1963] 1986, 57) has referenced the existence of both felt and enacted stigma, these women either anticipated or directly experienced the policing of the boundaries of maternal responsibility. By frequently demonstrating the way in which their decisions were responsible, the women interviewed were answering a felt or experienced accusation that as disabled mothers with genetic disabilities, they might be thought somehow irresponsible for having children. Even the women who had not directly encountered an accusation of parental irresponsibility for their reproductive decisions appeared acutely aware of their tacit accountability for such decisions and the negative evaluations of their disabilities embedded within them.

For Annabella, this accusation of irresponsibility did become vocalized, and thus directly experienced, shortly after she announced her engagement and hopes for future children to her friends and relatives:

> It was shortly after we'd got engaged and I was showing my ring to some of my mother's friends and one said, "well that's very nice, dear, but they won't allow *you* to get pregnant, will they?" and it was then that I started to think that people were having a really hard time imagining that I could ever be a mother. Because I've got SMA, I could never be mother material . . . and I suppose it was because they thought I could never look after one [a child] or that if I had one it would be like me, you know, that it would have my disability.

As Annabella's experience illustrates, her SMA disqualified her from being seen as "mother material" on assumptions that first she would be unable to provide adequate care for a child (owing to her own disability), and second that any child she would have would inevitably inherit her disability, which was presumed to be an unquestionably negative trait. As SMA is a recessively inherited condition (meaning that *both* parents must be carriers to produce an affected child), the chance of Annabella having a child with SMA would be medically defined as small; however, she felt that it was assumed that she would *automatically* pass on the condition to any child she would bear. Kallianes and Rubenfeld (1997, 209) have argued that these ideas form part of a broader social resistance to the idea of disabled women reproducing, which is underpinned by a "politics of eugenics" (Waxman 1993, 6). The idea that a woman with a genetic disability may knowingly reproduce and risk producing a child with the same disability as herself is understood to not only be a harm against the child (by inflicting an unnecessary disability) but also as a harm against society, which must then support that child throughout its life.

Although these women reiterated some notions of maternal responsibility, there was evidence in the interviews that they did not passively accept the judgments embedded within these discourses. Indeed, the women's very experiences of having a disability, the basis of their disqualification from the sphere of reproduction, could paradoxically be used by them to deflect and transform these discourses, altering the meaning of both motherhood and disability in positive ways.

EXPERIENTIAL KNOWLEDGE AND THE TRANSFORMATION OF MATERNAL RESPONSIBILITY

During the interviews, the women talked in depth about their experiences of growing up with SMA, and there was evidence that the knowledge acquired from living directly with SMA was considered to be a valuable resource, not only in relation to reproductive decision making, but also in managing day-to-day challenges. These women did not regard growing up with SMA in a society that does not always provide appropriate or adequate support for people with disabilities as a wholly negative experience. Instead, they noted many positive elements. As Annabella commented,

> I suppose in a way it's a gift to be born with a disability because you understand things and experience things that people, in a million years, wouldn't be able to understand and it enables you to see another side of people. You can understand so many levels, being discriminated against, knowing what that feels like, being in pain, not being able to do things. And you can say to people "yeah I know *exactly* how that feels."

What is particularly important about the way in which the women presented their experiences of SMA was that they conceptualized disability experience as producing a *bounded* form of knowledge. For Annabella, experiences of living her life with SMA enabled her to lay claim to a privileged perspective on life because of her particular disability. Experiential knowledge of SMA for Annabella was not something that could be transferred to another person simply by talking about it; it had to be lived through and experienced from the inside. By defining her knowledge of SMA as something inaccessible to "outsiders," Annabella was able to undermine the authority of others' judgments of her and to discount their standpoints on the basis that they could not be truly informed about what life with SMA was like.

The relevance of experiential knowledge to reproductive decision making has been widely emphasised by disability rights supporters, and more recently its consideration in genetic counseling has been proposed (Etchegary et al. 2008, 123). Writers such as Fletcher (2002, 27) have specifically called for more information about the lived realities of disability to be made available to prospective parents facing decisions about selective termination following fetal diagnosis. Disability-rights supporters deem that medical advice is overly focused on the complications associated with any given disability rather than the positive aspects of life that can be achieved by a person living with that disability. Indeed, websites such as AnSWeR use interviews and photography to address this perceived gap between medical representations of life with disability and the realities of people currently living with the conditions being screened for. For the interviewees, having direct knowledge about life with SMA provided them with a unique and exclusive resource with which to challenge and transform discourses surrounding disability and motherhood.

EXPERIENTIAL KNOWLEDGE AS EMBODIED KNOWLEDGE

Lena is in her twenties, has SMA Type III, and hopes to have children in the near future. For Lena and her husband, the process of undergoing genetic testing in preparation for childbearing was not a priority, despite it being strongly recommended to them by health-care professionals. Although Lena recognized that prenatal testing can offer benefits to some people, she felt that selective termination or PGD would not be an option to her in the event of her husband being found to be a carrier of SMA. For Lena, experiential knowledge of SMA was central to this decision:

I suppose actually in hindsight now, SMA's been a positive thing really. I think that a lot of sort of what I've done and what I've achieved have been hugely down to sort of having the personality to overcome the problems that have come along with SMA. Um I think when you sort of know your own experiences and when you think about having children and whether they will be affected by SMA, the way I look at it is, "well I've coped and I'm fine with everything" so, you know, it's not all bad. I mean there're always going to be a certain amount of people who feel it's irresponsible to bring in a child into the world knowing that they're going to be disabled or because you're disabled yourself, but they tend to be the people who have no experience of disability themselves, they don't know what it's like and it's just their perceptions . . . and that's just part of the harshness of life and I don't take a lot of notice of them.

By distinguishing between others' "perceptions" and her "own experiences" Lena was able to resist the discourse of responsibility that she felt others applied to her as a disabled mother and potentially the mother of a disabled child. Abel and Browner have referred to this form of experiential knowledge as "embodied knowledge" (1998, 310) as it encompasses an individual's subjective knowledge of their lives and their bodies. For Lena, defining her embodied knowledge of living with a genetic disability as being "not so bad" (or even positive retrospectively) enabled her to understand and represent her decision as responsible. SMA for her was not harmful or undesirable (as others may suggest), but a condition that instead instilled character and around which a happy and fulfilling life could be built.

As well as a positive image of what a person's life with SMA could be like, Lena also challenged the idea that someone with SMA would not be able adequately to parent a child, particularly a child with SMA, by drawing on her experiential knowledge:

I mean I think a child with SMA would be really lucky to have a parent with SMA really, because as someone with the same disability, you already know about the sorts of obstacles you're going to come across, getting into schools and the surgery . . . things like that, and you already know about how to get round them . . . you know where to look for help and support and you've already made those sacrifices in your life and live with the restrictions that can come with it. You don't get upset when you can't take your child on holiday because there's nowhere accessible, because you never had those holidays yourself, you know? So I just think I'd be a lot more confident and have a hell of a lot more insight than, say, an able-bodied parent who has a child with SMA, you know, who didn't even know what it was before the child was diagnosed.

Lena was aware that others might regard the decision to risk having a child with SMA as irresponsible. However, by drawing on her own life experiences, she was able to redefine the boundaries of parental responsibility and justify her own standpoint on parenting with SMA. Being in the privileged position of knowing SMA "from the inside," Lena felt that she had the authority to rewrite the discourses of responsibility, over and above those who might define her as "irresponsible."

Some women's experiences of SMA, however, rather than offering them reassurance about the life a child or parent might have with disability, instead served as a warning. Indeed, while Lena's experiential knowledge of SMA enabled her to redefine discourses of maternal responsibility and reproductive rights, Rachel's experiences of growing up with SMA and witnessing the sacrifices her parents made to support her led her to believe that her responsibility would be to prevent the birth of a child with the same disability. This was not because of her own negative life experiences; rather *because* she had had a positive experience growing up with SMA she felt that she would have a responsibility to provide the same level of support that her parents had provided for her:

At the end of the day, I wouldn't want to have a child that has the same disability as me. Not because I think their life isn't as valuable, or that they wouldn't have a decent quality of life, because they would, but I think that my parents could give me as normal a life as possible and I don't think that I could do that for a disabled child because of my own disability. My parents were able to do what they did for me *because* they were able bodied. That wouldn't be possible for me and a child with SMA to do together. So if I knew that I had a risk of having a child with SMA I would feel a bit irresponsible . . . to go ahead and have the child

. . . because I would want to know. I wouldn't want to risk that they would have SMA.

Rachel's firm belief that a child with SMA needs "two able-bodied parents putting the work in" and her subsequent desire to prevent any future children she may have from inheriting SMA, however, had to be negotiated alongside her belief that she would not feel able to terminate a pregnancy affected by disability.

> R: I don't think I'd abort a child because of a disability, but maybe that's because I have one. But I also don't think abortion should be ruled out either because if I were to have a child with a disability, I couldn't give them the life that I would want them to have. But I don't think I could do it.
> Interviewer: Why do you think that?
> R: Well, what would that say about life with SMA if I could do that [undergo termination for SMA]? It would just be the same as someone getting rid of me, wouldn't it?

Rachel's experiential knowledge served as a warning as to the physical work involved in raising a child with a disability, which she felt exceeded her abilities, but it also simultaneously identified her with the fetus diagnosed with SMA. A decision to terminate a pregnancy affected by SMA, therefore, would not only be a statement about her responsibility as a prospective mother, but also about the value placed on life with SMA, including her own life. Rather than simply offering her a resource with which to make sense of, and justify, her reproductive choices, therefore, Rachel's experiential knowledge introduced another level of complexity to her reproductive decision making. Through having SMA, Rachel's choice about having a child with the same disability was transformed from a personal one into a broader statement about "life with SMA." Writers on the issue of disability and selective termination have referred to this unease as the "expressivist objection" (Edwards 2004, 418): the idea that selective termination communicates a negative evaluation of the lives of people currently living with the condition (Asch 2000, 236). For Rachel, experiential knowledge of her disability, and her identification with it, meant that new and competing responsibilities complicated her repro-ductive choices, creating a situation that she felt could only be resolved by avoiding reproduction with someone who was a carrier of SMA. Rather than clarifying reproductive decisions, therefore, as in the case of Lena, Rachel's experiential knowledge led to the juggling of competing and con-tradictory discourses and the introduction of new forms of obligation.

CONCLUSION

These three women's accounts demonstrate the ways in which "insider knowledge" of a disability can be used to disrupt and redefine the dis-courses of responsibility that currently serve to exclude women with disabilities from the sphere of reproduction. Although these women experienced their disabilities in contrasting ways and arrived at different reproductive decisions, all three used their lived experiences of SMA in order to demonstrate their own reproductive responsibility, and further-more to deflect the critical talk of others, reaffirming the authority of those who live directly with SMA over and above the judgment of "outsiders." While these judgments could be experienced as "felt" or "anticipated," all of the women nevertheless were acutely aware of the negative ways in which their disabilities were perceived by wider society and thus how the decision knowingly to continue with a pregnancy affected by SMA could be defined as "irresponsible." The basis for their resistance to such dis-courses was the claim of a privileged perspective on SMA gained through living intimately with the condition. Indeed, highlighting the positive aspects of life with SMA enabled the women to understand and represent a hypothetical decision to continue with a pregnancy affected by SMA as both appropriate and responsible.

While experiential knowledge of SMA enabled the women who took part in my study to circumvent traditional discourses of responsibility, however, the reproductive choices they faced were also constrained by competing factors. Women with genetic disabilities may in fact experi-ence a perceived need or obligation to reaffirm the value of their own lives and the lives of those who share their disability (the expressivist objec-tion) by opting *not* to terminate affected pregnancies selectively. Although negative evaluations of life with disability may be used by prospective parents to justify selective termination, for women with privileged access to embodied knowledge of that particular disability, reproductive decisions are not grounded in *assumptions* about life with that disability, but on lived realities. If women with genetic disabilities view their own lives positively, it becomes harder for them to evaluate the life of any potential child affected by the same disability any differently. This evaluation poses fundamental challenges to the widely held belief that life with disability is a wholly negative experience, one best to be avoided, and that it can limit and constrain the reproductive choices women with disabilities feel able to make. Reproductive decisions made by women with genetic disabilities become transformed into political statements about life with that particular disability and the value attached to it.

Women with genetic disabilities may find themselves in a unique position in relation to reproduction. On the one hand, barriers to reproduction may be especially pronounced for them in the context of the increased acceptability of genetic technologies and the expectation that women with genetic disabilities *should* use them to prevent the transmission of their disability. Although prenatal screening decisions about terminating or continuing with a pregnancy may be made by prospective parents unfamiliar with life with disability, the women in this study suggested that their claim to a bounded, embodied, and intimate form of experiential knowledge of life with disability gave them a privileged perspective on such reproductive decisions. Their knowledge had the capacity to introduce new complexities and obligations to such decisions, but it also provided them with discursive pathways out of the negative evaluations of their reproductive decisions made by others and enabled them to challenge, in an extremely profound way, the assumption that disability is always, and fundamentally, a negative experience.

3

Stalking Grendel's Mother

Biomedicine and the Disciplining of the Deviant Body

TERRI BETH MILLER

In the ancient tale *Beowulf*, it is the monster's mother, rather than the monster itself, that is the hero's true nemesis. If Beowulf figures as the harbinger of a stable new sociality, the retreat from the nomadic tribalism of old, then Grendel's mother may be seen as his antithesis, the antisocial, antifoundational disruptor of communities. Grendel's mother is the source of heterodoxy, of aberrance and chaos. Her body breeds violation; it mocks pretensions to predictability and control. From it issue beings that explode the foundations of the society into which they come. Her greatest threat, however, is simply her fecundity, her capacity to produce endless variation, her flagrant rejection of the norm. Grendel's mother is profoundly difficult to kill, and Beowulf himself, that legendary warrior-king, nearly dies in the attempt to do so.

Today, scientific metanarratives, predicated upon reason and technological progress, have usurped the socializing function of ancient myth and legend. But the fear of Grendel's mother haunts us still. In a July 22, 1991, broadcast on Los Angeles's KFI Radio, talk show host Jane North ignited a controversy that would ultimately result in FCC charges of false reporting. The broadcast, according to the complaint, perpetuated numerous erroneous stereotypes as scientific fact. The topic under discussion on that July evening was whether Bree Walker, a respected local television anchor, had the right to carry her advanced pregnancy to term, despite having ectrodactyly, a congenital deformity of the hands and feet. The FCC would ultimately dismiss the case, and Walker, despite being compelled to resign her anchor position on the grounds that she had been rendered "too political" by these events, would go on to give birth to an ectrodactylic but healthy son. The debate elicited by the broadcast, however, brought to the fore long occluded issues concerning the reproductive rights of disabled women, the valuing and devaluing of so-called deviant bodies, and the social construction of parameters of the normal. Above all, the Walker/North controversy presaged a dilemma that has gained prominence in this age of seemingly requisite prenatal screening and ubiquitous selective abortion over, as Ruth Hubbard (2006, 93) so poignantly phrases it, "who should and who should not inhabit the world."

In this chapter I will examine practices of prenatal screening and diagnosis, reading these interventions as bound in a complex network of biomedical discourse and clinical intercessory praxis, in which contemporary modes of reproduction are increasingly imbricated in an aggressive effort at communal self-definition through a parsing of the boundaries of the "human." Within such a context, I argue, the ascendance of prenatal examination and intervention may well be understood as the coopting of the bodies of the pregnant woman and her fetus into a system of clinical discursive practices authorized solely for the regulation of bodies. Although naturalized and neutralized through the discourses of rationality and beneficence, such a system obscures what in reality is, as Foucault would have it, the subjugation of individuals through disciplinary processes. The intercessory practices of biomedicine render potentially deviant bodies docile through remediation or extermination, reifying an image of "normal" society by virtue of that which it disavows.

The regulatory norms, which undergird prenatal screening methods, are highlighted most poignantly when the body of the pregnant woman is itself "deviant." The outcry elicited by the specter of Walker's pregnancy offers an unusually pointed glimpse into often subterranean attitudes toward disabled sexuality and reproduction. These attitudes typically remain underground because the disabled are infrequently seen in the public eye and, when they do appear, it is rarely within the context of reproduction. As Abby Wilkerson notes in her essay, "Disability, Sex Radicalism, and Political Agency" (2002), issues of sexuality and reproduction typically are assumed irrelevant for the disabled individual, medical practitioners naturalizing this construct through such means as the failure to discuss birth control methods and disabled sexual function with their patients (34). Far more often than not, the discovery of parental genetic anomaly or fetal defect occurs within the walls of the examining room; because the bodies of many pregnant women give no outward sign of potential fetal anomaly, it is the pathologized discourse of the clinic that must textualize a woman's body and that of the fetus as deviant.[1] When the expectant mother already carries the signs of abnormality on her body, however, as in the case of Bree Walker, she does so within the context of a double transgression: the disabled pregnant woman exceeds cultural boundaries both in her corporeality and in the reality of her reproductive sexuality.

This refusal of disabled sexuality derives from an understanding of the deviant body as unstable, resistant to control, and infectious. The result is a complex binary that situates disabled women's sexuality, in particular, at one of two ends of a spectrum between wholesale asexuality and profligate promiscuity. The move to desexualize the disabled woman's body operates as a mechanism of containment and control, sanitizing a body that is always already textualized as volatile and contagious. Ascribing sexual respectability to only the most socially privileged in a society excludes the disabled from the realm of normal sexuality, thereby situating not only disabled sexuality, but also reproduction, within the domain of the deviant.

These views of disabled sexuality proceed in large measure from a fear of the potential fertility of the deviant body. Based not only in norms of able-bodiedness and cognitive fitness, but also in racist tropes of ethnic hygiene developed in the eighteenth and nineteenth centuries as a

---

1. I will abandon the use of quotations to denote problematic terminologies, such as "deviant," "anomalous," and "ab/normal," not because I wish to embrace or endorse standard usages of these terms, but merely to avoid a distracting cluttering of the page with such hedge signals. While this paper touches upon the contested histories of these terms, a more complete discussion of them is neither possible nor desirable here. I deploy these terms, therefore, in full recognition of their problematic nature, not without my own reservations regarding their use, but in the absence of any culturally recognized alternatives.

precursor to modern eugenics movements, this paradigm reads the body of the Other as a threat to established social norms by virtue of its capacity to propagate itself. Within this scheme, the devalued body possesses an almost infinite reproductive capacity. In his decision from the infamous 1927 *Buck v. Bell* case, in which the US Supreme Court ordered the sterilization of a developmentally disabled woman, Oliver Wendell Holmes characterized Carrie Buck and women like her as "those who already sap the strength of the State," arguing that, "in order to prevent our being swamped with incompetence, . . . [it] is better for all the world if . . . society can prevent those who are manifestly unfit from continuing their kind" (qtd. in Bowman, 1977, 125–26). In the face of such a perceived threat, practices such as forced sterilization, selective abortion, and euthanasia come to be seen as nothing less than a means of rescuing society from imminent ruin.

The proscription of reproductive choice by limiting sexual agency to those society privileges as normal in fact reflects an attempt at social self-definition through a form of communal boundary marking—only those deemed "fit" are approved to produce others like themselves. As Jackie Leach Scully (2002) has demonstrated, the construction of normality is always an act of interpretation, one based upon social constructions and paradigms of right action in the world: "Bodies, in the way we understand them, are not pre-given in some objective reality but are specific, variable and historically contingent constructions" (54). The "normal" body in ableist Western societies is based upon Enlightenment concepts of the autonomous, rational individual; such a body, according to this concept, is capable, productive, and independent. In its solidity, it is able to carry out the dictates of the reasonable mind, to conceive rational projects, and to bring them to fruition independently of others. In its self-actualizing capacity, the body is the perfect instrument of the well-ordered mind. As Cornell University's Laura Purdy notes in a letter advocating the selective termination of anomalous fetuses, "the primary reason we value health is because healthy persons enjoy a sense of well-being and are able to carry out plans normally" (qtd. in Walker et al., 1976, 31, emphasis added). For Purdy, as for countless others, the healthy body, and its functions, is inextricably linked to cultural concepts of the norm.

However, as disability theorists have shown, because this body does not and cannot exist outside of the coercive discourses that imagine it, the trope of the normal depends upon its binary Other, the deviant body, for its existence. The devaluing of the disabled body affirms a fallacy of disabled experience as intractably tragic in order to reinscribe the hegemonic cultural paradigms of an ableist society. This reified image of "abnormal" corporeality both creates and insists upon a singular ideal of "correct" embodiment as its antithesis. Thus, the abnormal becomes the means through which the normal defines itself, the normal operating as an illusory benchmark against which all members of society are measured. Foucault ([1975] 1999, 51) writes: "The norm . . . lays claim to power. . . . [I]t is an element on the basis of which a certain exercise of power is founded and legitimized. . . . [T]he norm brings with it a principle of both qualification and correction. The norm's function is not to exclude and reject. Rather, it is always linked to a positive technique of intervention and transformation, to a sort of normative project." In other words, this "normative project" depends upon the figure of the Other for its success. The objectification of bodies makes possible their classification according to this imagined standard of normality and legitimates and naturalizes biomedical strategies of examination and intervention, Foucault's methods of "qualification and correction."

The tyranny of the norm obtains in issues of reproduction insofar as the burden of responsibility falls upon expectant mothers to produce children who conform to the established ideal. This sense of responsibility, according to theorists as diverse as Marsha Saxton (2006, 111), Gail H. Landsman (1998, 80), and Rayna Rapp (1998, 46), has only intensified in the wake of technological advances that have rendered intervention or termination not only possible but expected. For Landsman, the birth of a disabled child operates socially as the delivery of "damaged goods" into a culture (77). Further, Shelley Tremain has adopted Foucauldian models of biopower as a framework through which to understand the increasing reliance on prenatal technologies. According to Tremain (2006b, 36), "biopower ensures that impairments are generated in utero." These screening technologies extend practices of subjugation, exclusion, and normalization by allowing surveillance and disciplining processes to occur before birth. As a result of clinical examination, the fetus is rendered simultaneously visible and (biomedically) describable. Indeed, the fetus's visibility makes such description possible because, as Foucault explains, "their visibility assures the hold of the power that is exercised over them" (1977, 187). He continues: "It is the fact of constantly being seen, that maintains the disciplined individual in his subjection [and] . . . holds [him] in a mechanism of objectification" (187).

For Tremain, the objectification of the fetal body activates the process of its subjugation through the trope of impairment. According to Tremain, impairment is a preeminently social construct, but one that has been naturalized not only in biomedical but also in cultural discourse (including the discourse of disability theory) as a biological descriptor. In this construct, Tremain reads prenatal diagnostic practices as a means of exercising power over the fetal body by naturalizing its supposed deviation from the norm.

Such a communal appropriation of reproductive praxis has a long-established history, and the discourse of childbirth is always already saturated with implications for the overall social well-being. Within this context, as has been noted, the birth of an anomalous child constitutes a social harm. Again, a quote from Purdy is telling here. She writes, "a society of healthy persons is apt to be more prosperous and satisfying to live in than would be a similar society of unhealthy ones" (qtd. in Walker et al., 1976, 31). This forging of a nexus between the health of the state and that of its citizens has a haunting precedent. As Ruth Hubbard (2006, 96) notes, such was also the language of Nazi Germany, where eugenic measures were conflated with health measures: "the people who designed these policies . . . looked on them as sanitary measures, required in this case to cure not individual patients but the collective—the Volk—of threats to its *health*" (emphasis added).

The seemingly dichotomous relationship between the autonomous Enlightenment subject and the collective *Volk* finds its link in pragmatic economies founded upon individual production. Various disability scholars, including most notably Lennard Davis (2006), have shown that the ascendance of the ideal of normalcy as the capacity for self-actualization seems to coincide with the birth of capitalistic industrial societies, in which the normal body came to be construed as the laboring body (Foucault 1977, 25–26). The discourse of disability as social burden is predicated upon a reading of deviant bodies as those that drain a society's finite resources. A 1925 genetics textbook supports this view, describing many physically and cognitively disabled individuals as "always on the border line of self-supporting existence and whose contribution to society is so small that the elimination of their stock would be beneficial" (Groce and Marks 2000, 819). As Susan Wendell notes in "Toward a Feminist Theory of Disability" (2006), the textualization of disability as unremittingly parasitic still prevails in the construction of resources-as-charity, which in turn places the disabled in a "double bind." She explains: "They have access to inadequate resources because they are unemployed or underemployed, and they are unemployed or underemployed because they lack the resources that would enable them to make their full contribution to society" (246). Such a formulation remains, Wendell argues, because it enables the continued denial of the socioeconomic factors that curtail disabled individuals' opportunities for economic, cultural, and political engagement. Once again, tropes of normality situate disabled disenfranchisement within the body of the individual.

In addition to its nationalist and socioeconomic derivations, tropes of normality also assume a great deal of their power from an intrinsic fear of the natural body. The image of the norm persists because the disavowal of the disabled body helps to occlude the lived reality of the "normal" body, with its inherent vulnerability to injury and illness, its ever-present capacity to join the ranks of the disabled, as well as its consistent failure to live up to the standards of correct embodiment. The vitriol with which the disabled experience is rejected, even to the point of an almost eugenics-like insistence upon controlled reproduction, reflects fear of the inherent instability of the human body, of its multiform nature, which not only engenders a plethora of genetic variations but which itself undergoes myriad transformations in the course of a single lifetime. Susan Wendell (2006, 250) describes the heroic tenor ascribed to medical practice in this culture in her assessment of doctors as "heroes of medicine," a role our culture projects onto them "because *we* want to believe that someone can always 'make it better.'" She continues: "As long as we cling to this belief, the patients who cannot be 'repaired'—the chronically ill, the disabled and the dying—will symbolize the failure of medicine and more, the failure of the Western scientific project to control nature. They will carry this stigma in medicine and in the culture as a whole" (250).

This process of stigmatization is redoubled in force when it occurs prenatally, as the fetus's status as a human being and a member of a family and social group has typically not yet been publicly validated. Into this void rush biomedical stratagems of intervention and containment. Practices of genetic screening and selective abortion, as advocated so vociferously in the Walker case, attempt to control for the intrinsic variability of the human body by asserting that, through the power of medical science, humanity has at last attained the ability to decide which corporeal manifestations are unacceptable and to intercede when it sees fit.

The debate over prenatal screening and selective abortion, now conducted in a context of what some bioethicists and disability theorists refer to as "genohype" (Holtzman, qtd. in Wilson, 2006, 70), the unquestioning faith in the potential of genetic medicine to identify and remediate (or eradicate) "undesirable" human conditions, extends a centuries-old Enlightenment-based discourse of the body as eminently describable, malleable, and containable through the inexorable march of scientific progress. In this paradigm, the disabled body comes to be read as anomalous at the core level of biology; it is textualized as a defect to be either corrected or exterminated through medical intervention. By situating reproduction squarely within the discourse of biomedicine, mothers and fetuses become the subjects of a "quality-control" orientation to childbirth (Rapp 1998, 46), exemplifying what Foucault (1977) has identified as the disciplining of the subject through the production of the "docile" body: this docile body is one that "may be subjected, used, *transformed, and improved*" (136, emphasis added).

Prenatal interventionist and rehabilitative strategies are becoming increasingly prevalent because aggressive processes of classification, remediation, and eradication may appear more easily accomplished and more readily justified than in circumstances of assisted suicide or medical neglect, for the former are read as occurring before the "undesirable event" (e.g., the birth of a "defective" human) has transpired. Advances in prenatal screening not only have enabled the detection of existing fetal anomalies but also, through genetic testing, have made possible the identification of as yet unmanifested defects. With few options for treatment, the fetus is usually aborted. Though records are typically not kept, Rapp's studies suggest that up to 95 percent of parents choose termination following a positive genetic diagnosis (1998, 62).

Indeed, the advent of sophisticated technologies of prenatal screening, combined with this growing reliance on selective abortion, have entangled women's reproductive decision making in a complex web of biomedical and sociopolitical discourses with which expectant mothers may have little experience and in which they likely exercise only limited autonomy. The issue of the right of women, disabled and nondisabled alike, to bear so-called "defective" children is imbricated in a social context that devalues and dehumanizes the disabled body through a process of biomedical appropriation. Prenatal screening techniques enable this process of appropriation by discursively reconstructing the fetal body according to the parameters of the medical model: the fetus ceases to be human, or at least a human *in potentia,* and becomes instead a "flawed genetic text" (Wilson 2006, 68), a recognized pattern of biological anomalies, a syndrome described in a medical journal.

The wholesale co-opting of the fetal body into the realm of clinical discourse constitutes a further example of Foucauldian discipline insofar as the fetal body is subsumed beneath discursive practices. Foucault describes this process as the introduction of "individuality into the field of writing," which occurs when an individual is made into a "case" through diagnosis (1977, 189). In this way, Foucault explains, "description (becomes) a means of control and a method of domination . . . the examination as the fixing, at once ritual and 'scientific' of individual differences" ([1975] 1999, 189–92). The pathologizing of any fetal body that cannot upon medical examination conform to probabilistic measures of the norm becomes, in Foucauldian terms, "a case." This distinction in turn enables that body to be absorbed into a sequence of diagnosis/(potential) termination, a process Garland-Thomson argues is "an aggressive intent to fix, regulate, or eradicate ostensibly deviant bodies . . . inviting the belief that life with a disability is intolerable" (2006, 264).

This conjoining of diagnosis and (potential) termination obtains even where the child is carried to term because clinical praxis typically demands that a parent consciously make the decision *not* to terminate once diagnosis has been made, often requiring mothers to waive their right to abortion in order to prevent lawsuits. In an interview with Larry King, Walker recalls her own experience of being called into the physician's office to "discuss the options" after an ultrasound revealed that her first child, a daughter, would also have ectrodactyly: "I looked at him thinking, 'This is a conversation that the medical community and the social science community had with women with disabilities that are congenital. There is an automatic conversation that you're going to be expected to choose abortion'" (B. Walker 2004). As Hubbard (2006, 100) notes, the requirement to waive one's right to an abortion legally once a positive diagnosis has occurred is in itself a coercive act, one that simultaneously isolates the mother. The medical community, as Davis notes (2006, 236–37), distances itself from the inevitably undesirable outcome that is the birth of a defective child and places the burden of responsibility squarely upon the mother's shoulders.

Moreover, diagnosis furthers the coercive and appropriative tendencies of prenatal intercession insofar as biomedicine's co-opting of the fetal body within discourses of pathology activates an estrangement of the fetus from its mother. This occurs because, as Foucault notes, hegemonic discourses are predicated upon the disjuncture between the expert and those upon whom the expert's knowledge/power operates (1977, 199). Within this paradigm, the expert alone has the capacity to comprehend—and command—the fetal body. The language of medicine enjoys the authority to name, measure, and interpret the body of the fetus for both the family and the community into which it may come. By incorporating the body of the fetus into medical discourse, the fetus loses its relational status as a potential member of a familial and social group and comes to be known solely by descriptors of the clinical, particularly those which accord with the diagnostic model. This diagnostic paradigm ignores the multiplicity of human subjectivity beyond the hospital room—the future child's place within its family, its community, its religious group, its nation—and situates the fetus solely within a practice of clinical surveillance and intercession.

In the presence of such a diagnostic label, tropes such as Garland-Thomson's "intolerab[ility] of disability" (2006, 264) activate a paradigm based upon the rights of the child not to be born burdened with a defect. The effect of this discourse, as Landsman (1998) notes, is the reification of the diagnosis/termination corollary. She explains, "the discourse of rights is increasingly applied to the fetus, often positioning it in an adversarial relationship to the pregnant woman and resulting in surveillance and regulation of women's bodies" (79). In addition, as Shelley Tremain (2006a) notes in her analysis of the political implications of sexual assignment surgery in the case of intersexed children, such "culturally condoned" practices naturalize the outcomes of normalization (190). In other words, "best interest" discourses conceal their aggressively prescriptive judgments by couching them within a framework of altruism and care.

Far more potent than the coercive potential of the discourse of biomedicine, however, is this capacity to naturalize the fetal/maternal estrangement that it actuates. The highly problematic model of objectivity and nondirection within which biomedicine operates occludes the profoundly regulatory nature of biomedicine's interpretive imperative. In the unequal relationship between clinical practitioners and patients and their families, the discourse of the clinic is highly privileged (Rapp 1988, 146, 150), and the readings it provides of the fetus's body often are paramount, particularly where there is a void of information in the mother's life on the lived reality of disability (Saxton 2006, 106). At this juncture, medical readings of disability assume preeminence and, as numerous studies have shown, such understandings, based primarily upon a biologically determined, diagnosis-oriented understanding of the fetus's future, advance a view of the child's life that is almost always inordinately grim (109). Thus, in the guise of choice, parents may be led to perceive selective abortion as the only alternative to accepting for their child the cruelty of a living death.

Despite biomedicine's increasing efforts to appropriate processes of reproduction and to subsume mothering practices within the discourse of the clinic, however, families of disabled fetuses and infants are learning to redefine disability beyond the parameters of the diagnostic label. According to Rapp and Ginsburg (2001, 534), this attempt at redefinition occurs, most fundamentally, as a process of extending existing understandings of kinship. For Rapp and Ginsburg, kinship exists primarily within the context of a preexisting familial narrative. The impending birth of a disabled child temporarily disrupts this narrative structure, and discourses of fetal pathology and the diagnosis/termination sequence have frequently stepped into this breach. Increasingly, though, families are learning to restructure the family narrative without recourse to diagnostic definitions. Further, such a redefinition, according to Landsman (1998, 82–83), frequently necessitates a two-stage process in which familial intervention vocally rejects clinical paradigms even as it demands the public recognition of the child's status as human. This recognition typically occurs in the context of honoring traditional rituals of childbirth—baby showers, homecoming receptions—which may be absent with the birth of a disabled child. Such acts of recognition are a means of validating the child as a contributing and valued member of a family and a community (85–86).

By redefining the boundaries of kinship, not only is the "anomalous" fetal body sanctioned, but also the experience of mothering a disabled child is vindicated. In the appropriative discourses that pathologize the fetus, the expectant mother may find herself estranged not only from her child but also from her own body. Disability theorists, particularly those rooted in phenomenology, have long described the ways in which clinical praxis estranges the patient from her embodied experience. Barbara Katz Rothman (1992) has identified the unique sense of loss and guilt that a woman undergoing selective abortion may experience: "What others had lost was a baby who was expected. What mothers lost was the baby they had" (S13). While for other members of the family and community the fetus did not yet exist as a human being until recognized experts had authorized it as such, for the expectant mother the corporeal reality of the child was already an undeniable and omnipresent fact. Cultural attitudes and clinical practices, however, conjoined to deny the lived experience of her body. By expanding the notion of kinship as advocated by Rapp and Ginsburg and by honoring the rituals of motherhood as proposed by Landsman, the harms perpetuated upon women by biomedicine's false discourse of choice and empowerment may be reversed, as the community, the family, and the clinic come to recognize the lived experience of a woman's body and validate the multiplicity of forms embodiment may take.

Such an expanding definition of kinship will likewise extend the boundaries of community, potentially paving the way for what Lennard Davis (2006) has identified as an ethics of care of the body that is founded on principles of, in Davis's terms, "dismodernism." Dismodernism, according to Davis, is an understanding of the body as contingent, vulnerable, incomplete, and interdependent (239). Disability theorists have frequently demonstrated that modernist concepts of the normal body belie the reality of human experience. Increasingly, these theorists, including Davis, have attempted to read feminist theory in order to remake a model of subjectivity that is based upon interdependence. Such a reformulation would have tremendous impact upon the selective abortion debate because paramount in the discussion of the termination of "defective" fetuses is the assessment of the extent to which the potential child is likely to place a burden upon its family and/or community. Because the Enlightenment trope of the autonomous self is itself a fallacy—every living human being at some point or another has depended and will again depend on other human beings—feminist and now disability theorists assert the need to revalue interdependence and to valorize a communal caregiving ethic. When dependence is acknowledged as a reality common to all human life, caregiving practices will no longer be disparaged and those being cared for will no longer be devalued or dehumanized (Garland-Thomson 2006, 265). Instead, these theorists argue, such a reformulation would bring about the kinds of social reforms, including increased assistance for the disabled and their care providers and improved accessibility in the community, that would refute the fallacy of the "norm" and validate the endless variations of human corporeality.

In the years since the radio controversy, Bree Walker has remained in the spotlight, continuing her decades-long advocacy for the disabled and appearing in various television series, including most notably her role as the ectrodactylic Sabina, the Scorpion Lady, on HBO's *Carnivale*. Her two children, Andrea and Aaron, both of whom share her condition, are now young adults, navigating a world not designed for embodiments such as theirs. But they are also active, vital, contributing members of a family, a community, a nation. And they are, in the final analysis, the children of a mother who did what thousands of mothers nationwide are learning to do when the right of their child to exist on this planet is called into question: raise a hue and cry and demand that that the dignity, the value, and the humanity of their children be acknowledged in no less certain terms than any other child who is brought with love and celebration into the embrace of a welcoming world. As for Grendel's mother: despite reports to the contrary, she is alive and well, presiding over her watery kingdom, that place of liminality and metamorphosis, of flux and flow. Despite science's best attempts to ferret her out, she remains elusive, undetectable by even the most sensitive of instruments. She is the unexpected event, the freak occurrence, the defier of all odds. The most potent of technologies is powerless to destroy her.

4

Uneasy Subjects

Disability, Feminism, and Abortion

CYNTHIA LEWIECKI-WILSON

Scene: A disability studies forum at Miami University in 2004. The room was filled to capacity with over 175 students, faculty, and staff spilling out the back doors. At the front, a panel of seven faculty and graduate students presented a short video on disability studies and disability activism and facilitated audience discussion. An older woman, a faculty member and mother of a disabled son, spoke from the floor. At the very back of the room a young man wearing a T-shirt sporting a Republican logo stood up and asked in a challenging voice: "What about abortion? Shouldn't all disability activists be pro-life? I have a little sister with Down syndrome, and I feel strongly that she has a right to live." Disquiet and unease filled the room—women seated in front turned in their seats to glare over their shoulders at this interloper, and a murmur of disapproval, not quite audible as words, filled the air. The woman continued to speak over his question without pause.

Perhaps no single issue intersects with disability and feminism more uneasily than the politics of abortion. As feminists, we champion the right to reproductive control. As disability studies scholars and activists, we analyze and work to change the attitudes, policies, and politics that stigmatize, discriminate, maintain barriers, or fail to provide adequate support for the disabled. The two roles exist in tension and even clash in the case of selective abortion. This scene illustrates our tendency to silence our discomfort.

Technoscience has produced a domain of genetic-reproductive knowledge and practices that regulate and shape women as subjects. Technologies of the self, such as birth control, genetic testing, and abortion, have been instrumental in constructing a more autonomous female subjectivity. These technologies are both products of scientific rationality and producers of it, enlarging the arena for exercising rational motherhood by saturating institutions, knowledge-formation, and decision-making with rational "choices" based on genetic information and technological intervention. In addition to science, public rhetorics of abortion overtly shape attitudes and actions through religious, legal, and popular exhortations, and also through silence.

Defined by Aristotle (1991, 36) as "the available means of persuasion," rhetoric presumes agents and motivated ends—its goal is to move an audience to a particular action or a reorientation of belief. From the admonitions of religious and political groups, to legal language and court rulings, to news coverage and everyday exchanges, the rhetorics of abortion circulate talk about women and disability, and these commonplace, embedded arguments exert their influence and wield power. As Sharon Crowley (2006) argues, rhetorical commonplaces are consequential, shaping and limiting how we may respond through the way that arguments are constructed and identities are understood. Commonplaces convey embedded beliefs about who merits civil rights, how far social responsibility extends, or what may be future possibilities. "Commonplaces are known to all who participate in the communal discourse in which they circulate, and because they are widely accepted, rhetors may use them as discursive sites from which to launch arguments that are not so likely to be met with general approval. . . . [However,] commonplaces are part of the discursive machinery that hides the flow of difference" (71).

Crowley argues that those in the liberal wing of civic debate have accepted binaries that separate the rational and emotional, public and private, fact and value. In their championing of rationalism, they have ceded the possibility of debating values and ethical actions to fundamentalists who are not shy about using emotions tied to single issues to argue on absolute and universal grounds. The young man posed his question, for example, as a binary choice, reinforced by the term *pro-life*, implying that if one is for abortion, one is against life for the disabled. Faced with the difficulty of explaining that disability activists can be both for the disabled and for abortion rights, many on our disability studies panel simply ignored him. We chose silence because, in truth, there are complications to holding these two views, complexities that would have made a short explanation difficult.

A fuller explanation must start by affirming that reproductive control has been a significant element in women's ability to secure individual rights—even while it is also important to note that women's rights also improve with access to education, food, health care, and paid labor (Shah 2010). Moreover, the availability of abortion is not always empowering for women. Abortion can be an instrument of state power (regulating the number of allowable births, for example) or of patriarchal power (pressuring women to select and carry to term only male fetuses). A greater array of reproductive technologies also increases demand for insuring the normativity of offspring. Knowledge gained through genetic sequencing and fetal imaging invites the pressure for self-policing. Cultural rhetorics of abortion circulate arguments about "the health of the fetus," "avoiding pain," or "reducing the burden of care," while genetic tests and counseling presuppose that some will choose to abort a fetus identified as "defective" as a rational health-care decision. Women who resist these medical procedures come to realize that the emphasis on "choice" can feel like coercion. As detailed by Felicity Boardman in "Negotiating Discourses of Maternal Responsibility" and Terri Beth Miller in "Stalking Grendel's Mother" (both chapters in this volume), women at risk for carrying disabled fetuses, whether or not they choose to go ahead with their pregnancies, often encounter hostility. Pregnant women have faced even more overt demands than merely self-policing to ensure normalcy or reduce risk. For example, there have been laws proposed that would make it a crime to select genetically for deafness (Bryan, Blankmeyer-Burke, and Emery 2006) and attempts, some successful, to criminalize pregnant women who are drug users (Boyd 2004).

Many disability advocates have argued that widespread negative attitudes toward disability are reproduced in the rhetoric of selective abortion and contribute to the stigmatizing and devaluing of people with disabilities, painting their lives as tragic or a burden on the nondisabled, or promoting the belief that to be disabled is to have a life not worth living. Disability scholars such as Ruth Hubbard (2006) and Marsha Saxton (1984, 1999, 2006) trace the connections between birth control, abortion, and eugenics and argue that today's genetic-technological regime, including prenatal screenings, imaging, genetic testing, IVF and embryo selection, as well as selective abortion, all contribute to the drive or dream of eliminating disability, and as such have a eugenic undercurrent. Shelley Tremain (2005) contends that notions of impairment and disability are actually constituted and materialized through technoscience practices, so that fetal testing and screening are technologies that produce disability where—in prebirth—they once did not exist. Tremain and others also argue that if genetic markers for queerness were found, then selective abortion would threaten fetuses so marked. Mark Sherry (2004, 772) concludes that "the threat of eugenics therefore hangs over queers and disabled people alike."

In contrast to feminist disability scholars, bioscience sociologist Nikolas Rose (2007, 69) disagrees with the view that contemporary reproductive technologies can be understood as a kind of new eugenics. Rose holds that only state policies of the 1920s, 1930s, and 1940s, aimed at policing and improving the stock of a nation's population and based on a now-outdated theory of the gene as a unit of inheritance, should properly be called "eugenic." Rose argues that what is now emerging is a contemporary "molecular biopolitics" (15), whose key concepts are the quest for individual perfection, continually improved vitality, and reduction of risk through molecular manipulation. He argues that the technosciences are producing "an innovative new ethics of biological citizenship and genetic responsibility. Our somatic, corporeal, neurochemical individuality now becomes a field of choice, prudence, and responsibility" (39–40). For Rose, technoscience is not an instrument of the state apparatus, not a political rationality, but an exercise of personal rationality in the era of the neoliberal subject, though he does not use this term. Indeed, Rose explicitly rejects political critique and even celebrates "the economies of vitality" (6), for instance, stating, "In the eugenic age, mental disorders were pathologies, a drain on a national economy. Today, they are vital opportunities for the creating of private profit and national economic growth" (209). He thus understands the newest biotechnologies as contributing to the emergence of the neoliberal subject and global markets.

As Lisa Duggan (2003) argues, neoliberalism emerged unevenly beginning in the 1970s and continued to the present to become the predominant American political philosophy—with its key ideas such as limited government, market discipline, competition, personal responsibility, privatizing of public institutions and issues, upward redistribution of resources, global competition, and neoimperialism. Its rhetoric "promotes the privatization of the costs of social reproduction, along with the care of human dependency needs, through personal responsibility exercised in the family and civil society—thus shifting costs from state agencies to individuals and households" (14). Neoliberal rhetoric uses, one could even say co-opts, cultural and identity politics, "organiz[ing] material and political life" through categories like race, class, gender, while "actively obscur[ing]" (3) the sociopolitical forces causing inequality, all the while celebrating multiculturalism as private equality.

Duggan's point about identity politics suggests why disability rights and abortion rights are not opposites, but together make up a tight and complex braid of intertwined issues enmeshing and constructing the liberal and neoliberal subject. Just as disability feminist critiques of selective abortion do not lead their proponents to antiabortion politics, as the young man in the opening scene seemed to wish, critiques of medical technologies do not lead the disabled to reject medicine. Both women and the disabled have come into view, have become visible and gained voice, through identity politics. Yet Duggan's critique suggests the political limits and tensions in claiming and gaining neoliberal subjectivity.

The fault lines and tensions in the laws affecting women and the disabled are discernable even in a brief review of late-twentieth-century US rulings related to reproductive rights and disability rights. Reproductive rights rulings helped establish liberal subjectivity for women, giving them a way toward achieving abstract disembodiment. While these rulings maintained some of the liberal welfare state's right to regulation, they widened the scope of privacy and located issues of embodiment within this zone, thus contributing to the neoliberal trend toward privatization.

Disability legislation also embeds tensions between the private and public spheres—for example, in the ADA's recognition of the need for public accommodations as a way to achieve individual rights—but it also reverses the trend toward privatizing the social supports for embodied differences.

SUBJECTIVITY AND EMBODIED DIFFERENCES

For many millennia, women occupied a position similar to that of the disabled. Both were disqualified from public citizenship and full rights by their bodily differences from the supposed "universal" and "able" male body, which itself was an idealized, abstract body (Dolmage and Lewiecki-Wilson 2010; I. Young 1990). A woman's ability to be in control of her reproduction allowed her for the first time in history to lay claim to abstract embodiment (i.e., not to have to be defined by the specifics of female embodiment, with all its messy dependencies and blurring of borders). Although a woman's access to the abstract universal subject position may not be complete and only partially achieved (and her class, race, and national membership have much to do with this), even a partially disembodied subjectivity gave her some distance from the disabled position.

In contrast, the disabled are by definition marked in some way as particularly embodied—deemed to have "special needs," individual conditions that render them nonabstract and vulnerable, dependent. As many in disability studies have pointed out, this view is the result of a fantasy of wholeness, an act of the nondisabled person's distancing and marking off of certain bodies as "not me," in the shoring up of an able-bodied, normative identity. Disability studies, instead, understands *disability* not as particular conditions or impairments in people—we all have those—but as arising from the relation of a body to its environment, as that relation is interpreted by culture. What constitutes a disability, then, is culturally and historically mediated and unstable, changing across cultures and time. Throughout an individual's life course, as well, human embodiment is unstable and shifting, with periods of vulnerability for all. Yet, denial and fear of vulnerability lead people to construct rigid lines between health and illness, able and disabled, the autonomous and the vulnerable, normal and abnormal. In the same way, although all people at some point in their lives are vulnerable and dependent, labeling women as essentially so and therefore as essentially different than men was both a founding move in the fantasy of the autonomous subject and a justification for women's inequality.

These two groups, women and the disabled, have experienced different forms of exclusion and oppression based on perceptions of bodily incapacity, but saying that is not to claim that these two "groups" (women and the disabled) are the same nor altogether separable. Women with disabilities benefit—that is, gain autonomous subjectivity—through access to reproductive control, just as nondisabled women do. Women who are pregnant and nursing experience embodied differences that need accommodation, as do people with disabilities, if only for a limited time. Overall, however, while the legal right to, and technologies of, reproductive control have brought real and important benefits to women, including disabled women, these practices can contribute to a culture of compulsory normality, an environment hostile to embodied differences.

SELF-OWNERSHIP THROUGH BODILY CONTROL

A woman's right to reproductive control over her own body is a technology of the self; these are, as Foucault (2006, 177) describes them, "technologies that permit individuals to effect, by their own means, a certain number of operations on their own bodies, their own souls, their own thoughts, their own conduct, and this in a manner so as to transform themselves, modify themselves, and to attain a certain state of perfection, happiness, purity, and supernatural power." It would not be far-fetched to claim that the rights to and availability of birth control, and its extension in abortion, were the defining technologies of self that enabled women to change their perceived status as biologically determined bodies marked by nature as inferior, weak, and needing protection to individual and free agents deserving inclusion on an increasingly equal footing with men in the last half of the twentieth century. In achieving individual rights, women abjected the vulnerable and contingent elements of female embodiment, and this exclusion enabled them to move from being a sign of nature to taking their place as citizens within culture (noncontingent abstract individuals who exert "choice").[1] By controlling their own fertility and spacing or forgoing pregnancy, women were able to mimic more closely the (illusionary) transcendent subject position of men (autonomous, needing little social support) and thereby gain access to work and careers. In the United States, the women's rights movement was not successful in passing the Equal Rights Amendment (ERA), but the more women adapted their subjectivities to seem more like those rewarded by the liberal market economy (a process of abstraction and disembodiment), the more successful they were in making inroads into this formerly excluded territory.

First proposed in 1923 by suffragist Alice Paul, the ERA, which sought to guarantee women equal treatment under the constitution, took almost fifty years to garner congressional support. In March 1972 the Senate and House of Representatives passed the ERA, initiating a ten-year, ultimately unsuccessful, effort at states' ratification. Just ten months later, in January 1973, the Supreme Court ruling in *Roe v. Wade* made abortion legal in the United States. The ERA, with its emphasis on "sameness" treatment, would have also contributed to the construction of women as abstract liberal subjects, but without specific language about embodied differences this constitutional amendment—if it had passed—would likely have led to Supreme Court rulings to sort out what constitutes "sameness." Meanwhile, abstracting embodiment seemed the way forward, and US feminists fought to overturn laws once on the books protecting pregnant women from the dangers of certain jobs on the grounds that such laws created inequality and pregnancy discrimination in the workplace and hindered women's advancement and equal pay.

In contrast, according to constitutional law expert Laurence H. Tribe (2008, 134), *Roe* asserted a "principle of self-ownership" and a zone of

---

1. My argument on abjection differs from one made by Tobin Siebers (2008, ch. 3), wherein he critiques Judith Butler's concept of abjection. Siebers argues that under Butler's theory disabled bodies living in pain are foreclosed and excluded as narrativizable subjects. He wishes, instead, to restore realism, to narrate and represent the impaired body for political effectiveness. Unlike Siebers, I am not arguing for better representation of identity politics (whether for the fetus or for the woman), but for a new politics and ethics of alliances and interdependency.

privacy that could not be intruded upon by the state without "compelling justification." In the 1992 Supreme Court decision reaffirming *Roe, Planned Parenthood of Southeastern Pennsylvania et al. v. Casey,* the majority opinion noted in upholding this precedent that "the ability of women to participate equally in the economic and social life of the Nation has been facilitated by their ability to control their reproductive lives." The outcome of increasing equality for women could thus be said to result from a law specific to a woman's particular embodiment, allowing her the freedom to terminate her pregnancy in the first two trimesters. But *Roe* also maintains the government's regulatory interest: "We, therefore, conclude that the right of personal privacy includes the abortion decision, but that this right is not unqualified and must be considered against important state interests in regulation." In short, *Roe* both addresses and privatizes a woman's unique embodiment and also asserts the state's right to regulate that embodiment. So while the right to reproductive self-control sidestepped the problem of trying to legislate sameness equality, it nevertheless enshrined tensions about the state's right to regulate "personal" decisions.

As Duggan notes (2003, 67), for a short period in the late 1970s and early 1980s, an alliance of activist feminists, the Reproductive Rights National Network, fought for access to abortions for poor women and against compulsory sterilization of women deemed "unfit," and advocated for lesbian women's rights to mother. However, this effort stalled in the more conservative 1980–90s. As neoliberal policies and values expanded in the Reagan years, popular feminism retreated to a narrower plea for individual equality and the right to compete. Instead of transforming the political landscape by advocating for and gaining widespread public assent for supporting human vulnerability—through such things as pregnancy leave; government support for prenatal care, delivery, and the period of nursing; child care; and universal health care—US women in the 1980s moved into the public world, more like abstract, Enlightenment and neoliberal subjects, by "privatizing" these needs.[2]

2. See Young (1995, 198): "The issue of a right to pregnancy and maternity leave, and the right to special treatment for nursing mothers, is highly controversial among feminists

ADA: INDIVIDUAL RIGHTS AND PUBLIC ACCOMMODATIONS

Whereas the Equal Rights Amendment for women died because enough states did not ratify it within the ten-year period, civil rights laws for the disabled were successfully passed in roughly the same period—the Rehabilitation Act of 1973, the Education for All Handicapped Children Act ([1970] 1974), the Individuals with Disabilities Education Act (IDEA) (1990), the Americans with Disabilities Act (ADA) (1990), and the Amendments to the ADA (2008)—although disability rights progress has not been a smooth march forward. Disability legislation has also been limited or complicated by Supreme Court rulings that narrowed definitions of disability, the reach of federal law, or the scope of redress. The ADA has brought many benefits to disabled Americans, but it also contains tensions—between sameness and difference equality, and individual rights and public accommodations. The goal of the ADA is to eliminate discrimination and provide "equal opportunity" in employment, housing, public transportation, and public accommodations. On the one hand, it presents disability as a social construction; it notes the social stigma against the disabled, does not blame the disabled themselves for their unequal treatment, and seeks remedies through public accommodation. In part, the law states:

> the continuing existence of unfair and unnecessary discrimination and prejudice denies people with disabilities the opportunity to compete on an equal basis and to pursue those opportunities for which our free society is justifiably famous, and costs the United States billions of dollars in unnecessary expenses resulting from dependency and nonproductivity. (ADA 2009)

On the other hand, the language and principles emphasize the rights of autonomous individuals to be treated equally so as to compete and cast "dependency" as burdensome and even un-American. Still, the ADA does acknowledge embodied differences.

---

today. . . . [T]he application of a principle of equal treatment on this issue has yielded results whose effects on women are at best ambiguous and at worst detrimental."

These two impulses—guaranteeing sameness of treatment or difference of treatment—have led to conflicting Supreme Court rulings. Anita Silvers (2006) argues that court rulings affirming sameness of treatment for disabled and nondisabled (equal civil rights) benefit the disabled more than those that consider the disabled as a vulnerable class needing special protections. Yet many millions of people with disabilities will not be able to work, even with increased accommodations, and will remain dependent on care and decisions at least in part made by others. Rather than "the opportunity to compete on an equal basis," these disabled "others" would benefit from a public culture supporting vulnerable embodiment and networks of interdependent care. In contrast to Silvers, Ruth O'Brien (2005, 2) argues that the ADA is potentially radical because it recognizes the differences of human needs. She argues that the ADA's philosophy could help "bridge the classic divide between individual rights and collective action," noting that labor laws promoted by unions have "not served women well" (5).

THE RHETORIC OF CHOICE

If women have not been served well by labor laws, neither have they— nor the disabled—been well served by "choice" rhetoric. "Choice" rhetoric does not acknowledge the tensions in reproductive rights and disability laws and instead offers a simple but seductive promise of control and mastery of embodiment. And "pro-choice" rhetoric actually helps to consolidate the opposite, antiabortion position by mirroring absolutism and individualism. As antiabortion advocates claim the rights of the fetus absolute, pro-choice supporters counter with arguments about the rights of the woman. The language of both sides construct her as a person with individual control over her body, and decision making as an exercise of individual will, rather than as a relative and contingent judgment—perhaps arrived at collectively—involving the balancing of interests of interrelated others.

With a visible interiority made possible by the sonogram's gaze, the pregnant woman's relation to self is increasingly an alienated relation to an interior "other," once hidden but now revealed. The fetal "subject" threatens to overshadow the thin framing substance of the mother's exterior subjectivity. So although technoscience bestows on her a greater ability today to shape her subjectivity through control of reproduction (she can opt out of childbearing or select or even design her offspring), it also pits two competing "subjects" against one another, both with dueling claims of autonomy and individual rights. This imaginary scene plays out a tug of war between competing "individuals," restaging the patriarchal ideology that feminists have criticized.

In place of dualisms ascendant in patriarchal and rationalist ideologies, such as mind and body, reason and emotion, postmodern feminists such as Margrit Shildrick question "the taken-for-granted stability of human bodies, the body that can be safely forgotten by the transcendent subject, [which] has flourished only in conditions of denial and exclusion. The erasure of maternal/corporeal origin, for example, that necessary move which has enabled the erection of a completed autogenic disembodied subject . . . relies on the notion of corporeal stasis, of a body that is fixed and transparent to the knowing gaze" (2002, 121). Severing the maternal/corporeal relatedness between self and other is an original foreclosure that founds the autonomous subject. In contrast, Shildrick proposes a feminist and disabled, postmodern notion of embodiment: "once, however, it is admitted that both social and biological bodies are not given, but exist only in the constant processes of historical transformation, then there are only hybrid bodies, vulnerable bodies, becoming-bodies, cyborg bodies; bodies, in other words, that always resist definition, both discursive and material" (121).

"Choice" rhetoric does not answer to this more fluid and interdependent concept of embodiment. It marks a retreat from civic debate about human interdependency and mutual responsibility for vulnerable embodiment. In addition, it deflects attention from the privileges of class and race. While only those of a certain class and level of wealth have choices, the rhetoric of choice does its work—it contributes to the ascendancy of private sphere politics and antidemocratic policies and may even foster a racist imaginary, in which people of color are believed to be bankrupting the country by seeking public services. As Patricia Hill Collins (1998, 35) argues, a "new politics of containment" is driven by a reversal of the idea of the public sphere. "Public places," Collins writes, are seen as "devalued spaces containing poor people, African-Americans, and anyone else who cannot afford to escape," while "privacy signals safety, control over one's home, family, and community space."

As a result, "choice" functions positively only for some citizens. The poor and disabled have few or no choices, but depend upon the increasingly meager social services of the public sphere. They are more likely to live in public housing and, and if they have access to health care at all, to rely on public clinics. Private health plans compete and fend off universal national health care by advertising benefits such as the right to choose one's doctor. Whereas upper-middle-class women can opt to have technoscientific interventions such as embryo selection or embryo reduction paid for by private insurance, or can discreetly get morning-after medications from pharmacists, the poor with no coverage rely on (fewer and fewer) abortion clinics, where they face picket lines and in some cases unsanitary conditions. Indeed, high-priced technoscientific interventions have succeeded in becoming largely disidentified with abortion, which seems more and more equated with poor women. This is doubly ironic because, since the 1976 Hyde amendment, public monies cannot be used for abortion. Not only do state Medicaid programs, upon which many disabled depend, not fund abortions, but they have also cut the availability of life-preserving services for disabled people while promoting end-of-life directives for them. Indeed, the furor raised by Sarah Palin and other right-to-life conservatives over "death panels" during the health care debates of 2009 has some, albeit small, basis in that state Medicaid programs have declined to provide life-sustaining treatment for people with severe disability, and many forcefully push end of life directives on their clients, using rhetoric that frames the obvious correct "choice" as making the decision to decline "extraordinary" care. In sum, the idea that there can be a free "choice" is in reality a fiction for the poor and disabled.

Disabled people also lack privacy and often have their personal matters decided by social agencies. As Tobin Siebers (2008) reminds us, the disabled, often dependent upon attendants for bodily care and leading all too public lives in group homes, have little access to the kind of privacy that provides space for a sexual life. Historically, the disabled did not even have the right to sexuality or reproductive rights. And although they may no longer be sterilized against their wills, as laws once permitted in thirty-three states until the mid-1970s (Lombardo 2011), women and men with disability today still struggle to assert the right to parent or to retain parental rights, especially when the disabled parent is poor and relying on public social services.

In contrast, post-*Roe* middle- and upper-middle-class heterosexual Americans have their interests defined in terms of the private sphere—freedom from government intrusion. The set of laws and court rulings supporting sexual freedoms—the right to engage in consenting adult sexual acts, the right to obtain birth control, and the right to undergo an abortion—grounded in the concept of a zone of privacy, of freedom from intrusion into personal matters, applies to heterosexuals only, however. *Roe* specifically excluded privacy protection to lesbians and gays. "Compulsory heterosexuality," as Robert McRuer (2006, 31) argues, "is intertwined with compulsory able-bodiedness." Both systems work to reinforce the dominance and naturalization of the "normal" as the way things ought to be and the people who rightfully ought to be privileged.

It may appear that only antiabortion rhetoric is antifeminist and antimodern,[3] urging a return to circumscribed biologically determined roles for women, yet pro-choice rhetoric, rulings, and practices also contribute to the consolidation of normality, a narrowing of possible subjectivities, and the devaluation and even erasure of queer and disabled bodies. In short, although I support the right of women to control their own reproduction, I was tempted to agree with the young man at the disability forum. If I could have fully developed my thinking then and there, I might have said that the discourses and practices of technoscience and the rhetorics of abortion shape neoliberal subjectivity by enforcing normative and competitive individualism. Especially by keeping public argument focused on the competing subjectivity of woman *versus* fetus,

3. In this chapter I purposely have not examined antiabortion rhetoric because I presume its antifeminist position is understood. I would add that "pro-life" positions are not necessarily pro-disabled, but that is a larger argument than the scope of this chapter allows.

debates about abortion conceal through this repetition the contradictions in and possible openings for changing the neoliberal system that we are currently exporting to the entire world. But I don't think this reply would have made him happy either.

BUILDING NETWORKS OF INTERDEPENDENCY

If, as Shildrick writes (2002, 121), "biological bodies are not given, but exist only in the constant processes of historical transformation," then there is hope that in changing economic, political, and ethical human systems, we also usher in new understandings of embodiment, so that the "rational" choice would no longer seem to be the elimination of nonnormative bodies. Disabled bodies, hybrid prosthetic bodies, and the mother/fetal dyad could be valued and supported in a network of interdependent relations. As Anita Silvers and Leslie Pickering Francis (2005, 45) argue, caring for those in society who cannot contribute to autonomous exchange relationships (e.g., infants, the ill and disabled, the aged) contributes to a wider social good because care builds what they call "trust relationships," and the flourishing of "trust relationships," they argue, creates "a climate of general confidence in the comprehensive embrace of justice."

While the direction for mainstream feminists has been to repudiate the vulnerable body and valorize independent agency, to downplay interrelatedness and responsibility to one another, and thus to dis-identify with the vulnerable and contingent body, whether the embodied duality of mother and child or the body needing prostheses, attendants, feeding tubes, or life-support systems, the challenge today is to think otherwise, constructing new rhetorics of interdependent embodiment and social responsibility that foster diverse freedoms, embrace difference, and promote justice.

Instead of rational argument, with its retreat from debates about values, Crowley (2006) recommends rhetorical argument, in which claims are not based on a universal, rational ground but on an ethical preference. Rhetorical argument is about proposing values, persuading others about values, and finding rhetorical resources for creating motivation to mutual action or goals, even out of disparate values and goals. Rhetorical argument is not about finding common ground but about forging alliances for a particular purpose at a particular time. So it does not erase differences but seeks to understand and articulate the intersections of difference that might be mobilized for a particular purpose.

Without making disability or feminism transcendent categories, I believe a critical awareness of their intersecting interests can promote these goals. "What we might call a critically disabled position," McRuer (2006, 30) writes, "would call attention to the ways in which the disability rights movement and disability studies have resisted the demands of compulsory able-bodiedness and have demanded access to a newly imagined and newly configured public sphere where full participation is not contingent on an able body." In rejecting compulsory able-bodiedness, the challenge forward is not to reject technoscience, nor to reinstate compulsory motherhood, nor tie an ethic of care to female subjectivity alone, but to build, instead, a global ethic of and commitment to mutual interdependence, social justice, and personal possibility.

PART TWO

Refusals

Contesting Diagnoses and Cultural Scripts

The four essays of part 2 address and resist the power of stock stories—for example, cultural scripts about who should mother or how one must mother, or medical diagnoses that may or may not result in helping the disabled. Each author counters the narrative power embedded in these cultural scripts with her own narrative, challenging biases against women with disability having children, offering alternative ways of mothering, and calling into question the familiar themes of strength, able-bodiedness, and discipline-as-care in medical discourses. Collectively, these counternarratives speak powerfully about the ways that cultural attitudes and practices enforce identities, and they also demonstrate that it is possible to develop one's agency in resistance to such formations.

In "'What Does It Matter?' A Meditation on the Social Positioning of Disability and Motherhood," Samantha Walsh recounts her dialogue with another woman wherein her visible disability is assumed as an inevitable and insurmountable obstacle to bearing or parenting children. Although Walsh does not desire children at this moment, she wants to protect her right to choose. As she confronts such stigmas against disabled women, she argues for the right of women with disability to parent and also challenges metanarratives of motherhood and personhood.

Kristin Lindgren's account of giving birth and mothering with chronic illness both offers a critique of mothering practices and voices a hope for an alternative model of parenting.

In "Reconceiving Motherhood," she makes visible the extent to which common cultural perceptions and daily routines of mothering emphasize health, strength, and agility as necessary prerequisites for successful parenting. In contrast, she describes her own experiences bearing and raising two children with her husband. Lindgren proposes an alternative model of parenting and a set of "embodied practices of care," which she hopes will open up new conversations about both disability and motherhood.

In "Refusing Diagnosis: Mother-Daughter Agency in Confronting Psychiatric Rhetoric," Abby Wilkerson identifies the tensions between cultural pressures to socialize children and discipline their bodies and minds, and parents' efforts and desires to avoid imposing normativity or stigma on them. Wilkerson recounts a period when her daughter was hospitalized for psychiatric treatment and details how the medical diagnosis of her daughter's mental well-being was weighted with cultural and social prescriptions about her behavior and appearance. Wilkerson contends that advocating for a child may mean rejecting treatment in order to resist the compulsory able-bodiedness that can harm a child, and she argues that parents must be permitted to participate fully in medical decisions.

In "Diagnosable," Julia Miele Rodas explores the complexities attendant to life at the margins of disability. For Rodas, the choice to occupy this border space emerges as a result of competing concerns about her independence, her identity, her ability to act collectively and to agitate for change, and a responsibility to herself, her children, and others in the community. Throughout this chapter, Rodas reflects on her self-described "ambiguity," both acknowledging and contesting a range of perceptions on the merits and drawbacks of seeking a diagnosis as disabled.

5

"What Does It Matter?"

A Meditation on the Social Positioning of Disability and Motherhood

SAMANTHA WALSH

"*Listen, you don't want kids anyway, so what does it matter?*"

There was a conversation-ending silence as these words tumbled out of the mouth of the woman painting my nails on a bright Saturday morning at a local spa.[1]

We had run out of things to talk about. In an effort to keep the conversation going, I simply brought up the fact that my friend who, like me, has no children at present and still considers herself one, depending on the day—my friend who is young and has not yet started a career—my friend who lacks financial and material resources—is pregnant. She and I share the same inherent sense that we lack the life experience, knowledge, and wisdom to raise a baby, but we differ in our desire to have children in the future. I do not see myself as being a mother because currently mothering is not something I feel compelled to "do." In bringing up the subject of my friend's motherhood to the esthetician, I expected that we would whimsically discuss the joy and anxiety experienced in preparing for the birth of the baby. I, being without child, assumed that we would talk about hypothetical baby names, or the experience of raising a child and what I imagined it would (or would not) be like.

---

1. In the interest of protecting the identity of those involved, the setting and beauty service provided has been changed.

Throughout my visit, the woman painting my nails and I did discuss what it would be like for me to raise a child, but not in the sentimental way I had expected. The conversation almost instantly turned into a discussion of how I would manage in "my condition." I am visibly disabled, receiving my manicure from the comfort and style of my wheelchair. The woman very factually informed me of the mayhem that would ensue should I give birth. She conceded that my mother or some other person would have to take care of a child for me.[2] I quickly became agitated at the thought of my disability being a master status that would bar me from motherhood.[3] I protested. Her response came in a tone sounding only the alarm of having upset a customer, rather than any concern that she had oversimplified a complex and deeply personal issue. She stated, "There are just some things you can't handle. Listen, you don't want kids anyway, so what does it matter?"

What does it matter . . . indeed? Although the dialogue was short, what the conversation produced socially was the understanding that disability is not something that should intersect with the experience of motherhood. My relationship to motherhood is framed by my experiences as a young disabled woman, a scholar and activist, and as someone contemplating her own fertility. I find myself caught between the demands of my culture and my interpretation of those demands. It seems as though I must perform the intersectionality between my gender and disability; for example, I feel compelled to have children to prove my capacity and capability as mother. However, I do not currently understand myself as having a profound need or desire to have children. It is this tension between my lived narrative and my sense of obligation to confront the commonsense

2. In saying that my mother or some other person would have to take care of the baby, the esthetician was assuming that I would have to be removed from any role of parenting. She was not suggesting that parenting would be taken up in community with my mother and other people around me.

3. William Hughes coined the term "master status" in 1945. The term is used to describe the phenomenon of one person being understood as completely defined through one social identity (Curra 2000, 26). For further discussion of master status as it relates to disability see Albrecht, Fitzpatrick, and Scrimshaw (2003, 301).

understanding of the intersectionality of my identity as a disabled woman that unsettles me; it is this tension and the manifestation of it in the conversation above that provides the opportunity to interrogate and reflect on motherhood and disability from my social location.

The esthetician's belief that motherhood and disability could not exist together was revealed through our conversation in the nail salon; in the short time I was there it quickly became obvious that their mutual exclusivity was to her a self-evident fact. Our discussion made me wonder: what it is about disability that unsettles conceptions of motherhood within contemporary culture? Furthermore, what is it about the inference that I would not be able to be a mother (despite not wanting a child to begin with) that I find so unsettling? To explore these questions one needs to think about how we culturally take up disability, personhood, and what it is to be a woman and a mother.

According to Rod Michalko (2002, 69), in contemporary culture disability is defined as something that renders life unworthy or inferior and becomes situated as the antithesis of normal. Disability, Michalko notes, is something that must be silenced as a way of masking the unnatural "nature" of normalcy, a socially constructed concept. Disability becomes something that is kept far away, overcome, or removed. Michalko points this out by discussing how disability is situated in language. He says, "In fact such people, 'normals' [people not identified as disabled], often say, 'I don't even think of you as disabled,' or, 'You know, I sometimes don't even notice her disability.' And visibly disabled people, themselves, tacitly acknowledge their disability, often saying things like, 'I am a person, just like you. Treat me as a person.'"

These examples of the "treat me as a person" remark illustrate the sense that disability negates personhood. Tanya Titchkosky (2003) also comments on the presumed need for person-first language ("person with a disability"), which illustrates the commonsense understanding of disability as something gone wrong. She notes that this narrow perception of disability as something gone wrong, without an analysis of disabling cultural or social factors, allows for a version of disability—understood as erasing personhood—to permeate contemporary culture. She writes, "Representing disability as something arising from biological abnormality, organic misfunction, or bodily inability, restriction, and limitation consequently leads to, and is based upon, the assumption that disability is an individual incapacity—an inability to do things" (15). Titchkoksy acknowledges that disabled people "do not do some things in the ways that non-disabled people do, or may not do some things at all," but also insists that, "disability highlights how things are 'normally' done [and] the background expectancies that order this doing in a culture" (15). Furthermore, she notes, the fact that people with disabilities must constantly remind others that they are people first "highlights the sorry state of affairs of living in a culture whose conception of people is such that 'disabled people' do not quite fit, and the contrary thus remains something of which others need to be reminded" (24). For Titchkoksy, even this reminder—embedded in phrases like "persons with disabilities"—has consequences, for it suggests that disability and personhood or the self can be isolated from one another (24).

There is a cultural need to separate disability as a way to preserve or create personhood. According to this cultural understanding, disability is something that inhibits my personhood, so much so that I cannot model what it is to be a person to another person. My conversation with the salon worker serves as a microcosm for the cultural understanding of disability—disability is never understood as intersecting with, or in this case shaping and molding, the way in which I would mother. Herein lies the reason the inference that I as a disabled woman could not mother matters to me, despite the fact that I do not currently want children. The sense that I could not mother because of my disability suggests that disability somehow negates the validity of my personhood. Motherhood is understood culturally as the central performative act of being a woman and reaffirming life. For me there is something disturbing about the inference that I cannot mother. I feel it is an inference that shakes the foundation of my personhood. As a disabled woman I want disability to be treated not as something that occasionally disturbs the "normative" order of things, but rather, as something that is taken up as a valid way of being in the world. I want disability to be treated not as something that negates personhood but as something existing within in it.

In "Sex and Death and the Crippled Body: A Meditation," Nancy Mairs (2002) illustrates the societal divide between disability and motherhood.

Mairs uses the example of her able-bodied daughter, who is in her twenties and conceiving a child using fertility drugs. This conception is considered to be a joyous occasion and a testament to the positive use of medical technology. She acknowledges that infertility is a problem in and of itself but questions if she would be met with the same joyous response if her daughter had cerebral palsy.[4] Furthermore, she questions whether or not her daughter (if disabled) would even be allowed the resources to conceive. Mairs contends that "disabled women might have an easier time finding someone to help them end their lives; lives assumed by their very nature to lack quality, than enlisting the corps of medical personnel required to resolve my daughter's infertility" (160). Mairs elaborates her point,

> No one ever questioned the appropriateness of [her daughter] Anne's desire for a baby. In fact she'd have raised more eyebrows had she chosen not to reproduce. Suppose, however, that she was exactly the same woman except with cerebral palsy. Would the nurse practitioners and doctors who consider Anne's inability to conceive a treatable problem and muster their arsenal of scopes and dyes and hormones and catheters be just as eager to rush to her aid? I have my doubts. Her infertility might even be viewed as a blessing. (160)

Mairs illustrates the social tension experienced by disabled women, using the example of access to reproductive technology as well as being acknowledged as a valid candidate for motherhood. The use of this example is poignant to the discussion of disabled women and motherhood. Motherhood is understood as a hallmark of being a woman. For the disabled woman to be excluded from this hallmark of womanhood brings into question her social location as a woman. Is she socially understood as being a "real" woman? Irony and tension again rear their heads as disabled women struggle to be understood as entitled to the opportunity of motherhood. On the other hand, other able-bodied women (or more accurately, women perceived as able-bodied) may struggle to be understood

---

4. CP is a medical name for a type of disabled embodiment (ironically, the condition I identify as having).

as women despite not being and/or not wanting to be mothers. The tension becomes a struggle to reaffirm one's personhood and to qualify in the expected enactment of gender.[5]

This tension is manifest in my outrage at the inference that I could not mother. I want to have control over my body, I want to perform my gender, and I want to partake in the rituals and decisions that mark the passages of life within North American culture. The notion of control, gender performance, and the hallmarks of rights of passage could all be points of discussion unto themselves; they are all important elements of my participation in society. It is through this desire that I am able to identify with disabled scholar Anne Finger as she recalls when she ceased taking birth control and eventually conceived a child after reading a "devastating" medical report on what her life as a disabled person would eventually become. She reflects on the "accidental" conception saying, "I wanted to make myself anew. I needed to have control over my body: Instead of letting it grow more frail, letting it lose its power, I wanted to make it grow, to do more not less. I wanted my power to be *physical*" (Finger 1990, 18).

While Finger wishes to maintain and create a physical power, I relate to Finger's need to have control, produce power, and create herself anew. I want my body to be culturally perceived as valid the same way that Mairs's able-bodied daughter experienced her body. I want my body to have "power" in the sense that I want to struggle with cultural rights of passage such as childbirth. I want to struggle with those choices embraced *in* my body, not through the separation of myself from my body, not in the erasure of the "disabledness" of my body, but with it. I want my body to have that power of choice, of discernment, of experience.

I, like Finger, also want to create myself anew, but not in the literal sense; I want to be understood through a new cultural lens. I want disability and its relationship to motherhood to be understood differently. I want the casual conversation about my hypothetical child to embrace and be reflexive of my embodiment. I want the very idea of disability and

5. This discussion on the performance of gender is animated by the work of Judith Butler's *Gender Trouble* (1990b).

motherhood to be used as an occasion to delight in rethinking how we as a culture understand disability and motherhood. Rather than uttering the words, "Well . . . there are some things you just can't handle," "I don't know, . . . listen you don't want kids anyway, right? So it doesn't matter," we, as a culture, need to have conversations about what it is to mother (have children) and why we want or do not want to mother. These questions and conversations matter regardless of one's own intentions to mother. They are questions that should be posed not only to individuals but also to our collective culture.

6

Reconceiving Motherhood

KRISTIN LINDGREN

In September 2005, a twelve-foot-high marble statue entitled *Alison Lapper Pregnant* was installed temporarily on the fourth plinth in Trafalgar Square, joining permanent statues of Admiral Nelson, King George IV, and two generals. This statue, by the British artist Marc Quinn, shows a naked, pregnant woman with no arms and shortened legs. It began as a life-sized sculpture Quinn created from a body cast of his friend Lapper, herself an artist, when she was eight-and-a-half months pregnant. The larger work—thirteen tons of Carrera marble—was commissioned by a committee charged with selecting a series of artworks to be displayed on a rotating basis on the fourth plinth. The public debate about the statue revolved in part around whether this representation of Lapper belonged in the company of naval heroes and generals. In *The Guardian*, Brendan O'Neill (2007) opined that the statue celebrates "the distortion wrought by nature on a woman's body rather than of that woman's contributions to public life and society . . . [it] celebrates what nature, in all its arbitrariness, does to humans rather than what we do to shape, lead and transform the world around us." The editor of the *British Art Journal* called it a "repellant artifact;" another critic declared that "Trafalgar Square should be a place where men who have served their country should be honored" (Lyall 2005). Other commentators saw the work as a Venus de Milo for our times, a contemporary reinterpretation of public statuary and an overdue recognition of the beauty of disabled bodies.

The lively conversations that followed the statue's unveiling—conversations that took place on blogs and listservs as well as in traditional media—echoed cultural debates about the proper subjects for art, such as the debate spawned by the *Sensation* exhibition at the Brooklyn Museum of Art in 1999, in which another of Quinn's works was displayed. They also recalled recent debates that had no obvious connection to the arts, such as those about breastfeeding in public places and about reproductive and adoptive rights for women with disabilities. And they gestured back to much older debates about private and public spheres. Ultimately, these conversations raised the question of whether in the twenty-first century disability, pregnancy, and motherhood can be seen not only as acts of nature but also as acts of culture, embodied practices that might, in O'Neill's words, "shape, lead, and transform the world."

An article about Quinn's statue in *The New York Times* was accompanied by a striking photo of the statue and another one of Lapper herself with the statue in the distance. In this photo, Lapper's five-year-old son is leaning against her, half-sitting on her lap, both of them supported by her wheelchair. The photo is less artful and less sensational than the statue, but in some respects it is just as striking. It captures, framed by the very public space of Trafalgar Square, both an outsized representation of a disabled mother-to-be and, in the foreground, the mother herself, cheek-to-cheek with her son. Looking at these photos, and reading the *Times* article and other coverage of the statue's unveiling, I was first of all engaged by conversations about the relationship between art, public monuments, and disability. But I also wanted to know more about one of the stories behind the statue, the story of Lapper's pregnancy and motherhood. I had some very basic questions: How did she change diapers? What kind of personal assistance and childcare arrangements did she have? Did she and her son, doing errands, living their lives, attract as much attention as the statue?

I have a private stake both in Lapper's story and in these public debates surrounding the statue. As a disabled mother of two sons, I daily confront preconceptions, including my own, about disability and motherhood. Because my disability is invisible, my maternity does not challenge aesthetic standards or cultural mores in the way that Quinn's statue and Lapper herself do. Invisibility does, however, challenge assumptions about disability. Both disability and motherhood are often marked and validated by their visibility—the missing limb or uneven gait as evidence of disability, the swollen belly or toddling child as evidence of impend-ing or actual motherhood. Without visible, bodily proof of either state, we're subject to claims of fraud. The accessible-parking sticker and the paperwork preceding adoption don't carry the same persuasive force. Yet when disability and maternity register visibly in the same body, they sometimes create a visual and cognitive dissonance, as if one can be either a mother or a disabled person—not both at once. The writer Denise Sherer Jacobson, who has cerebral palsy, describes the looks of amazement she encountered when she was out and about with her infant son, David. One elderly man approached her apologetically, saying: "Excuse me, I know I'm staring . . . I've certainly seen a wheelchair before, and I've certainly seen a baby before. But I've never seen the two of them together. You've just made my day" (Jacobson 1999, 133). The reactions to *Alison Lapper Pregnant*, both negative and positive, register a similar amazement. In contrast, when disability is largely invisible, visible evidence of maternity often trumps signs of disability, and the generally positive cultural asso-ciations with motherhood often neutralize the generally negative associa-tions with disability. This process makes it hard to be seen—and hard to see oneself—as a disabled mother. The spectacular visibility of Lapper's pregnant, armless body, jarring to many, was fascinating to me.

I had never imagined myself as a disabled mother. When I became pregnant with my first child, I was healthy and nondisabled. In the early months of parenting, the fatigue from interrupted nights was so mixed up with the fatigue of what would turn out to be a long-term illness that I didn't realize I was ill. The bodily dramas of pregnancy, birth, and parent-ing masked the other changes taking place in my body. Later, when I was coming to terms with the daily realities of chronic illness, the transforma-tions of illness and those of pregnancy and motherhood seemed phenom-enologically related. Both pregnancy and illness involved the redrawing of bodily boundaries and incorporation of an other into the self. Both motherhood and illness required learning new ways to use my body and to interpret bodily signals. Both demanded a crash course in taking care of physical needs. As a new mother, I solved problems one at a time, muddling through the fog of exhaustion and milky elation. Although I was already experiencing symptoms of illness, I certainly didn't think of myself as a disabled mother, and I had no awareness of other mothers who might be confronting issues similar to mine.

The second time around, my husband and I thought long and hard about what it would mean to have another child. By then I had been through several cycles of partial recovery and relapse, and my body had found a fragile stability. My son was in kindergarten, relatively independent and beyond the stage of needing a lot of physical care. I had returned to work part-time. Could we return to the chaos of life with a newborn? Did pregnancy pose risks to my health? Did my illness pose risks to a growing fetus? Was taking on unknown risks to me or a baby fair to our six-year-old son? How would we afford childcare, assuming I wouldn't be able to work for some time after the baby was born? What if the baby also had health issues or disabilities that required special care? Were we uniquely qualified to raise a disabled child or uniquely positioned to be overwhelmed?

Grappling with this decision, we had very little information to go on. There was no research on the medical or practical implications of my illness for mother or baby. I couldn't think of anyone I knew who had a chronic physical illness and had raised a child. Although I had read many accounts of living with illness and disability, I wasn't aware of any books on the subject of illness and mothering. The ubiquitous *What to Expect When You're Expecting* didn't tell me what to expect. Finally my ob-gyn threw me a lifeline: she had a patient with an illness similar to mine who had recently had a baby. I had a long conversation with this new mother, and then with another new mom she knew, and eventually with several women around the country. Embedded within the stories they told were the stories of other women, a mother lode of interconnected narratives that I shared with my husband and my doctors. In conversation with these women, we practiced a version of what Arthur Frank (2004, 209) has called "thinking with stories." Drawing a distinction between thinking *about* and thinking *with* stories, Frank writes: "Thinking with stories involves a hermeneutic of mutual engagement; a story is one aspect of a complex of nested relationships that remain in process. Thinking with stories involves taking one's own place in that process." It was only through our engagement with the stories of other women that my husband and I were able to make the decision to have a second child.

Our decision about parenthood was a private one, made in consultation with my internist and ob-gyn. It had little to do, on a conscious level, with cultural representations of maternity or disability and everything to do with medical information, practical details, financial and emotional resources. Nonetheless, it required a fundamental reconception of motherhood. I had to jettison idealized images of motherhood that I had probably held since childhood. The truth is, since I became ill shortly after my first child was born, I never fit the picture of motherhood I had envisioned, which featured me hiking miles with my baby in a backpack, both of us munching on homemade organic snacks. As a working mother, I probably wouldn't have conformed to this image even if I'd remained healthy. But choosing to become a disabled mom required, for me, a sometimes painful rethinking of what it meant to be a mother. Recalling the poet and dancer Neil Marcus's comment that "disability is an art . . . it's an ingenious way to live" (Marcus 1996), I began to imagine disabled motherhood as an art requiring special skills, adaptability, and inventiveness.

When I became visibly pregnant, I attracted the usual benevolent gazes and questions from strangers. As my six-year-old proudly pushed me in a manual wheelchair during a visit to a local arboretum, we received looks of smiling approval. (Isn't it sweet that this boy is giving his pregnant mom a chance to put her feet up?) Before becoming pregnant, I had often attracted quizzical looks on the rare occasions when I used a wheelchair. (Why is this woman using a wheelchair? She looks fine to me.) Now, my pregnant body was the dominant visual icon and narrative, one that erased the meaning even of such a prominent marker of disability as a wheelchair. And because pregnancy is sometimes considered to be a form of disability—after all, most pregnancy and maternity leave policies use the language and terms of disability leave—there seemed to be no inherent contradiction between the two, no visual dissonance.

Yet the prospect of caring for a newborn was daunting. It made me newly aware of all the physical tasks I could no longer perform. Getting up at night to feed or comfort a baby is a basic requirement of motherhood; with my first child, the blur of nighttime awakenings seemed to be motherhood itself. Now, I needed ten hours of uninterrupted sleep to function at all. My stamina was limited. Being a mother, especially a mother of a young child, involves many physical activities of care: feeding, bathing, snuggling, steadying an early walker, running after a toddler. I took comfort in knowing that disabled mothers are endlessly inventive about accomplishing these tasks, alone or in partnership with another caregiver. Disability highlights the physical demands of motherhood, but it also engenders creative solutions. Sometimes the solutions involve using our bodies creatively: Alison Lapper, I learned, changed diapers with her feet. Sometimes the solutions are technological ones. A hard-of-hearing friend talks about her fear of not being able to hear her children if they awaken and cry out during the night, a fear easily banished by a vibrating baby monitor that alerts her to their cries. Often the solutions involve the physical assistance of family members or paid caregivers, and the attending redefinition of the tasks of motherhood. In this age of working mothers and rapidly evolving reproductive technologies, maternity is constantly being redefined. Even so, disability puts pressure on the notion of motherhood, requiring mothers to negotiate not only physical tasks but also cultural expectations about what mothers do.

When my younger son was born, I needed a great deal of help, both because of my chronic illness and because complications after a C-section consigned me to weeks of bed rest. Apart from daytime feedings, I couldn't care for him during the early months of his life. As a mother, I was akin to a dairy cow; my job was to make milk. While my husband readied my older son, Anders, for school, Janie Johnson appeared at our door to take care of me and baby Elias. Every morning she delivered a freshly bathed, sweet-smelling bundle to me for a 7:00 a.m. feeding. Then she put him down for a nap and prepared a nursing-mother breakfast: oatmeal and fruit, eggs and toast, orange juice and tea, delivered on an elegant silver tray. While juggling mommy care and baby care, Janie managed the daily traffic of visiting nurses and friends dropping off dinner. When my older son came home from school, she turned her attention to the details of his day and gradually coaxed him into holding his baby brother. She struck a deal with him: she would touch his pet cricket, despite her deathly fear of insects, if he would hold his brother, who at the time seemed to him about as desirable as a cricket in the house did to Janie. I couldn't believe my luck in finding such a loving, creative, and efficient caregiver. Any mother of a newborn, disabled or not, would thrive on such care.

But care costs money. While my postpartum complications entitled me to visiting nurses paid for by health insurance, my chronic illness entitled me to paid help for neither myself nor my baby. Because I worked part-time I had no maternity leave benefits or, for that matter, benefits of any kind. My husband's job provided our health insurance. We were dependent on my mother-in-law's generosity and financial well-being to pay for Janie's help. Once I recovered from the delivery, I was able to care for Elias myself for a few hours in the afternoon and evening. My husband did night duty from the beginning. The infrastructure of assistance we required was far less than what many people with disabilities need on a daily basis, but it demanded that we adjust to the realities of parenting with a chronic illness and recognize the importance of financial resources and loving, trustworthy caregivers.

Hiring Janie seemed to me an entirely different transaction than paying someone to care for my baby while I worked. When I was working, I interviewed numerous caregivers, carefully checked references, left detailed instructions. When I was in bed and needed care for myself and my child, I felt much more vulnerable. I didn't have the energy to interview lots of people or write out daily instructions. I had to entrust my baby and myself to someone I barely knew. And yet I had to be alert and attentive enough, even when I most needed care, to ensure that my baby was receiving the care he needed and that Janie, too, was thriving and not being stretched beyond her own capacities. As many working mothers know, an expanded circle of caregivers can enrich the life of both the child and his parents. But disability introduces a different dynamic into the relationship between mother and caregiver, especially when both mother and baby are receiving care.

In *The Question of David*, one of the very few book-length narratives chronicling the experience of a disabled mother, Denise Sherer Jacobson (1999, 129) discusses at length her struggle to find suitable caregivers. Both she and her husband have cerebral palsy, and their adopted infant son, David, exhibits some early signs of CP. Some of the caregivers who work in their home, Jacobson feels, undercut her authority as a mother and employer. She wonders, too, about the effects on David: "Would he learn that he had to rely on someone else? Would he think less of me as his mother if I weren't always part of the picture? . . . [A] working mother could solely care for the physical needs of her child without too much bother. For me, many of those physical needs took the time and energy of a five-mile uphill run." Mothers who are ill or disabled often rely on what philosopher Eva Feder Kittay (1999, 107) calls *doulia:* relations of "nested dependencies" through which caregivers also receive care. These relations, ideally, are based on respect for the agency and well-being of everyone involved. Kittay calls for a conception of *doulia* that situates it not just in individual relationships but also in social institutions and socially recognized principles of care and justice. For disabled mothers, the private, intimate acts of maternal care take on a public dimension when they are embedded in other caregiving relationships. Much like the nested stories that shaped my reproductive choices, these nested relationships of care call attention to interdependency and mutual engagement. They challenge us to reimagine caregiving as an act that has the power to transform social institutions and cultural expectations.

Disability falls between the cracks of my public identities as teacher and mother. Not because I conceal it, though its invisibility does grant me the luxury of choosing when and where to disclose my illness. At work, even colleagues who know I live with chronic illness assume that I work part-time because I'm involved at my kids' school. At their school, fellow parents assume that I miss a lot of school activities because I have a demanding full-time job. Some of my friends simply don't see or understand my physical ups and downs or the complicated, artful dance that illness and mothering require. Because we have fashioned a household schedule and pace that accommodates illness, it is often invisible even to my family. I need to sleep until mid-morning, so my husband has always managed the morning routine and shepherded the kids off to school. In turn, I supervise homework, piano and cello practice, and bedtime. After my kids are in bed I leave each of them notes about the next day's schedule, notes they read over breakfast, in my absence. To them, this routine is perfectly normal, and indeed it seems a fair division of labor. But I resist, sometimes, the way our carefully choreographed routines render my illness invisible. I want my children, especially, to see and embrace the creativity and flexibility that disability demands.

My boys are now sixteen and nine. They attend a school filled with robust, athletic kids who garner championships and trophies. With few exceptions, the only visibly disabled kids at their school are injured athletes with temporary casts or crutches. I worry about the dearth of disabled kids in their daily lives. Still: disability is normal to them. Because of my involvement in disability studies and disability arts, they have grown up meeting Deaf poets, blind scholars, stand-up comics with cerebral palsy. When my older son first saw *Finding Nemo,* he reported excitedly: "Mom! It's about disability!" When my younger son was asked if he would like to buy a gift for me for Mother's Day, he said, "Yes! A book about disability," as if disability were simply an interest of mine, one among many, which of course it is. I like to think that when my sons someday encounter changes related to disability or aging in their own bodies, these changes won't seem as scary and foreign as they initially did to me. But if they are more knowledgeable about and accepting of disability, it will be not only because their mother has a chronic illness but also because of their exposure to the larger world of disability arts and culture.

It is crucial that our private negotiations with disability and motherhood enter the public spaces of art, literature, and policy. These negotiations can easily remain invisible, cast as issues for mothers and families to figure out on their own. But our private acts of mothering, of giving and receiving care, are inevitably shaped by social contracts and cultural norms. And, in turn, embodied practices of care can shape and reshape these norms. Attending to the experiences of mothers who are ill or disabled opens up new conversations about both disability and motherhood, revealing, among other things, the extent to which the idea and the daily realities of mothering have depended on health, strength, and agility. Yet alternate models of mothering can be hard to find. In the era of the memoir, and amid a proliferation of personal narratives about illness and disability, published accounts by disabled mothers are rare. Anne Finger's *Past Due* (1990) and Jacobson's *A Question of David* (1999) are notable exceptions. This literary absence reflects the discomfort or surprise many still experience when faced with the visual or narrative juxtaposition of disability and motherhood. How do we make this juxtaposition visible—at once more everyday and more celebrated? For starters, we need to place it in plain sight. The marble artifact *Alison Lapper Pregnant* is no longer installed in Trafalgar Square, but the conversations engendered by the statue continue to circulate, a testament to the power of public art and debate to nudge us toward imagining disability and maternity in the same body, the same story.

1

Refusing Diagnosis

Mother-Daughter Agency
in Confronting Psychiatric Rhetoric

A B B Y   W I L K E R S O N

My daughter Lauren has a sizable cynical streak, but there are injustices against herself or others that she will not tolerate, even when the odds are stacked against her.[1] In her adolescence, her talent for art extended to her own self-presentation, which was unique enough that people took notice. And if a mother is any judge, she's beautiful, even though the pursuit of beauty has never been her prime operating concern in life. The story of Lauren's psychiatric hospitalization confirms that a seventeen-year-old girl who is attractive yet apparently uninterested in being pretty can still get attention for her looks. It also suggests that there may be times when a mother concerned with her daughter's mental health may need to refuse diagnosis (not *a* diagnosis, but *any* diagnosis) in order to foster that health.

1. I am indebted to Cynthia Lewiecki-Wilson for insightful comments that greatly benefited this article. I also thank listeners at the Radical Philosophy Association, University of Minnesota Bioethics Seminar Series, Temple University Philosophy Department, and the Washington Ethical Society for thoughtful responses to early versions of this paper, as well as the Artivism group of Washington, DC (particularly Urooj Arshad, Margo Kelly, Cindy Newcomer, and Grace Poore), Melissa Burchard, Julie Elman, Cayo Gamber, Lisa Heldke, Robin Meader, Peg O'Connor, Pam Presser, Karen Sosnoski, and Dan Williamson. Both Lauren and my partner, Pat McGann, made many useful suggestions that benefited the paper. Most of all, I thank Lauren for her insight and for her courage, as well as her generosity in permitting me to tell my version of this story.

Disability studies, scholarship on illness narratives and medical rhetoric, and gender studies can all be enriched by exploring the significance of refusing diagnosis. Mothers of children targeted for psychiatric treatment face the challenge of assessing the purposes, motivations, and potential consequences of interventions. We hope a proposed remedy will relieve our children's suffering (if indeed they are suffering), remove obstacles to their flourishing, and ultimately foster their agency in the world (Ruddick 1995). Yet a remedy can also participate in, or even constitute, regimes of normalization that privilege some minds and bodies, some ways of functioning, being, and appearing, while stigmatizing others that cause less suffering than proposed interventions, or may even be positive and healthy variations. Psychiatry is one of the chief enforcers of "compulsory able-bodiedness," a norm overlaid at the same time with social ideologies of race, class, and gender, along with sexuality (as invoked by the term's echoing of Adrienne Rich's notion of compulsory heterosexuality [McRuer 2006, 1, 6]).[2]

Mothers, entrusted with the cultural role of prime socialization agent for their children, are often conscripted into enforcing compulsory able-bodiedness even though it frequently does not serve their children—or themselves—well. Advocating for a child's interests may sometimes mean rejecting treatment in order to resist the compulsory able-bodiedness that can harm a child. Adolescent psychiatry robs adolescents of agency by constructing them as subjects who generally cannot be trusted to represent their own experiences and interests with authority, especially when their perceptions and behavior are seen to violate social boundaries such as those structuring compulsory able-bodiedness. When the rules of psychiatric rhetoric prevent mothers from participating along with doctors in constructing meanings regarding our children, we are denied agency as well. Medical rhetoric shapes knowledge, the meanings that can be shared among doctor, patient, and parent, defining what can be expressed

---

2. I use the term "compulsory able-bodiedness" to encompass norms of mental/emotional ability—an appropriate framing given the hegemonic medical model of mental illness as chemical imbalance leading to brain dysfunction.

and acted upon, what is relevant and irrelevant. When crucial knowledge becomes inexpressible under these terms, saying no to psychiatric discourse and the compulsory able-bodiedness underlying it may become the most coherent option and the best exercise of agency for a parent on an adolescent's behalf.

The case study considered here took place in the late 1990s, reflecting events that continue to shape adolescent psychiatry. Julie Passanante Elman (2008, 200) argues that the 1990s, designated "The Decade of the Brain" by presidential proclamation, witnessed the development of a discourse of "neuroparenting" based on medical perceptions of adolescence as a pathological stage of brain development. I take up her argument to consider the implications for mothering illustrated by the case study. As Elman shows, in 1990s neuroparenting discourse, parenting itself becomes increasingly medicalized, as teen brain development is understood as far too unruly to be left solely to the inexpert attentions of parents. The traces of these influences can be seen in Lauren's story, reflecting a larger and ongoing historical trend.

During the 1980s and 1990s in the United States, psychiatric hospitalization became increasingly common as a response to teens in conflict with their environment. From 1980 to 1984, adolescent psychiatric hospitalization in private facilities quadrupled, with rates continuing to rise through the 1980s (Weithorn 1988, 773). Between 1990 and 1999, in Washington State for example, psychiatric hospitalization as a proportion of all adolescent hospitalizations rose by about 50 percent, from 14.5 to 21.5 percent (Garrison et al. 2004, 781). Psychiatric intervention into speech, behavior, thoughts, perceptions, emotions, and identities, particularly at such a formative stage as adolescence, has long-lasting effects on individuals and far-reaching social influence. The benefits that many people have derived from psychiatry do not undo its harms to others.

HAIRSTYLE OR DIAGNOSIS?

When our seventeen-year-old daughter asked to be hospitalized, my partner, Pat (her stepfather), and I did not have to be told she was in trouble. About four years earlier, when we had moved from Chicago to Maryland,

Lauren struggled with leaving friends behind and making new ones in an unfamiliar environment. Then came academic struggles, which were unprecedented for her. Her classmates had, unlike her, made the transition to changing classes the previous year, leaving her to learn on her own how to cope with this new level of organizational demand, which proved to be too much for her. She began acting out.

A year after the move, we enrolled Lauren in an alternative school with an intensive therapeutic component. There, she was diagnosed with attention deficit disorder and medicated with Ritalin. The drug initially seemed to help, but when she eventually began to abuse it, we stopped it. She returned to the high grades she was used to getting before the move, though the school did not offer the academic challenge she needed. Eventually she was asked to leave, after one disciplinary infraction too many (applying black lipstick to a transgendered classmate, as it happened), and we enrolled her in the neighborhood high school.

Here her lack of organizational skills (still not developed at the alternative school because of its small size and highly structured program) undermined her aptitude, and her frustration level soared, undoubtedly fed by the substance abuse we did not know had continued. She had recently come out and had to endure homophobia from some classmates and teachers. She began skipping classes and could not tolerate our efforts, or those of the tutor we hired, to help academically. Most of her friends were in the magnet program, occupied with academic achievement and other efforts to get into the best colleges possible. Lauren spoke of being alienated both from school and her friends' attachment to academics and future career paths. She was truly overwhelmed, and nothing we were doing seemed to be helping.

For the two weeks before Lauren was admitted to the hospital, she was jumping out of her skin at home, begging us to let her get out of the house. We had reluctantly allowed her to stay with friends, with frequent phone calls home, as well as many calls between her friends' parents and us. We discovered that she had also sometimes panhandled for subway money.

Under the rules of her insurance at the time, patients had to be in imminent danger of harming themselves or someone else to justify psychiatric admission. Lauren was neither suicidal nor violent to others, nor has she ever been, but the doctors evaluating her for admission construed her "running away" and panhandling as dangerously self-destructive. I did not consider Lauren to have "run away," but I acquiesced in the construction of her behavior as dangerous—and therefore diagnosable—in hopes of getting help for her distress. I did believe Lauren to be in some kind of danger, but one that had less to do with being out of a place she was expected to occupy and more to do with how she would situate herself in a troubled and troubling world—a subtle but important distinction. I would soon learn, however, that while an ostensible danger to self was what got her into the hospital, her visible nonconformity signaled a perceived brain dysfunction that could keep her locked up for an indefinite period of time and medicated for the rest of her life.

In adolescent psychiatric hospitalization, the central concern is "stabilizing" the patient through medication, in a highly structured environment depriving her of her own clothing, controlling communication with friends and family, and mandating additional behaviors while forbidding others. These "privileges" most people take for granted outside the hospital must be earned back in sequential stages. Participating in psychotherapy (typically a group program) is usually mandatory, but medication and the privilege system tend to be emphasized far more.

Once Lauren was admitted to the adolescent ward, her hair became the immediate focus. I learned of this and many other details of her stay through several phone conversations a day with her and various staff members, as well as through visits. Lauren's straight brown hair hung several inches past her shoulders, with many strands trained into dreadlocks, and a large section in back tangled together—her "uni-dread," as she called it. On top of her head and in back she kept sections of hair pinned up with many small gold safety pins, which had become firmly entwined in her hair. Many times when I was out with Lauren, other teenagers and young adults would compliment her on this distinctive creation. In the hospital, however, patients are never allowed access to "sharps," so Lauren had to take the safety pins out immediately. Those she could not remove, a nurse cut out, along with the attached sections of hair. Lauren was required to sign a contract to wash her hair daily, and for the first two days a staff member stood by the shower and watched to make sure she did.

Next, Lauren's psychiatrist ordered treatment for head lice, along with a gynecological exam, CAT scan, and MRI in order to rule out medical problems. I asked whether she had discussed these plans with Lauren, who was anxious about medical procedures, even having her blood pressure taken. The doctor had not and acknowledged that Lauren had the right to refuse the procedures, but she wanted her to have them. I asked about the lice treatment. The doctor acknowledged that it was not routine, nor was there any indication of lice, but considering how Lauren's hair looked, she felt she had to avoid any risk to the other patients and the staff.

Lauren refused all medical tests except a urine screen for drugs. This meant she would not be taken off "Safety," the highest level of restriction, nor would she earn the privilege of wearing street clothes rather than hospital-issue pajamas and paper slippers. The doctor told me that for adolescents this privilege was an especially powerful incentive to comply with hospital demands. She was confident Lauren would submit to the tests. I told her that given Lauren's fears and her awareness of the right to refuse, she might well continue to do so. The doctor—paradoxically acknowledging and at the same time disavowing the psychiatric assumption of control—replied, "If that happens, I'm not going to get into a pissing contest with her. She can stay at Safety Level, it's up to her."

Soon two men entered Lauren's room, introduced themselves as the infection-control team, explained "in scientific terms" that her hair was unhealthy, and then asked her permission to examine it. She refused, but they went ahead, explaining they had to cut all her hair off because it was a health hazard. She refused again, and after some argument they left. Lauren told me that the hospital was feeling less and less like a safe place for her. Later the doctor conceded to me that the situation "may have been mishandled," but she neither apologized to Lauren nor spoke to her of the situation at all.

Lauren told us she felt the hospital was not benefiting her. She was also tired of doctors, nurses, and other staff constantly asking whether she had a boyfriend. I too had been asked this about her over and over; without fail, it was one of the first things that each staff member in the long parade of those we met would ask us.

A couple of days later, the doctor called Pat and me in for a meeting, when she notified us that she had reached a diagnosis of schizotypal personality disorder, which is biologically related to schizophrenia, perhaps a milder form of it. She noted that Lauren "disorganizes under stress," and that her "running away" was most likely a way to "fend off the feeling of losing her mind." Thus, Lauren's "defiant mode" seemed to be a way of organizing herself. Furthermore, people with this disorder are more vulnerable to anxiety, and tend to attribute their problems to their environments. Perhaps this accounted for Lauren's failure to examine why she was hospitalized—"running away"—despite the "supportive environment" of the ward. Qualifying the diagnosis as provisional, the doctor nonetheless recommended risperidone, an antipsychotic drug, along with the Ritalin that Lauren was seeking, although we did not realize it at the time, and an antidepressant. The doctor expressed how sorry she was to give us this diagnosis, saying she would rather a child of hers had cancer than a personality disorder (clearly reflecting social hierarchies of ability that position the mentally disabled as extra-abject).

Over the weekend, I spent many hours going over the diagnostic criteria for schizotypal personality disorder in the *Diagnostic and Statistical Manual of Mental Disorders,* or *DSM-IV* (1994, 645). Five of nine "diagnostic features" must be present to confirm the diagnosis, yet after seriously considering them, I could not see how a single one applied to Lauren.

I then tried to learn more about risperidone (or Risperdal, its trade name). Its risks include tardive dyskinesia and extrapyramidal effects— uncontrollable movements of the limbs, face (including drooling), neck, and trunk. Mouth, tongue, and breathing can be affected. These effects are irreversible, but "merely cosmetic," the doctor assured us. She recommended it because the risk of these side effects is lower than with older antipsychotics. (Later we would learn that the drug had not yet been approved for children or adolescents, and that its risks are more significant than originally assumed; successful lawsuits against the manufacturer would soon come as well.) I was concerned that the three recommended drugs, each with its own set of significant effects and risks, could interact in unpredictable ways, and it could be difficult to determine which drug was doing what. Given my own holistic approach to health, if the goal was stabilizing Lauren emotionally (in itself an unsettling locution cast in the passive voice), I had a hard time believing that introducing three such powerful chemicals into her system at once would accomplish this.

We met with the doctor again, asking which of the *DSM* criteria in her view described Lauren, and she cited the following six:

> (2) odd beliefs or magical thinking that influences behavior and is inconsistent with subcultural norms (. . . in children and adolescents, bizarre fantasies or preoccupations)
>
> (3) unusual perceptual experiences . . .
>
> (4) odd thinking and speech . . .
>
> (5) suspiciousness or paranoid ideation
>
> (6) inappropriate or constricted affect . . .
>
> (9) excessive social anxiety that . . . tends to be associated with paranoid fears rather than negative judgments about self. (1994, 645)

I expected her to cite "(7) behavior or appearance that is odd, eccentric, or peculiar" (645), but she did not.

According to the doctor, Lauren's failure to earn the "privilege" of wearing her own clothing set her apart from other adolescent patients, clear evidence of a disordered personality. Perhaps most important, the doctor reemphasized that Lauren's "failure to make an alliance with her caregivers" supported the diagnosis. In the doctor's year and a half on the ward, only one other patient had not connected with caregivers, and that patient was "severely disturbed." The doctor found Lauren's suspicions and criticisms of her caregivers, and failure to criticize herself, characteristic of the paranoid thinking and denial of personal responsibility associated with the disorder. Lauren's own initiation of her hospitalization was irrelevant because of these "failures" on her part.

Deeply troubled by this diagnosis, I countered that the "paranoid" behavior the doctor was describing had been a direct response to how Lauren was being treated on the ward. The doctor replied that a patient's responses to hospital life are appropriate diagnostic measures, because personality remains stable across all domains.

Finally, I asked for evidence of "odd beliefs or magical thinking that influences behavior and is inconsistent with subcultural norms."

The doctor answered: "Her hair."

"Her hair? But that's a hairstyle, not a belief."

"No, it's a *belief*. She believes that it's appropriate to wear her hair that way."

At this point, it was impossible to deny that conventional appearance (and the compliance it may seem to represent) was truly the fundamental concern. We declined the risperidone. As for the Ritalin, we reluctantly agreed, despite our knowledge—and the doctor's—that Lauren had abused it in the past. Perhaps we were clinging to the fantasy that somehow it would "work" this time, or that the antidepressant, which we also agreed to, would support her efforts not to be miserable. And perhaps it was simply too difficult to contest every recommendation of the psychiatrist.

The next day, when we returned Lauren from a short visit off the ward, an attendant insisted on strip-searching her, despite Lauren's distress and my protests. When I asked to be present for the search, I was refused. I called the nurse when we got home and was told that the search was performed despite Lauren's "failure to cooperate," and that she was "fine."

The next morning, Lauren called begging me to get her out. The attendant had been rough and disrespectful, making no secret of her anger. Lauren felt violated in the hospital.

I phoned the doctor, who defended the appropriateness of the searches, the humaneness of the staff, and the tolerability of the procedure, which she felt was "no big deal." However, the doctor recommended a residential facility because Lauren was "resisting treatment" in the hospital (although the doctor would note in the chart that Lauren's condition on discharge was "stable"). She seemed surprised that we did not comply, warning us to expect further episodes of "running away" and specifying what hospital to bring her to when (not if) this occurred and how to involve law enforcement. Without residential treatment, the doctor admonished, Lauren would become a "street person."

HAIR-RAISING ANARCHY

Rather than seeing these events as isolated instances of bad medical care, owing, perhaps, to one doctor's inexperience with particularly nonconformist adolescents, I take this case study and the conflicting perspectives it illustrates to exemplify what is fundamentally a broader rhetorical struggle, one structured by compulsory able-bodiedness. Rhetoricians Chaim Perelman and Lucie Olbrechts-Tyteca specify the basic condition for addressing an audience in a genuine effort to persuade: "The indispensable minimum for argumentation appears to be the existence of a common language" (qtd. in Segal 2005, 91). Medical rhetorician Judy Segal observes, "Two people are not engaged in a properly rhetorical process if only one of them really speaks the language of exchange." She goes on to add, "Another condition for rhetoric . . . is mutual respect" (91).

Segal applies this framework to an analysis of "the problematic nature of end-of-life conversations between medical professionals and patients/ family members" (2005, 92). My case study indicates similar problems in treatment conversations in adolescent psychiatry. Interactions between doctor and patient/family are framed as a process of mutual exchange and persuasion that facilitates informed decision making and patient and parental consent, but in reality such a severe imbalance of rhetorical power exists that a context of coercion is created. When Lauren and I attempted to find a common language, to use the language of the ward to address psychiatrist and staff concerns and to seek agency, whatever we said could only be heard as further evidence for Lauren's pathology. Medical discourse rendered personal meanings not merely irrelevant but incoherent, so pathological as to justify intrusive and risky interventions. Indeed, in cases such as this one, psychiatry scrambles identities containing any nonconformist element into fundamental incoherence, along with the intersubjective knowledge a mother shares with a child. At the same time, the neuroparenting model effected by the "decade of the brain" (Elman 2008) intensifies the psychiatric stripping of authority from a mother's perspective when it does not coincide with, or it actually contests, medical conclusions.

For the psychiatrist, Lauren's appearance was the outward sign of a profound internal disorder, especially because she also refused to comply with medical authority, thus placing herself outside the realm of reason as the medical world defines it. However, despite my comment to the doctor—"it's a hairstyle, not a belief"—Lauren's appearance, and her hair in particular, expressed a visceral, aesthetic, and principled rejection of rules and institutions that she sees as punitive, arbitrary, and unjust, at the same time that it functioned within larger social patterns of meaning-making beyond her intentions and inclinations. In other words, rather than marking some fundamental incoherence, her style functioned lucidly as a language, one which the psychiatrist and others on the ward refused to hear because it violated the ableist terms of *their* language for describing her and her behavior.

Lauren's messy and unwashed hair clearly signaled a class defection, distinguishing her from the ranks of the tidy and well-washed middle class. If conformity—the pursuit of normalcy—is the most important of middle-class habits, hygiene is clearly its most basic aspect. The medical demand that Lauren shampoo her hair daily expressed a judgment that she had failed to accomplish middle-class notions of respectability through her appearance and behavior.[3] The racial associations of Lauren's partially formed dreadlocks may also have signaled a transgression of social boundaries that a middle-class white girl is expected to observe.

Lauren's stylized refusal to prettify herself was also unintelligible as a coherent expression of identity because it violated boundaries of gender and sexuality, exhibiting an aggressive femaleness rejecting the limits of girlhood gender identity. The psychiatric panic surrounding Lauren's anti-pretty stance suggests a deep cultural need to see all adolescents as successful heterosexuals-in-progress, and girls as decorative and decorous surfaces for male pleasure, thereby maintaining heteronormativity (also

---

3. Philosopher Iris Young writes of respectability norms originating in nineteenth-century notions of morality that she argues still shape class boundary consciousness: "Respectable behavior is preoccupied with cleanliness and propriety, meticulous rules of decency. . . . The body should be clean in all respects. . . . All manners come to be associated with bodily decency, restraint, and cleanliness" (1990, 136–37).

reflected in the rhetorical ritual of the boyfriend question—its priority for every staff member suggests a cultural fixation bordering on obsession).

In virtually every problematic decision during Lauren's stay, the notion of safety, whether hers or others', functioned as a rhetorical trump card. And safety was generally construed in ways that problematized any behavior that did not conform to social norms, while procedures of the ward (such as the routine strip searches involving actions that elsewhere would be recognized as assault) were immune to charges of risk. When the psychiatrist perceived a behavior or choice of Lauren's as unsafe, but my understanding as her mother differed, my perception carried no weight. I had not realized that when I acquiesced in the rhetorical construction of Lauren's staying with friends as having "run away," this language would take on a life of its own. No matter how many times I explained that Lauren had our permission to be with friends and that we always knew where she was, once "running away" was written on the chart, staying with friends was on its way to becoming an ineluctable sign of extreme brain dysfunction.

Within the rhetorical framework of the ward, words could lose their ordinary meanings and applications. "Failure" became a term that could meaningfully be applied only to patients (a linguistic phenomenon often remarked upon in medical rhetoric and bioethics), as in Lauren's "failure to make an alliance with her caregivers." Patients had "rights," which in ordinary usage do not entail punishment when exercised, but on the ward, claiming them, as Lauren did in refusing some procedures, could result in "losing privileges." It could be construed as defiance—"a pissing contest."

Rather than rejecting the doctor's diagnosis outright, I attempted to approach the situation as a context of persuasion, working through the *DSM* criteria with her and exchanging observations about their appropriateness or lack thereof. Yet these attempts at rhetorical engagement were irrelevant because the rules of the game stipulated that as a layperson, I could only hear and repeat the language that had been given me. Because of the dominance of the medical model (despite the ostensible context of family participation in decision making), I could not formulate insights or create meanings that would be heard by the doctor.

One consequence of the epistemology grounded on the rhetorical framework of psychiatry is that the problems of those whose appearance is conventional may be too easily overlooked, while those who take up nonconformist practices and styles may be too readily pathologized—a dangerous notion of mental health, for the conformists and the nonconformists alike. The doctor described Lauren as far more troubled than any others on the ward—including those whose very survival was at risk from late-stage eating disorders and multiple suicide attempts. Perhaps anorexia could be seen as at least congruent with gender norms, if exaggerated, in a way that Lauren's "extreme" behavior could not be. Moreover, anorexia and bulimia are nothing if not rituals of hygiene, closeting or even attempting to eliminate the messy excesses of embodiment.[4] In contrast with the neat and tidy anorectic girls, the cultivated chaos of Lauren's appearance was taken as far greater pathology. This preoccupation with surface prevented any recognition that all of these adolescents could have been responding in different ways and with varying resources to some of the same pressures, or that pathology could ever be located in society, in so-called "normal" expectations rather than in individuals.

Shortly after Lauren left the hospital, we discontinued both of her prescriptions and she never took them again.[5] She did not return to her high school, and although at her instigation we worked together to create a home schooling program, these efforts did not succeed. She spent some time in a rural commune in Virginia and then in squats in Manhattan, eventually heading west to live among the gutterpunks of San Francisco. Pat and I worried constantly about her, but after her hospitalization we had decided that locking her up was not the answer to her problems—a decision we have never regretted. I believe this decision helped us to maintain her trust, which in turn helped her to remain in regular contact and seek our help when she needed it. We may not have been parenting in anything like the ways we had imagined we would be at this time in her

4. Many thanks to Cayo Gamber for this point.

5. Careful research and preparation should be undertaken before withdrawing from psychotropic drugs, since it can be a risky process.

life, but it was our best understanding of what our daughter and her situation called for. Lauren is doing well now, and is enrolled in college where she is studying art and has written on these issues; antipsychiatry activist Fritz Flohr's website http://www.gayshamesf.org/againstpsychiatry .html features some of her artwork and writing on the abuses of psychiatry. She also managed to confront her substance abuse on her own, largely because of heart symptoms she quite plausibly attributes to her Ritalin abuse.

I do regret, deeply, that none in the long array of mental health professionals we saw ever helped us to confront the medication abuse triggered by their prescriptions in the first place. Not long before Lauren's hospitalization, in desperation I made the futile gesture of taking her to a (single) twelve steps meeting. I knew there was a problem, yet the professionals she encountered at the hospital and afterwards led her and us in every direction but this one. I now know how irresponsible we were, along with these professionals. It was sheer luck, along with the strength that Lauren somehow called up, that prevented an outcome that could have been far worse—and was, for many of the friends and acquaintances she made in her traveling days.

One reason Lauren is where she is today is her access to rhetorical frameworks that allowed her to see herself in ways other than the psychiatric definition of her—including feminism, the consumer/survivor/expatient movement, queer liberation, and other activist discourses, as well as holistic healing discourses. My own access to these and to disability studies and other scholarly critiques of medical discourse certainly facilitated my contesting the diagnosis and proposed treatment, which despite all these resources was surprisingly difficult.

We need to open up rhetorical spaces for talking back to medical discourse not simply because its recommendations to individuals can be inaccurate and damaging, but more fundamentally because it authorizes us to avoid some dangers while overlooking others; it certifies conventional bodies as safe, social and political conformity as medically superior, while positing disorderly and nonconformist bodies as a danger both to self and the social order and therefore in need of containment. Its rhetorical constructions, in short, can endanger selfhood and agency.

At the same time, there is much to be learned from the groups who have attempted to use psychiatry and the medical system more generally to get recognition and help for their concerns. Medical discourse can sometimes function as a rhetorical tool for the social legitimation of human needs as people themselves define them; it is one of the most powerful resources for influencing society to acknowledge its obligation to respond to those needs. Talking back to psychiatry, which sometimes means taking up a diagnosis with caution and sometimes means refusing it, is an important form of moral and political dissent, one that rhetoric, disability studies, and narrative ethics can assist in and ought to encourage.

8

Diagnosable

Mothering at the Threshold of Disability

JULIA MIELE RODAS

I am at a meeting of my son's preschool co-op, and I have my fellow coop-erators in stitches.[1] I'm good at getting people to laugh—it's one of my strongest social skills, but the joke of the moment is a little complicated. During the past year, our teeny, privately operated, cooperative preschool has been fortunate to have the regular support of two Early Intervention specialists. For three or four days each week, these women have come into the classroom because two of our fifteen students have been diagnosed with disabilities for which the state is legally required to provide special services. As a result, the families involved in the school have benefited from the expertise and attention of these professionals, and our children have benefited from the presence of more educators in the classroom. At this parents' meeting, near the close of the school year, we become communally aware that the two students who have been responsible for bringing this benefit to the group will be moving on to new schools next

---

1. To the extent that the thinking in this chapter remains faulty, the deficiency is entirely my own, but where clarity has been achieved, it certainly would not have come without the assistance of Paul Longmore, whose conversation on the subject of power and ambiguous disability identity helped to challenge my own thinking and whose generosity as an interlocutor helped me to traverse this very difficult ground. I had intended he would see my thanks upon publication of this volume and that this essay would become food for further dialogue between us. Instead, with a deep sense of loss, I dedicate this piece to his memory.

113

year and that none of the newly admitted students has a disability that will bring special educators into our classroom. Suddenly, there is a realization that the preschool will be poorer as a result.

At this juncture, I propose that my four-year-old son is probably "diagnosable," that his language skills are idiosyncratic enough that we could likely use his unusual gaps and pauses as a means of enriching our school with another paraprofessional for the coming year. The suggestion is made with my usual deliberate affect, a kind of performative enthusiasm that may be read either ironically or as genuine. In this instance, the group understands this ambiguous emotive screen as humor. Ha, ha, ha. After all, what mother would deliberately choose to have a disabled child? Would willingly saddle her son with this label for the sake of some generalized, institutional advantage? What mother would even publish her child's disability to the group in this way? Certainly the identities of the disabled kids who are departing have been carefully concealed by their parents, a feat made possible by the fact that neither child is evidently disabled physically and by the social camouflage resulting from the naturally idiosyncratic behaviors of a group of three- and four-year-olds. "Julia," says one parent (and if I am not mistaken, it is the father of one of the disabled kids who is leaving), "you crack me up."

LOCATION, LOCATION, LOCATION

This is an essay about a hotly contested issue in the experience and theory of disability: the question of how to locate, talk about, and live with an ambiguous disability identity. Because many disabilities are not immediately evident, because many are progressive or create erratic episodes of impairment, and because cultural and political considerations factor largely into competing definitions of disability historically and globally, scholars and activists have been keenly attentive to how individuals locate themselves in relation to disability. Sociologist Erving Goffman refers in *Stigma: Notes on the Management of Spoiled Identity* ([1963] 1986) to the act of "impression management" and the need shared by many stigmatized people to "exert strategic control" over image and personal information (130). The impetus behind this nearly universal human tendency to mask perceived difference, to "cover," as Goffman puts it, is amply explored in Rosemarie Garland-Thomson's *Extraordinary Bodies* (1997), which describes the perceptual fusing of atypical persons in the architecture of the freak show, indicating that the "spatial arrangement between audience and freak ritualized the relationship between self and cultural other" (62). According to this framework, the freak, often represented by a disabled person, occupies the most stigmatized possible social identity, one that—as Goffman indicates—most individuals seek to avoid, if at all possible. Speaking to the sweeping harm of such covering strategies, however, Simi Linton's politically charged *Claiming Disability* (1998) observes that "both passing and overcoming take their toll. The loss of community, the anxiety, and the self-doubt that inevitably accompany this ambiguous social position and the ambivalent personal state are the enormous cost of declaring disability unacceptable" (21). Linton writes about the relationship between queer and disabled identities, focusing on the empowerment and relief that arrive with "coming out." Indeed, the influence of her argument is evident in disability writing of the last decade, where coming out stories abound. Georgina Kleege's *Sight Unseen* (1999), Jim Knipfel's *Slackjaw* (1999), Steven Kuusisto's *Planet of the Blind* (1998), Dawn Prince-Hughes *Songs of the Gorilla Nation* (2004), Ryan Knighton's *Cockeyed* (2006), and many other autobiographical narratives attest to the power and importance of "claiming" disability.

More recently, theorists have approached ambiguous disability identities with greater ambivalence, testing the unstable ground of an identity with an increasingly broader definition, passing in and around the indefinite area of liminal disability identity. Brenda Jo Brueggemann's piece "On (Almost) Passing" in *Lend Me Your Ear* (1999) frets productively over her cultural place as both hearing and d/Deaf. And more recently, Tobin Siebers's discussion of "Disability as Masquerade" in *Disability Theory* (2008) discusses instances in which disabled people might be inclined to exaggerate impairment to clarify for others the needs and expectations of an individual who is not visibly disabled. And this debate continues to attract the passionate attention of disability scholars and activists, in part, I think, because of interactions like the one at my co-op meeting. It's not always simply a matter of stepping up and claiming a concealed self, but a process of questioning and discovery that leaves us continually unsure of who exactly we are and where precisely we belong.

For me, the exchange with my fellow parents is characteristic of my place within the group. Charged with a sadness that is momentarily inexplicable, I leave the meeting feeling depressed and anxious. To begin, this is not the first time I've sounded off about disability at one of our parent meetings. Earlier in the year, I had urgently resisted the cooperative's implicitly defining diversity as characterized by color, and I had strongly objected when a member of our admissions committee lamented that we did not get more applications from "diverse" candidates. I was appalled that this group of liberal and educated parents had such a limited sense of what diversity encompasses and equally appalled that anyone in the group felt that it was theoretically (or grammatically) possible for an individual to be "diverse." During those discussions—or perhaps it would be fairer to admit them as monologues—I had used disability identity and culture as a paradigm for understanding inclusion and diversity, thereby offending many parents in the group, especially, I think, the people of color who were there. To link race identity with the typical deficit understanding of disability entertained by most in the group was an unpopular maneuver. Raising the issue of disability again now, even in what most understood as this joking manner, rewarmed a subject that was already fraught with discomfort.

There is also this: despite the unpopularity of my stance and the soapbox approach that turned off many in the group, I'm actually right. Disability has made a powerful contribution to the diversity of our school, not only in the form of attendant paraprofessionals, but more immediately by adding to the explicit individualism in the classroom; by helping to generate a sense of allowable and desirable difference; by demanding creative teaching practices; by exposing students, teachers, and families to a more complete range of learning and personality styles; and by affirming the sense that conflict and resolution are natural and valuable aspects of human interaction. As an institution, the cooperative should be seeking to include any form of diversity that our staff and physical plant can accommodate. But while the school has benefited from the inclusion of students with disabilities, this point is far from being universally acknowledged.

Even the parents of the children with disabilities seem not to recognize that the presence of disability has been a positive factor. For them, disability appears to be a private issue, not a social, political, or cultural one, and the parallel between the benefits of a racially diverse school setting and one that includes people with disabilities is not fully appreciated by the group. Part of the bad feeling I have after the meeting is due to this very conventional misreading of disability—the statements I've made at the meeting about getting my son diagnosed can be understood only as a kind of joke. The cooperative's reading of disability seems persistently rigid and negative; my own advocacy notwithstanding, no parents really feel okay about saying their kid has a disability, and no one really appears to see how disability contributes positively.

When one of our teachers leaves and I become involved in the search for a replacement, I encounter the same resistance: the search committee actively and openly seeks a candidate of color, but does not fully embrace other diversity factors. When I again broach the subject of disability, I feel like a broken record. The others point out that our building is not wheelchair accessible, but to me this stance points to the reductive definition of disability shared by the others. My words seem to mean nothing but have become merely an irksome refrain from that offensive woman who is always sounding off on the same tired subject.

And now we come to the heart of it, my own sense of social isolation as a mother. The relationships between the other cooperating parents seem warm and convivial. We all share a progressive political, social, and educational agenda. As a mother and an educator, my feeling is that this is an ideal environment for my son, and yet . . . there is something about this monthly meeting that leaves me ill at ease. The truth is that I am not well-liked by the group, and I know it. I am funny, usually consciously so, and my remarks often make the other parents laugh. No one is pointedly unkind and I am not deliberately excluded, but I sense a difference. Tonight's meeting speaks volumes. I can crack people up, but the laughter is not entirely a sign of pleasure. The others are laughing, in part, because I make them feel a little uncomfortable, because they can't tell for sure when I'm being serious and when I'm joking. I talk too much; I talk out of turn; I fail to respond to the social cues that tell me that others are done with the subject. They wonder if there is something "wrong" with me, and I share their wonder, but—while I identify with disability identity in broader terms—I do not want to reduce myself to a label for the social convenience of my peers. I imagine the conversations in the homes of the various families after the meeting, or worse, the exasperated comments the parents must make to one another at drop-off and pick-up time, over coffee, on play-dates: she's so neurotic, so obsessive, so obnoxious, so condescending; she can never just let it drop; her son seems very sweet, but it's such a hassle to deal with her.

In fact, no one can quite define the social idiosyncrasy essential to my character; I am sociable and can talk easily with those I've just met. I can come up with chitchat at a party or speak with ease in a professional setting. I am genial, pleasant, full of fun. I make friends easily, and I'm good at interviews. Maintaining social connections, however, has always been more of a challenge. After a while, most people begin to sense that there is something inexplicably strange. I am hard to get along with, emotionally unavailable, always on my own schedule, unreasonably impatient with bureaucracy, disproportionately outraged by workplace inequities; I don't demonstrate quite the right interest in the personal lives of my acquaintances. I am moody, unpredictable, persevering, inappropriate, and persistently ironic. In short, I don't play well with others. Until I became a mother, these aspects of my social experience never underwent much self-scrutiny. In recent years, however, the emergent sociality of my six-year-old daughter and my four-year-old son has become an area of unforeseen intellectual interest. As I have recognized likenesses between the two of them, between them and myself, and within the context of my greater family, I have begun also to see the sociality of my entire family matrix in a different light. And as I myself have been confronted with the social aspects of motherhood—the expectations of the "mommy group," the playground, the schoolyard, and the monthly co-op meeting—I have also begun to think much more about a category I call "diagnosable."

As I live in and speak from this indefinite space, unsure if my experience warrants a "claim" to disability identity, I consider Goffman's observation that "the most fortunate of normals is likely to have his half-hidden failing . . . creating a shameful gap between virtual and actual social identity" ([1963] 1986, 127); I wonder, in fact, whether my intellectual occupation with disability encourages me to misread what Goffman might call the "failing" of a "normal" so that I can stake a false claim to disabled identity. At the same time, I feel entertained and empowered by my own "disability masquerade," if such it is, enjoying the fruitless attempts of outsiders to locate and define my interest in and connection to disability. Like the disabled person who relies on a prosthetic "prop" to create a desired identity, I exaggerate or dramatize my own sense of difference, creating "a temporary confusion of the public mind," making for myself "a brief moment of freedom in which to assert [my] independence and individuality" (Siebers 2008, 110–11). Thus, by creating for myself (and for my son) an intangible disability identity—not diagnosed, but "diagnosable"—I simultaneously claim kinship with disability and disown the social stigma and medicalized reduction in those conventional readings.

THE EMERGENCE OF ASPERGER: FROM CLINICAL CATEGORY TO ICON OF POPULAR CULTURE

The *DSM*, as it is widely known, is an acronym for the *Diagnostic and Statistical Manual of Mental Disorders* (1994), a professional tool of the American Psychiatric Association and the diagnostic authority recognized by government institutions and insurers. Mental health professionals use the criteria and categories established by the *DSM* to assign psychiatric labels that allow for various forms of intervention and therapy. Although many agree that it is a valuable document, most users also understand that diagnostic criteria are fluid and that the diagnostic process is fraught with subjectivity. The latest additions and changes to any authoritative medical text will reflect not only new medical discoveries and greater scientific understanding, but also changes in our culture. Whereas it was once believed, for instance, that deaf people were "idiots" and that people having hallucinations were "possessed," the approach and attitudes of human culture have shifted, and we now collate and define unusual behaviors and experiences with labels like social anxiety, Tourette syndrome, and attention deficit hyperactivity disorder. The most recent edition of the *DSM* (the *DSM-IV*, published in 1994) naturally signals the values and perceptions of our cultural moment in myriad ways. Among these is the addition of a clinical category called "Asperger's Disorder."[2] Understood by most clinicians as a kind of "higher-functioning" autism, the Asperger category creates a diagnostic envelope for persons who might hitherto have been considered "eccentric," those who are socially remarkable or who prefer to be alone, people with intense interests and preoccupations, those who are prone to overstimulation or emotional outbursts. Most significantly, the inclusion of Asperger as a discrete category in the *DSM-IV* allows for the diagnosis of those who are considered to be socially impaired, but who otherwise have strong verbal skills, an arena in which people with "Autistic Disorder" (what some think of as "classic autism") are considered to be clinically deficient.

The introduction of Asperger into the *DSM* as a distinct category has met with abundant controversy, including criticism that these criteria do not encompass a genuine clinical category. Scholarship in the field reflects this conflict: one paper appearing in the *Journal of Abnormal Child Psychology* asks quite directly: "Does DSM-IV Asperger's Disorder Exist?" (Mayes, Calhoun, and Crites 2001); another—"Asperger Syndrome or High-Functioning Autism?" (Schopler et al. 1999)—teases out the diagnostic debate. This controversy is fueled in part by what many see as an untenable ambiguity in the Asperger criteria, one that has fostered an enormous surge in diagnosis. In some respects, the Asperger category has been seized as an opportunity, and its ambiguity has been exploited by a range of interpreters, including parents seeking to name the quirky ways

---

2. Asperger was added to the *DSM* with the fourth edition, published in 1994, although there is no strong basis for differentiating the clinical and theoretical descriptions of the two physicians—Leo Kanner and Hans Asperger—who first described what both termed "autism." When the *DSM-5* is officially released in May 2013, it is expected that "Asperger's Disorder" will be subsumed within the diagnostic criteria for "Autism Spectrum Disorders" (ASD). In keeping with preferred practice, this essay adopts deliberately less-exploitative language, altering the typical use of possessive forms to create more neutral terms: Asperger (syndrome), Down syndrome, and Tourette syndrome. Indeed, some prefer not to use upper-case letters in naming these identities, thus removing the lived experience of psychosocial idiosyncrasy one step further from named medical authority.

their children interact with the rest of the world. A decade ago, Asperger was virtually unheard of; now, suddenly, Asperger stories abound. *Forrest Gump* (1994) and *Rainman* (1988) were merely the thin end of the wedge. A divorced friend indicates to me that her ex-husband has Asperger syndrome, then one of my cousins is diagnosed. An article in the December 2001 issue of *Wired* identifies it as "geek syndrome" (Silberman 2001) and offers an almost clubby take on the diagnostic spike in Silicon Valley. The shelves of my neighborhood bookstore are teeming with autism-related titles: *Songs of the Gorilla Nation* (Prince-Hughes 2004), *All Cats Have Asperger Syndrome* (Hoopmann 2006), *The Curious Incident of the Dog in the Night-Time* (Haddon 2004), *Nobody Nowhere* (Williams 1992) and *Somebody Somewhere* (Williams 1995), *With the Light: Raising an Autistic Child* (Tobe 2007), *Aspergers in Love: Couple Relationships and Family Affairs* (Aston 2003), *The Boy Who Went Away* (Gottlieb 1998). It would seem that the opening up of diagnostic possibility has made life on the autism spectrum marketable, even sexy.

RESISTING DIAGNOSIS

As inclusion on the autism spectrum has become increasingly acceptable, I have begun thinking more seriously about the benefits and disadvantages of diagnosis, of defining myself, and my children, in clinical terms. Walking home in a funk from a co-op meeting, feeling isolated and insecure, socially inept, I take comfort in running through the diagnostic checklist. Even this activity, I tell myself, this proclivity for list-making and checking, for ordering and organizing, is clinically significant. I wonder what an expert would say?

I began to ponder this question soon after my first child was born. I was finishing my dissertation and had done some general reading on autism as part of my research. It was Oliver Sacks's essays, especially—*An Anthropologist on Mars* (1995) and "The Autist Artist" and "The Twins" (1985)—which initially got me thinking about the presence of autism in my own greater family. As a group, my relatives certainly manifest quite a number of social peculiarities, but these have been so fundamentally a part of our family culture and history that I had never really examined them in psychosocial terms. With my reading of Sacks's descriptions of autism, I began to see my family in a different light, illuminated by the clinician's lamp. The giftedness I saw—and of which there is plenty— seemed to dovetail with Sacks's descriptions of "islets of ability," a classic autistic "symptom" indicating unusual talent or skill, but in an isolated area or areas; what I had before seen as selfishness now looked to me like the failure to form a "theory of mind," a blind spot attributed to autistic individuals by some clinicians who argue that it prevents autists from ascribing true thought and feeling to others. (This theory is deplored by many who claim autistic identity.) Our habit of speaking our minds, throwing convention to the wind, instead of establishing us as counterculture people, now looked suspiciously like the disinhibition of the socially clueless. One family member, brilliant and accomplished, offered advice on mastering appropriate social behavior from her own experience, saying: "I just ask myself, 'what would a normal person do?'" As Hans Asperger (1991, 58) observes regarding one autist, "Social adaptation has to proceed via the intellect."It took a bit longer (years, in fact) for me to notice that my own behavior was also somewhat atypical and to see reflected in myself the unusual affect, contact, and sociality I had already observed in other family members. Through my daughter's play, her personality, her habits, I slowly gained insight into my own. Influenced, no doubt, by my own personality and parenting, my daughter's tastes and behaviors reflected many of my own. Together we played "store" with all kinds of toys, a game primarily of sorting, organizing, and lining up; I was fascinated by her developing powers of abstraction and keen to consider with her the endless possible principles of categorization, an autistic gift specifically acknowledged by Hans Asperger: "They are good at logical thinking, and the ability to abstract is particularly good" (49). Her ability to focus and to remain intent on such tasks was frankly astonishing, and I would often observe her and think of a photograph of myself as a child, sitting on a rocky beach, carefully filling a plastic bottle with small stones. To others, such activities might appear meaningless, rigid, or bizarre, but the pleasure of creating order in this way has always filled me with satisfaction and tranquility. Autist autobiographies often describe the peace and ease that come with ordering things: for example, Daniel Tammet recounts the pleasure of collecting ladybugs (*Born on a Blue Day*, 2007), and Donna Williams writes blissfully about the stockroom of the department store where she once worked and about her carefully preserved collections, scraps of fabric and stone treasured beyond all her other possessions (*Nobody Nowhere*, 1994). My daughter and I both loved the ritual of collecting and classifying and were disturbed, sometimes seriously, by the disarrangement of our "set-ups." My own bitter fury at minor infractions of citizenship—littering, for instance, or the edging of a car into the crosswalk—found a counterpoint in my daughter's life at school. She was profoundly attentive to school and classroom rules, terrified of misbehaving, and felt compelled to report children who disregarded regulations. "Little things," Hans Asperger observes of one autistic child, "drove him to a senseless fury" (1991, 51). With this emerging context, I increasingly saw the urgent needs and desires of little children as perfectly reasonable and was at a loss to understand how other parents could so easily thwart or dismiss feelings that seemed to me to be so evidently sensible. If my daughter's expressed need that only Mama can put the straw in her juice box, or her Mama's need to have only blue towels in the bathroom, is not harmful to anyone else, why can others not honor the internal urgency of these idiosyncrasies? My growing respect for my own idiosyncratic self is enabled, then, by my growing respect for my idiosyncratic child. But the occupation of this undefined identity leads inevitably back to the question of diagnosis.

Given the diagnostic climate and the inherently subtle and ambiguous nature of the Asperger category, I suspect that we are both diagnosable, but I feel unsure about what purpose diagnosis would serve. In my deepest moments of alienation, I think I might feel legitimized by the pronouncement of a doctor, but I also recognize that my ambivalent desire for diagnosis is a simple (and impossible) longing to be perfectly understood. My desire for medical definition (and my fainter desire to so define my children) offers the possibility of affirmation, but it also facilitates a greater threat.

For the labeling of disability effectively closes off opportunity, generates exclusion and misunderstanding, and leads to the dismissal of the person as an individual; all behaviors, feelings, and thoughts are ascribed to disability rather than to a more authentically understood self; the individual is patronized and those with whom she engages are exempted from the effort of genuine understanding. This one tag suffices to explain every aspect of a person's being. This is the central message of Goffman's *Stigma* and the foundation for the argument that claiming disability is our only politically acceptable alternative; bias abounds, and unless we self-identify, we participate in the rampant oppression of and discrimination against disability.

I feel stuck here, though, by competing concerns, especially as a person strongly vested in my independence and particularity. I do not wish to abandon or undermine the work of my peers, but I feel stronger and better acting out my resistance from the margin of the disability masquerade than I do by potentially acting collectively with my friends and colleagues who self-identify. My desire to remain in the indefinite, occupying the "diagnosable" space, is not so much an unwillingness to stand up politically as it is a desire to challenge the disciplinary and diagnostic boundaries of the conventional order. I feel that I perform as a kind of "trickster," inserting myself into the mainstream and rocking the boat in a way that would not be in my power if my identity made more sense to more people.

I do not want my resistance to diagnosis to be understood as entirely pure and political; my resistance is also reluctance, a fear that my colleagues in the disability community would reject a diagnosis so fraught with ambiguity. In the circle of professional friends with whom I most deeply connect, many are obviously marked by disability. Their evident physical difference legitimizes what they think and say about disability. As an apparently nondisabled woman, I have often felt insecure about my place in this community, about the validity of my contribution, about my role as what I have elsewhere termed a "satellite."[3] What if my being

3. The theory of the satellite relationship, briefly stated, is that in relationships between disabled and (ostensibly nondisabled) helper or caretaker figures, the latter, identified as the "satellite," relies on the power, authority, and authenticity of the "central" disabled figure in order to establish his or her sense of self. The fundamental instability of this relationship results from the fact that the "central" disabled figure is typically dismissed, rhetorically

diagnosed with Asperger read as a pathetic bid for legitimacy, a medical affirmation totally lacking in meaning or credibility for the larger group? As a person who has trouble connecting with others, I often anticipate the experience of rejection and exclusion. Even with one's closest associates, it sometimes seems better to keep people guessing, and therefore engaged, than to risk presenting oneself as a known entity, an interpretable figure, and therefore vulnerable to the critical judgments of others.

Despite the taint of mere insecurity, however, resistance to diagnosis has a real and legitimate place. It is a means of enacting a generalized resistance to medicine and medical authority, a refusal of the rhetorical gesture that frames a person as a "case." The way I am does not require intervention or reconfiguration or fixing. My obsessions and compulsions, my love of lists and collections, and my profound desire for order may sometimes be irritating, but these traits are also fundamental to my creativity, to my powers of abstraction, to my abilities as a researcher, and to my victories in the endless skirmishes against head lice, an inevitable feature of every mother's life. To be a nit-picker is not necessarily a bad thing.

Indeed, diagnosis has degenerated into an increasingly reductive gesture. Whereas the ambiguity of the Asperger criteria and the broad possible range of application create a sense of inclusion, a mingling of the categorically "normal" and the explicitly "disordered," any diagnostic approach to human identity is nevertheless fundamentally divisive, or, as Michel Foucault might have it, disciplinary. A great part of the beauty of Leo Kanner's (1985) and Hans Asperger's (1991) initial work on autism is its recognition of the multifacetedness, the originality, the rich inner life, the intelligence and creativity of the autistic individual, theoretical observations that have largely been lost in the clinical application of autism/ Asperger diagnosis and therapy. In fact, with the addition of Asperger to

---

and/or socially, leaving the satellite figure without a secure means of establishing his or her own identity. As a result, the satellite is both threatened and empowered by the disabled, and the disabled is both threatened (framed/imprisoned) and empowered (acknowledged as authentic and bearing authority) by the satellite, the two circulating in an endless contest for power, authority, and authenticity, even while they are both frequently dismissed by outsiders (see Rodas 2003, 2007).

the *DSM*, society seems increasingly apt to read the socially remarkable person in medical terms rather than implicitly accepting a wider range of human "neurodiversity," a term that emerged in the late 1990s and is associated with a political and cultural movement that sees autism as a "normal" part of human diversity rather than as a "defect" requiring "cure." I refuse to cede control of my identity to the powers of normalization and standardization. For my own sake, certainly, for the sake of my children, but also for the sake of my colleagues, my neighbors, and my fellow parents, I embrace an undisciplined space, rejecting the confinement of diagnosis and thus choosing to challenge the narrowing definition of human "normalcy."

The moment of discomfort, the questionable humor of my remarks at a preschool co-op meeting may bear their own fruit. Perhaps disability can be both fluid and political, ambiguous yet assertive, a way of being without having to be boxed in by a clinical authority and naming. It seems possible that the eccentric, undiagnosed parent can help to challenge our sense of convention, to stretch our boundaries of thought, and to augment our notions of diversity. I may not always play well with others, but my game still has its place in the human playground.

PART THREE

Narrativity and Meaning-Making

Rewriting Stories of Mothering and Disability

Whereas the essays in the previous section disassembled or countered many of the restrictive cultural scripts of parenting and disability, the essays of part 3 seek to recast stories of mothering and disability. These authors encourage readers to consider how narrative itself constitutes values and ways of understanding and living in the world that have real, material consequences. The authors express the belief that narrative also offers spaces for the rewriting of stories, the crafting of new versions of living, leading to social and cultural change. In this effort, creativity can be a way to exercise agency and demonstrates what feminist disability theorist Tanya Titchkosky (2007) has described as the power arising from acting "in that liminal space between subject and group, between the power that forms the subject and the subject's own power" (21).

In "Mothers as Storytellers," Linnéa E. Franits explores how "mothers construct narratives of disability and how disability can construct narratives of motherhood within relationships, be they maternal or not." Using an ethnographic approach, Franits examines a culture of "life-writing" as mediated by the author's experiences as well as cultural expectations, revealing the element of interdependence at the center of life-writing, of disability, and of mothering.

Rachel Robertson's "Sharing Stories: Motherhood, Autism, and Culture" describes her son, his diagnosis, and their relationship as chronicled within diverse contexts and frameworks. Weaving together narrative and critical analysis, Robertson brings together medical discourse, disability studies theory, scenes from her son at school, personal journal entries, cultural expectations, and a series of short stories authored by her son. In doing so, she not only reveals the misunderstandings and gaps between these various discursive communities but also offers the multigenre, multivoiced text as a way to increased social awareness and inclusion.

In a personal and embodied account of breastfeeding and recovery, "Nurturing the Nurturer: Reflections on an Experience of Breastfeeding, Disability, and Physical Trauma," Heather Kuttai offers readers a series of diarylike entries detailing the related experiences of pregnancy and childbirth amid her multiple, invasive back surgeries. Kuttai's narrative of pain and healing centers on the value and agency that a disabled mother gains through breastfeeding her child.

The final chapter in this section, "Vulnerable Subjects: Motherhood and Disability in Nancy Mairs and Cherríe Moraga," presents alternatives to the "self-reliant subject" in narratives about disability and mothering. Examining works by Mairs and Moraga, Suzanne Bost reveals a series of cultural beliefs and their limitations in our corporeal ideals and encourages us to imagine "other" viable ways of being.

9

Mothers as Storytellers

LINNÉA E. FRANITS

Motherhood and disability have always been inextricably intertwined for me, as I was born into a family where disability was already present in my sister's and therefore my parents' lives. You might say that I was born "wise," to use Erving Goffman's descriptor of people who are privileged by being closely associated with individuals who are discredited or stigmatized by a characteristic such as disability ([1963] 1986, 28). Disability is also part of my current daily experience, as I am the mother of a pre-adolescent boy who has a couple of diagnoses that "qualify" him as disabled. In this chapter, I explore how mothers construct narratives of disability and how disability can construct narratives of motherhood within relationships, be they maternal or not.

I tell some stories myself, but as an autoethnographer I also reveal my position within these stories, reflecting on how life writing is mediated by the expectations of culture as well as narrative scripts. By focusing on storytelling rather than the stories themselves, I hope to formulate a broader understanding of how narratives of disability and motherhood can construct each other.

THE POWER OF STORYTELLING

The word "storytelling," particularly when paired with motherhood, conjures up the iconic scene of bedtime-story sweetness where a small child is snuggled in the crook of a mother's arm while she rocks and speaks in soothing melody, perhaps reading from a book or simply relaying her own version of a story while gazing lovingly at her little one. These can be emotionally laden moments. On the other hand, adults rarely read aloud to each other in this culture, and if not a designated performance, their storytelling is generally a more unstructured activity that happens around a dinner table or other social gathering. These stories can be emotionally ripe as well, of course, and although they often develop spontaneously, these narratives can also become scripts we recite as the situation dictates. In their research on the relationship between narrative and identity, Debra Skinner and her co-authors remind us, "These constructions of meaning do not happen in a vacuum. People learn to tell stories a certain way, to come to particular points of view, through participating in a community of tellers and listeners" (Skinner et al. 1999, 489).

And so, when I was asked to write a short memoir for a graduate class I was taking, it was easy to decide which story I should tell. I chose the story of the medical crisis my son had on his first day of life; it has all of the elements of a "good" story framed so as to follow a satisfying, typical narrative arc. I have told this story countless times and in fact regularly share it with classes of students in the health professions who are learning about the same cardiac defect my son was born with. There is even a slick PowerPoint version with dramatic photographs of my little boy with a long incision on his infant chest. However, for my class, I was instructed to write this autobiographical piece and then read it aloud to my classmates, which was not the typical way that I tell the story. I was confident at first that this well-practiced essay would roll off my tongue and that I would be able to time my words just so in order to give the audience an opportunity to respond as expected, always surprised and often moved to tears. I have found during my multiple retellings of this story that my listeners are often primed to hear my story in a certain way, and their expectations and response have in turn shaped the way I tell the story. I have tended to build this narrative with a typical arc of rising action, and the audience climbs that pinnacle with me. Just as a ride on a roller coaster has an expected incline, and the surprise comes when that incline suddenly turns at the climactic peak and quickly descends, the peak or climax in this story I tell is known to me but not to my audience, and so while I have come to expect their surprise, I do not feel my stomach flip. I pause; they tear up.

This telling became completely different. I found myself becoming more and more moved by the words I was reading, to the point where my eyes welled up with tears, which eventually spilled out onto my face as I was overcome with sobs. I was a mess. My kind peers passed tissues my way, and the professor was gracious and gentle as I tried to regain my composure. I was perplexed by my response and struggled to figure out why this telling of the story was such a different experience for me than my typical presentations. For some reason, reading my written word aloud multiplied the emotional impact it had on me. The story was the same as it always had been, and I already knew the admittedly constructed happy ending. The words on the page were somehow more real, more powerful because of their written and then aural form. As I heard myself reading these words to my classmates I became a listener as well as narrator, a participant who received the story and who was not in control of the happy ending. The roller-coaster track had become unfamiliar to me, and the turn startled me as it did the rest of the group. I was reminded that the story of my son's birth and early life was not the one I had mentally written before it happened, the one that other mothers had told me to expect.

EXPECTANCY AND EXPECTATIONS

Although the genre of disability memoir has truly established itself (particularly over the last couple of years), narratives about bodies tend toward stories about people with extraordinary athletic skill or beauty, or in the case of disability memoir, the overcoming of a disability rather than people with bodily difference that require medical intervention or that require accommodation. However, narratives of pregnancy and childbirth can cross between these categories and are some of the most often told stories of corporeal life. In the same way that a woman's pregnant contour invites the touch of near strangers, the mention of a woman's pregnancy seems to incite the storyteller in many women, who purport empathy but may simply wish to tell their own amazing stories. And these stories are indeed amazing because the pregnancy/childbirth process is so. Women (and sometimes men) are free to describe the most intimate details of bodily functions without fear of being stigmatized for it because the narrative is well scripted and meets our preconceptions of what a story is expected to be.

My mother used to tell my own birth story to me in what became a tradition on each birthday. Because of her generation and old-world beginnings, she tended toward euphemisms in a kind of poetic way, saying "womb" instead of uterus and "labor pains" instead of contractions. Women in my age group who have grown up reading *Our Bodies, Ourselves* (Boston Women's Health Course Collective [1973] 1992) are often more comfortable with the biology of childbearing and can be even more descriptive when telling pregnancy and birth stories. Maternity allows gatherings of women to discuss episiotomies and vaginal topography or troublesome incontinence, topics not typically part of polite conversation in our ordinary social contexts. These grounded moments are not stigmatized because they are a part of the expected narrative surrounding childbirth in this culture.

But what of the narratives that do not fit these expectations? When a child is born and disability or illness is present, the story changes. The climax of the birth can be superseded by the "tragedy" of a diagnosis. This kind of a story is less often welcomed by those awaiting the expected resolution of "normal" childbirth and may not even be shared in the same way. When disability or illness is present, the new mother may be stripped of her "expert" status regarding her child as medical personnel busy themselves with often critical tasks. Health care practitioners take over in constructing the infant child's story. Some mothers and fathers share horrifying tales of physicians who recommended institutionalization of newborns diagnosed with disability. These stories and others like it are increasingly becoming part of disability narratives, as people with disabilities become more free or able to tell their own stories and to share the disheartening choices parents were asked to make. Most of the narratives about this kind of a choice are now being told by individuals who were not institutionalized and whose parents fought the recommendation to do so.

When a narrative about a birth does not traverse the expected arc (anticipation of the birth, to the climax of the birth itself, to the resolution of a healthy baby), there are alternative narrative scripts that mothers may choose that fall into what G. Thomas Couser (2008, 190) describes as formulaic "rhetorical schemes" in his discussion of narratives of disability. One of the most familiar narrative patterns is one where the individual with the disability is either cured or gets beyond his/her condition in some other way. This story always has a happy ending and is often strongly reinforced by those who receive it. The narrative of overcoming disability can be seen in mothers' stories of the resolution of "normal" life after the initial disappointment about a child's diagnosis and the salvation offered by professionals. Truthfully, this is how I have constructed my own story about my son's diagnosis shortly after birth; I tell the tale of his ability to overcome a severe cardiac defect and the intervention offered by medical experts. I do not mean to suggest that this story is inaccurate or that his life wasn't saved by medical expertise. Rather, I am compelled to tell the story this way because both the expectations of my listeners and expectations I have internalized are very powerful. There is more to the story than the details I typically include, but those that don't fit the prescribed shape I leave unsaid.

Sometimes, a mother feels the need to construct a narrative of disability that fits the listeners' expectations. This "wish fulfillment," as Simi Linton describes it, is fueled by the desires of people outside of the disability experience as well as people living disability narratives who have internalized those tropes and become characters in their own stories, rather than more authentic autobiographers (Linton 2008, 177). When my son was discharged from the hospital after his third surgery in a two-year span, I was asked by a friend of the hospital chaplain to submit an essay for a book of inspirational stories he was collecting to distribute to other families who were going through similar medical experiences. At first I was excited to have an opportunity to tell my son's story (or perhaps my own story), but I quickly recognized the impossibility of the task as set out. Although I can be spiritually reflective about my motherhood and my son's diagnoses, I really don't want to construct the story to insure that it inspires readers.

DISABILITY, THE SEQUEL

Some find it ironic that having grown up with a sibling with disability and spending much of my childhood longing for a more "typical" family,

I have a disabled son myself. Others frame it as a cruel injustice, and still others see it as fulfillment of a divine plan because I have been "prepared" to be a mother to someone with disability. None of these formulations really fit the stories I construct about my life experiences, although I have tried each on for size at times. More frequently, I examine my mother's position, culturally, historically and geographically, and how that may have dictated her actions and compare it to where I perceive myself to be. Some similarities between our situations are striking, but our stories are not and could not be the same.

My mother and I have each experienced the pain of watching a child undergo major surgery on multiple occasions, when medical fragility required that precious moments be spent in the antichildhood context of the hospital. We have each spent countless hours in waiting rooms anxious to hear the surgeon's assessment of an outcome of a procedure. We have felt the support of friends and family that go along with these medical crises and know that these are the dramatic stories that people want to hear. As a child, I sought the attention that my sister received during these periods of intensity and eventually learned that I could get some of that attention by telling her story. As a mother, I also learned to manipulate the story of my son's critical moments, sometimes for attention, sometimes for educational purposes, and sometimes just to tell a good story.

But in addition to my sister's acute neurological episodes and my son's critical cardiac status, each has what is characterized as a "developmental disability" that, because chronic, doesn't generate the same interest among the audience as a life-or-death operating room tale. In my sister's case, "mild mental retardation," and for my son, "high-functioning autism," these experiences are perceived as nonnormative states that are perhaps pitied but do not generate narratives that are as interesting to the public as dramatic hospital stories. I have presented the story of my son's cardiac condition to a number of college classes as well as academic conferences but have never been invited to speak about his autism. I conjecture that the narratives associated with a disability that will not be cured, or overcome, do not fit any template of popular disability narrative in our culture, and so these stories are not sought out. The daily care-giving associated with my sister's short-term memory difficulties or my son's anxieties about fire drill alarms doesn't provide as compelling a story for most, and so these narratives go untold.

MY MOTHER, NOT MYSELF

I couldn't begin to tease out where my experiences watching my mother construct disability narratives about my sister inform my own maternal authorship about my son's disabilities, yet I am confident that they are interwoven. Sometimes women say that they understand their own mothers better once they become mothers themselves, and one might think that especially true of mothers of children with disabilities. But disability complicates motherhood in very individualized ways. Eva Feder Kittay is perplexed by her own mother's unfathomable advice to institutionalize Kittay's daughter Sesha when her numerous disabilities were initially recognized. Kittay's emotional pain is palpable when she asks "My model of maternal love asking me to discard my child? . . . I couldn't comprehend it" (1999, 152). The only way that she could frame such a foreign sentiment was by delving a bit into her own mother's history with disability, which most likely included horror stories from the Holocaust, where revealed disability meant certain death in a concentration camp. Kittay understands that her mother wishes to protect her granddaughter with "preservative love" by hiding her away (163) but simultaneously maintains her own perspective to create a "protective circle" of support around her daughter rather than institutionalize her (Goffman [1963] 1986, 97).

As I have already mentioned, my mother's choice of words about childbirth clearly identified her as a product of her generation and place. Her vocabulary about disability was equally culturally positioned, and she unwittingly taught me the power of negative language about disability and how certain words could stigmatize. One particular story was logged in my brain when I was a six-year-old girl, sitting on the beach with my nine-year-old sister and my mother. A wind picked up and lofted our little clamp-on umbrella right off the webbed chair and into the sea; my mother did her best to jog after it as it somersaulted across the sand, rolling yellow with white polka dots, but she was unable to reach it. When the surf grabbed it and it began to move further towards the horizon, my sister burst into tears for fear of losing our stuff. She pointed and cried, repeating, "The umbrella! Get the umbrella!" That's when my mother shouted back at her with a short-tempered, almost mean, "Stop crying!" I was surprised by her sharp tone, which she rarely used and particularly not to my sister. But then I was even more surprised by her next statement, "People will think you're retarded or something!" I was shocked and perplexed and for the first time really wondered how my mother viewed my sister. Wasn't she "slightly" retarded? Isn't that how some people had described her? What was my sister anyway if not "retarded"? What word would she use? Then I recognized why my mother used that tone with my sister—she was embarrassed. She didn't want people around us to think of my sister as being cognitively disabled and particularly not that dreaded word—retarded. My mother was never ashamed to tell the story of my sister's neurological trauma and almost bragged about how well she recovered from brain surgery each time. Yet the narrative that accompanied the word "retarded" was not a story line my mother embraced. Even as I write this, forty years after this event, the word retarded is in the news as an ableist epithet being used in a major motion picture. Simi Linton includes the word "retard" in her list of "nasty words" in her discussion of how language related to disability should be reassigned new meaning, as defined by those living the narratives of disability (Linton 2008, 176).

My own choices to use the words autism or autism spectrum disorder when describing my son also depend on my audience, but I find them less stigmatizing than my mother did with the word retarded. I likely use these terms as shorthand, tapping into the public awareness about autism and the preconceived notions people have about what individuals with autism are like. Although there are plenty of misconceptions, I can explain some of my son's unusual behaviors with the simple phrase "he is on the autistic spectrum" worked somewhere into the conversation. Although I theoretically resist labeling people with diagnoses, in practicality I make use of labels to my son's advantage, such as in school to get the supports that help him to benefit from the instruction. Perhaps because autism is sometimes associated with purported savantism, or extraordinary talent, it is not as stigmatizing a word to use as words associated with subpar cognitive capabilities. It is not uncommon for people to ask me, once I've outed my son, what his extraordinary talent is. Admittedly, I use this opportunity to brag in a way mothers of typical children might brag about their kids' accomplishments, but I eventually wind up concluding that my son's skills in whichever area I'm discussing are really just a little bit above average. My listeners may desire a more dramatic climax to the story to somehow balance the perceived tragedy of the diagnosis of autism, but I take pleasure in the "normalcy" of the ordinary.

DEPENDENCE AND CAREGIVING:
HOW DISABILITY NARRATES MOTHERHOOD

Mothers construct narratives of disability for a variety of reasons and in a variety of ways, yet the disability experience can write stories of motherhood, too. The most obvious understanding of this is the way that disability in a person's life can shape or construct her motherhood. Caregiving for children with disabilities often extends beyond typical timelines, and the "dependency work" associated with motherhood can be a lifelong commitment when disability is present (Kittay 1999, 156). These characteristics enabled my mother to avoid the "empty-nest syndrome," as—in my sister—she had someone at home who depended on her in a childlike way for forty years. My mother's identity was indeed formed by my sister's needs, which in turn became my mother's need to be needed. In my case, my son is my only child, and so my entire experience of biological motherhood has been informed by the presence of disability as it has been defined in his life. It is not that I wouldn't have a story if my sister and son didn't have disability, but I wouldn't have this story.

Disability can also construct narratives of motherhood for anyone considered to be a caregiver. Although disability is often equated with dependency, this is not the most accurate description of the dynamic between the individual with disability and the caregiver. Just as motherhood can be constructed to include "othermothers," caregiving can be seen as an interdependent exchange between an individual with a disability and caregiver(s), including mothers. Eva Feder Kittay recognizes that the care her daughter requires dictates "distributed mothering," and she calls upon what I would identify as othermothers to accomplish this in her daughter's life (1999, 156). When othermothers participate in the narratives that disability constructs, the interdependence between the child with disability, the biological mother, and other caregivers becomes solidified. One of the women in Kittay's network of othermothers relays a sweet story of reciprocal learning between herself and Kittay's daughter, a story that Kittay uses to illustrate her idea of "care as labor and care as relationship" (157).

The demarcation between independence and dependence is generally determined by context, yet in this society we continue to subscribe to an either/or paradigm with little room for situations that don't fit either end of what is more likely a continuum between complete independence and dependence. The gray area of interdependency is rarely referred to in popular culture or in scholarship, but this is where most of us firmly live. This interdependency is often underacknowledged and can deprive caregivers, always giving and never receiving, of what they might need. Susan Wendell (1996, 142) discusses interdependency in light of an ethic of care and the reciprocity that it necessitates between the caregiver and the cared-for. While women who are mothers of children with disability are often privileged with this knowledge of interdependency and understand how it has constructed their experience of motherhood, othermothers should have access to this storyline as well.

Nurturing another human being can construct a woman as a mother, and the ability to nurture can construct a "good" or capable mother in the eyes of society as much as the perceived inability to nurture because of disability can steal the role of mother from a woman. Nancy Mairs struggles with this construction as she reflects on her diminishing capabilities due to multiple sclerosis. Although she does not want her children to become her caregivers, flipping the traditional roles, she recognizes that by allowing others to care for her, she can fulfill their need to be needed and thus reclaim the nurturing she desires to do. She concludes, "Permitting myself to be taken care of is, in fact, one of the ways I can take care of others" (1996, 83). She goes on to describe the power of her own storytelling as an act of caregiving, "Above all, I can still write, which for me has always been an act of oblation and nurturance: my means of taking the reader into my arms, holding a cup to her lips, stroking her forehead, whispering jokes into her ears. . . . With such gestures, I am taking all the care I can" (84). In recognizing the interdependent nature of these constructed stories, we can better understand disability experience as well as the venerated occupation of mothering and how one can construct the other.

10

Sharing Stories

Motherhood, Autism, and Culture

RACHEL ROBERTSON

*M*r. *Perfect, number 42, had a sister called Little Miss Naughty, number 2. They were playing together with his new sword. He took his sword and chopped off Little Miss Naughty's head. He was only joking. Then they swapped. Mr. Perfect was Mr. Naughty now. Little Miss Naughty took some blue paint and dripped it on herself so she was Little Miss Perfect. Then Mr. Skinny bustled up. He's tall and thin and yellow, number 35. He said, "Why are you playing here?" "We're not playing, we're just rescuing our paint," said Little Miss Perfect. "No cause to be rude," said Mr. Skinny. He didn't know that Mr. Perfect and Little Miss Naughty had tricked him. "Oh no," said Little Miss Perfect, "the paint is washing off!" Now Little Miss Perfect was Little Miss Naughty again.*

"That's a great story."

"But I don't know if it's a real story."

"Well, it's real to you and me."

"But it's not real like in the books."

"We could type it up on the computer if you want?"

"No, thank you."

THE PERSONAL STORY

We tell stories, my son and I.[1] We read them, we write them, and we talk them. It is our way of making sense of our life together, our separate expe-

---

1. Names in this essay have been changed to protect privacy. My son's stories are used with his permission.

riences having sometimes seemed so far apart. The son who once rode in my body, a little circle within a larger circle, only three years later seemed to have drifted far away, a small circle heading into wide emptiness. Now, at eight years old, he is much closer again. I imagine us as a Venn diagram, the space of overlap equaling the spaces on either side. Stories are one way we have reconnected. Together and separately we have shaped our daily life into story after story.

At the end of the day, which for Ben is 8:00 p.m. sharp, we climb into his bed under his blanket, me in my clothes, he in his pajamas. I take off my glasses and lay them on the bedside shelf next to his clock, his colored light, his drink bottle and his ten frogs. We lie cheek to cheek and he says, "You can tell what we did today," and I start like this: "Well, first we had breakfast, and then . . ." And after I have retold the day and we have talked over any confusing events or unmanageable feelings, he says, "We'll have a good time tomorrow, won't we?" and I say, "Yes, we probably will," because we mainly do have good times, even though every day my son faces difficult challenges and every day I feel the pain of witnessing his difficulties. Then Ben says "good night, mum," in a firm and final way that means I am dismissed, so I leave him to sleep and turn to my computer to share my account of our stories.

I tell my story because becoming a mother has taken me to places I never thought I would visit. I'm not just talking about places that mothers go or places that mothers of a child with a disability go; I'm talking also about visiting another culture, one that is profoundly challenging, even frightening, to me, but also illuminating and remarkable. I'm just starting this journey—I expect it to last the rest of my life. If I write about it as I go, it is probably because that is the only way I think I can understand what is happening. Perhaps I am trying to write what Rayna Rapp and Faye Ginsburg call an "unnatural history," a vision of our lives "lived against the grain of normalcy" (2001, 552).

THE MEDICAL STORY

There is a medical story about my son and me—one I both accept and resist. Like all stories, it has a subject, the child; subordinate characters, mum, dad, doctor, therapist; a plot, the "normal" developmental path;

metaphors such as theory of mind, central coherence, and executive function (see Biklen et al. 2005) and a title, Autism spectrum disorder.[2] Like
all stories, it is constructed, though this aspect is not foregrounded. And
like all stories, it reflects particular values. For a short while, I understood
my son through the lens of this medical story, but I soon recognized that
it was a partial and problematic story, one that could harm him as much
as help him. I say that I accept it in the sense that I accept the fact of
neurological difference (neurodiversity), and I accept that Ben is what we
can label autistic and I am what we can label neurotypical. I accept that
this will mean that Ben, an autistic person in a predominantly neurotypical world, will experience disability, just as a visually impaired person is
disabled by the world created for and by sighted people. In other ways,
though, the medical story is one I want to question, resist, reframe and
rewrite, and I hope that Ben will do the same throughout his life.

In Australia, for a child to be diagnosed as having an autism spectrum disorder, he or she must meet a number of criteria in the diagnostic
manual used by clinicians. The three groupings of criteria are: "Qualitative impairments in reciprocal social interaction"; "Qualitative impairments in communication"; and "Restricted, repetitive preoccupation with
one or more stereotyped patterns of behavior, interests or activity" (*Diagnostic and Statistical Manual of Mental Disorders* 1994). Medical descriptions
of autism almost always focus on this triad of social interaction, language
and symbolic play, and particular interests. You can read this as an accurate description of the results of neurological difference, or you can read
it as a manifesto of desirable behavior. For example, a "total lack of the
development of spoken language" (*DSM-IV* 1994) can be a self-evident

2. The term autism spectrum disorder is now used to refer to a range of disorders,
including autism, Asperger's syndrome, Rett's syndrome, and other pervasive developmental conditions. I use the term autism in this essay because it is the diagnosis my son
received. I describe autistic people using person-second language (rather than "person
with autism") following the reasons given by Jim Sinclair (1999) in "Why I Dislike Person
First Language" and in response to reading other autistic people writing about nomencla-
ture. Following common usage by autistic writers, I use the term neurotypical for those not
diagnosed with an autism spectrum disorder or other neurological difference.

example of deficit or a statement about how important spoken language is in our culture. You could argue that autism contests—or at least lays bare—some of the key values of our society: the desirability of certain types of social interaction, the importance of spoken language and conversation, acceptable forms of imagination, the relevance and importance of some activities over others.

Frog was unique. When he was in Tadpole School, the other tadpoles had to read the numbers from one to nine, but Frog could read numbers up to 1000. Frog liked water and put his head in a bucket of water. But it had detergent in too. Frog's eyes were very sore.

"Do you remember that, Mum? When I put my head into the bucket?"

"Yes, I certainly do."

"Do you remember that I could read numbers then, at kindy?"

"Yes, I remember."

"I was unique not technique."

"What's technique?"

"You know, mum, if you're not unique."

THE STORY OF THE "OTHER"

Six or seven times a day for two years, I would ask Ben, "Are you okay?" and he would answer, if he answered at all, "Yes." The way he said yes (the way he still says yes) had a slight nasal sound in front—"nyes"—as if he was hedging his bets just in case he should have said no. He didn't do this sound with any other word beginning with *y*, just with yes. Even though he always answered "nyes," I kept asking the question. I had no confidence in my own ability to guess his frame of mind from his actions or manner, and he didn't have the ability yet to convey in language his mood or feelings. In asking, "Are you okay, Ben?" I may as well have been crooning to myself, "everything's okay, everything's okay." It was a meaningless exchange, yet it meant something to me. It reassured me.

If we witnessed an autistic person repeating a question like that to another person and getting the same answer, regardless of the true situation, and continuing to repeat the question for months, what would we say? I think we would describe this behavior as "obsessive repetition" or "perseveration." We might recognize that it resulted at least partially from anxiety, but we would still categorize it as an "inappropriate" response.

It is apparent to me now that the premise on which I am asked to make judgments about my son's behaviors is a manufactured and very partial premise. Does he make appropriate eye contact when addressing others? Does he respond appropriately to peers who exhibit distress? Does he give and accept compliments? These are all questions I recently had to answer about Ben. Does he give compliments? I didn't actually know that giving compliments was an essential part of an eight-year-old's social repertoire. And what is an appropriate response to a distressed child? For Ben, standing back and watching may seem the right thing to do because that's what he would want another child to do for him. When Ben stands and watches a crying child without taking any action, do we judge this behavior as a lack of empathy, a fear of doing the wrong thing, a respectful acknowledgment of another's distress, a freezing of all his actions because of witnessing distress, or a practical response based on a belief that no action of his is going to make the other child feel better? Or do we try to stop judging behaviors on the basis of our own interpretations and acknowledge that we don't actually know the basis on which this behavior is generated?

It is a common trope in discussions about autism to describe the autistic person as an alien in our world or like someone from another planet. Autistic writer and scientist Temple Grandin describes herself as "an anthropologist on Mars" when she tries to understand the neurotypical world (Sacks 1995, 248). Other autistic people have used similar terminology (for example, Anna Hayward 2001; Jasmine O'Neill 1999; Jim Sinclair 1993). The metaphor of the alien is interesting because it suggests that we recognize some fundamental difference between neurotypical and autistic people. It also suggests that this difference is unbridgeable, that both neurotypicals and autistics believe they are like two different species. But what if we were to understand the differences between autistic and neurotypical people as a cultural difference instead? Rather than thinking of my son as an alien who landed on earth by accident, I could think of him as someone whose neurological makeup resulted in his belonging to a different culture. People parent across cultures all the time (for example, adopting children from other countries); it's complex but not impossible. This, I think, is my task as mother to Ben: to respect and understand autistic culture as much as I can and then to perform a kind of cross-cultural parenting. I need to help him understand neurotypical culture also, of course, because it is the dominant culture. Like many other parents of autistic children, I have become a kind of cross-cultural translator, explaining the world to Ben and Ben to the world, mediating and interpreting everything I see and hear.

Frog was very sad when he came home from amphibian school. "What's the matter?" asked Toad. Frog had to write 100 lines. He missed his lunch. "Why?" asked Toad. Frog had been very bad. He had rocked on his chair in class. "Oh, Frog," said Toad, "I don't think you are bad." Frog had an apple and the two friends had a fine afternoon.

THE CULTURAL STORY

"Look at me when I'm talking to you, please," commands Ben's teacher, Mr. A. "Now, where is your pencil case?"

Ben turns his face and stares at Mr. A. with goggle-eyes before saying, "I don't know." I try not to laugh. Then he drops his eyes to the ground again and leans away from the teacher. Mr. A. frowns. "Did you have it in the library?" he asks.

"I don't know," replies Ben.

"Look at me, Ben. You have to learn to get organized," snaps Mr. A., and Ben does a brief goggle-stare again before looking down at his shoes.

"Never mind," I intervene. "We'll talk about it at home, Ben."

I don't know how many times I've heard people tell Ben to look at them. It started when he was two and continues even now. I said it a couple of times myself before I realized how ridiculous it was. If I told Ben to look at me, he would turn both his eyes toward my face and then turn away again as soon as he was allowed to. It was an exercise in compliance.

He wasn't learning anything from looking at me, and I didn't learn anything from his face turned to mine except that he would obey orders. More recently, I have tried to explain to Ben why it is that people like to look at each other when they have a conversation: how we use facial expressions to help us understand words and how we can learn whether people are listening to us from seeing their eyes. I have also tried to explain to Mr. A. that autistic people can find seeing people's eyes and faces quite confronting as well as confusing, and that they may not be able to concentrate on listening and watching at the same time. But I don't think Mr. A. really believes the things I tell him. I don't suppose he'd tell a vision-impaired child to look at him, but he can't resist telling Ben to do so.

It's one of those things that mothering Ben has shown me: our culture has an obsession with eye contact. People seem unable to cope if you can't or won't look at them. It's one of the first things our early-intervention therapist tried to work on with Ben, even turning his head to make him look in a particular direction. When I told her that I wanted Ben to make his own choices about where he would look and why, she gave me her "being understanding with misguided but caring mother" face, a face with which I have become quite familiar over the years. Actually, Ben now makes eye contact with me quite regularly and will come over and study my face if he feels he is unsure about my mood. We may even share a joke or catch one another's eye in public. But he still needs to ask me about the meaning of facial expressions or nuances that other children of his age just seem to recognize. As for looking at Mr. A., well, who wants to look the teacher in the eye when he's cross?

There are many different ways we can interpret this eye contact issue. The interpretation we choose determines the action we take. If I decide that Ben's lack of comfort with eye contact is the result of what is described as "mind blindness" or the lack of a theory of mind, then I might decide to teach him some theory of mind "rules" (Howlin, Baron-Cohen, and Hadwin 1999). If I think it is about mono-channeling, then I might give him auditory integration therapy to encourage his ability to manage auditory data better. If I think it is just a behavioral tick or deficit that is part of the autism diagnosis, then I might train him to look people in the eye by giving him lollies every time he does. If I decide it's a cultural (or even a personal) preference, then I might let him continue to avoid eye contact. I actually don't know the reason Ben sometimes avoids looking at people's eyes. He hasn't told me, perhaps because he doesn't really understand the premise of (the norm implied by) my question. I've read and heard what other autistic people say about this, but the diagnosis of autism has been given to a very wide range of people with many individual differences, and so what others say may not be true for Ben.

The issue of eye contact is just one of many differences that may be defined as deficit or as cultural preference. Other differences include stimming (bodily movements such as flapping, tapping, or spinning, which are described as "self-stimulatory"); the preference for literal and direct language use; sensory and motor planning differences; a focus on routine or order; exclusive or specialized interests; and communication choices (some autistic people will write but not speak, others do not use symbolic communication modes at all).[3]

The notion of an autistic culture has grown out of the Internet and the autistic-run online communities that have developed over the past ten years. Autistic people who call for recognition of autistic culture generally focus on the need for society to accept neurological diversity, the need for autistics to be formally recognized as a minority group, self-determination, and the removal of discrimination, including the effort to find a "cure" for autism (Nelson 2004; Dekker 2006). Camille Clark (2006) explains on her Autism Diva website that autistics are not claiming that autism is a culture but that when autistics meet (online or in person) they share a particular culture.

The official United Nations description of culture says that "culture should be regarded as the set of distinctive spiritual, material, intellectual and emotional features of society or a social group, and that it encompasses, in addition to art and literature, lifestyles, ways of living together, value systems, traditions and beliefs" (UNESCO 2001). As more people on

3. David Goode (1994) has suggested that there are forms of nonsymbolic, alingual communication, and this may be a type of communication used by autistic people without verbal or nonverbal symbolic language.

the autism spectrum are being diagnosed, including parents with their children, and as autistic-led groups become more influential, it seems possible to me that autistic differences could be considered a minority culture. It is not just a matter of description. As Carol Padden says about Deaf culture, "To use a cultural definition is not only to assert a new frame of reference, but to consciously reject an older one" (Padden 1996, 85), in this case the older but still predominant medical model of autism as deficit. Like the Deaf community, gay community, and some indigenous communities in Western countries, the autistic community is not bounded and separate from other communities, but living among and within mainstream culture. Jim Sinclair (1993), in his influential essay "Don't Mourn for Us," says, "autism goes deeper than language or culture; autistic people are 'foreigners' in any society." But perhaps one day neurotypical people will have learned and changed enough that autistic people are not foreigners anymore but equal participants in a neurodiverse world.

Like all stories, this one is grounded in the personal. I don't know if it has any wider relevance. I realize that it's possible for me to contemplate the idea of autistic culture because of my particular experiences with Ben. If my son were nonverbal, I'm fairly sure I would be desperate to have him speak, culture or no culture. If he refused to eat anything but rice crackers and carrots or if his motor-planning skills were so poor that he couldn't get his body to obey him at all, I doubt I'd see these things as cultural issues. And it would have been no help to me to consider autism a medical and social construction during the four years I got out of bed nine or ten times every night to resettle Ben. It doesn't make me more patient when I have to answer the same question from Ben dozens of times a day for weeks on end. And it doesn't help Ben manage his extreme anxiety when faced with new people, new places, or a change of routine. So, I can see that for many autistic people and their families, exploring the cultural construction of autism is neither possible nor useful.

In suggesting that autism is a medical and social construction, I don't mean to imply that there aren't neurological and other differences or that these differences don't result in disability. I'm not saying that autism doesn't exist, but that how we define and describe it is a result of our beliefs about normalcy. As Simi Linton (1998) and many writers in disability studies have pointed out, normalcy is a creation that is dependent on the creation of its unequal opposite, abnormality or disability. Normalcy and disability are unstable and relational terms but are used as absolute categories. Douglas Biklen (2005) points out that most scientific accounts of autism treat it as a relatively stable concept that is internal to the individual. He compares this with the view that autism is a concept developed and applied (not natural or discovered) that can be viewed as a set of qualities among many. Foregrounding the constructed nature of autism, Biklen argues that "people classified as autistic as well as those around them . . . have choices to make concerning which constructions to privilege" (65).

The concept of autistic culture allows us to make these choices about how we describe and understand differences. To consider parenting a cross-cultural activity acknowledges the complexity of the situation and creates a space for mutual reciprocity. It allows us to move away from the belief that there is "normal" behavior and that our role is to teach our children how to perform normality.

Mr. Mischief, number 36, decided to have a drink of cordial. He poured some into two glasses. But when he took a sip, it was disgusting. He spat it out. The bottle spilt all over the table. Oh no, thought Mr. Mischief, I hope I don't get into trouble.

"Was I like Mr. Mischief when I did that?"

"Yes, I think you were. I think you knew it was red wine not cordial, didn't you?"

"How cross were you when I did that—cross, angry, very angry, furious, or enraged?"

"Well, I was a bit cross. It was a big mess to clean up so early in the morning."

"But you weren't enraged. I don't think you'd ever be enraged."

"Well, let's hope not."

THE HIDDEN STORY

"Mum, why is this wrong?" Ben pulls out a math worksheet from his school bag to show me. I can see that the teacher has put a red cross against two of the twenty questions. The first one asks: "What is the difference between nine and six?" and Ben's answer was "one is odd and the other even." I try to explain to him that this was a subtraction question and that, even though his answer was correct in one way, it wasn't the answer the teacher required. I'm not sure if he understands, but I move on anyhow. "This one is measurement. How long is this line? You wrote 6cm. I don't think it's that long. Let's measure it." The line is only 2cm. I notice, though, that Ben has no idea which line to measure, and he starts by measuring the line upon which he is supposed to write his answer. It's perfectly clear to me which line they intend him to measure, but I think it must be one of those examples of the hidden curriculum that Ben finds so tricky.

Many of the rules and instructions they give at school have underlying premises that Ben seems to miss. The rule "Walk in the undercover areas," which really means, don't run in the undercover areas, still confuses him, so that he asks at the start of every term, "Am I allowed to walk in the outside areas?" Similarly, "look to your classroom teacher for instructions" muddles him because he expects to see some instructions, and they have never yet appeared. When the Italian teacher told the class that next week they would be "taking a trip around Italy," Ben was the only child who rushed home in a panic about traveling without his mum. The first time the teacher took his photograph and said, "say cheese, please," Ben said, "No, thank you. I don't really like cheese."

It is not just about language, though. It happens with play as well. Other children seem to use some invisible signal to indicate which way the game will go, and they all move in the one direction—all except Ben that is. Even when they spell it out, "you chase me now, Ben," he doesn't quite get it, running in the wrong direction or running after a child but not tagging him or her. It's as though they know the secret and only Ben has no idea what's going on.

We don't have nearly so many muddles at home. I'm not sure whether this is because I am careful to explain things very clearly to Ben or whether it's just that he is able to predict from the context and from his knowledge of me what is likely to happen. He understands that language is not always used literally and can now identify the meaning behind many common turns of phrase, but he can't recognize sarcasm or irony. Although autistic children are supposed to find it hard to interpret others' feelings, intent, beliefs, and desires, I find that Ben quite often has a good idea of how I feel and what I want. If he doesn't know, he actually asks me, so that he probably knows more about my feelings than any other male I've met. The other day as I dropped him at school I said, "Ben, I'm having my hair cut today, so when I pick you up, you can tell me if it looks good." He said, "But mum, that might be false flattery so that you give me a treat."

Frog and Toad were in the park. Frog was on the swing when all of sudden, "woof" along came a dog. "A dog, a dog, run, hide," yelled Frog. He climbed on top of the slide. Toad said, "Don't worry, Frog. This is a nice dog, he won't hurt you." But Frog was scared. Dogs are very noisy and run around a lot. Then there was a bang and the dog was gone.

THE INSTITUTION'S STORY

It is assembly time at school, and Ben is going to win a merit certificate. He doesn't say much, but I know he is pleased. It's true that last term he won one as well, but that was for "trying to improve his handwriting," something that Ben doesn't see as important or valuable. The children all sit on mats on the concrete floor, and I sit on one of the benches, not far from Ben. One of the classes does a little skit. Then the student of the month certificates are given out. The children are rewarded for "courtesy and consideration in the classroom," "making great strides in class work," and "representing the school in the community." Each time another student wins an award, Ben bobs up and down on the mat, and occasionally he turns and looks at me, anxious that he won't get an award after all. I smile and nod at him. Then the principal of the local high school presents the Character Award, which is only given out every couple of months. Ben's classmate Jamie wins the award for "helping a friend in need." Everyone claps, and Jamie goes to the front to get his award. The principal asks him to tell everyone about "the friend in need." Jamie says, "His name is Ben and I'm teaching him how to play football." Ben bobs up and turns to look at me again. I smile and nod. Finally, after several more announcements, the weekly merit certificates are given out. Ben wins his for "showing improvement in his handwriting." Then the assembly is over; I wave at him as he goes back to class.

As I walk home, I think about what I've just witnessed. Ben has been labeled a child "in need" in front of the whole school community—students, teachers, and parents. He has been told that children who play with him need to be rewarded. And he himself has been rewarded, not for his positive, playful and generous character, nor for his remarkable memory, his excellent spelling and math, nor for the courage and persistence he shows every day; no, he has been rewarded for improved handwriting yet again. At a single stroke, the friendship between Ben and Jamie—which is based on mutual pleasure in each other's company—has been redefined as an unequal relationship of need and charity. Even if it was done quite unconsciously, which I expect it was, nothing changes the message this sends to Ben, his classmates, and the wider community. I can try to reframe this story for Ben but he'll still have heard the implication that his friendship is not valuable, that he is not his peers' equal. I realize that this is a story he'll hear many times in his life. These last few years, Ben has been surrounded by schoolmates who accept him for who he is and who accommodate his differences without judgment. As he gets older, I expect this to change and Ben's life to become more difficult.

I notice that I also feel a sense of humiliation, as if I have been shown up as a failure because my son is less competent and independent than others his age. Just as disabled children are considered lesser than nondisabled children, so, too, are their mothers. Gail Landsman has argued that the "diminished personhood of the child with disabilities" is linked to an experience of "diminished motherhood" for the mother (1999, 135). Because a mother's moral value rests on her association with a valued or "perfect" child, the mother of an unvalued child is not seen as "morally equivalent." I felt marked out at the school assembly, as if I had been given a public certificate of failure.

The loneliness of the mother of a child with a disability is possibly similar to the loneliness of the child. And if your child is autistic, that loneliness may be compounded by the difficulty your child experiences in social interactions of all sorts. The combination of this isolation with the challenges that living with an autistic child may present can be exhausting and dispiriting. But, like any movement into unknown territory, it can offer opportunities as well. When your experiences strip back all the window dressing of your society and you see with terrible clarity what it is your culture values, and that those values deny your son personhood— well, once you have admitted your grief and your fury, then your marginality becomes empowerment. You have your story and you're bound to tell it, one way or another.

During the weekend I tried to fly my new kite. At home I sat on the top of the wall and kicked my football. I jumped off the wall and flew off with it. The kite fell in the fish pond with the football. I swam in the pond. I was scared so I won a lot of medals and trophies!

THE MOTHER'S STORY

How do you parent across the cultural divide of autism? How do you prevent yourself from interpreting your child's behaviors in ways that are based on neurotypical culture? How do you respect your child's preferences but help him live in a world that won't feel that respect? I don't know the answers to any of these questions. Even though I have read many books and web pages about autism—by researchers, psychologists, medical professionals, autistic people, parents of autistic people, and educators—and I have learned many things from this reading, I haven't found one that gives me a road map for my journey with my son. This is probably good, because my son is an individual and so how I relate to him will be different from how other parents would relate to their children. Of the many different therapeutic models and approaches to autism, the one I feel most comfortable with is Stanley Greenspan and Serena Wieder's DIR or Floortime model (2006). By focusing on developmentally appropriate, individualized, and relationship-based play therapy, the Floortime approach seems to honor the differences of autistic people while not denying that autistic people want and can develop strong relationships with the key people in their lives. By trying to attune myself to Ben's needs and desires, by seeing him as a whole person and not a collection of deficits, by listening to his stories—whether verbal or nonverbal—without believing I can necessarily successfully interpret them: these are the ways I try to support and facilitate Ben's growth.

Put like this, as neat sentences on a page, it sounds possible, perhaps even easy. But it isn't easy, because so much about autism is challenging to a neurotypical like me. The sensory perceptions (seeing things I don't but not seeing what I consider obvious), the unusual bodily movements, the lack of small talk and white lies, the extreme interest in one or two things (like numbers or swimming pools) that aren't important to me, the need for so much time alone to regroup and de-stress, the superlogical approach to human problems, the desire for sameness, and the failure to consider relationships with others as the primary ordering principle of a life—all these things are confusing and worrying to me at times. Still, even as they worry me, even as I continue to identify myself as neurotypical and therefore an outsider, I have noticed that I'm beginning gradually to see the value of these differences. All my life, I've been missing things that Ben has shown me—the shape of shells, the number of petals on flowers, the color of swimming pools, the different types of clouds, the way some words have no antonyms, the number of words that are spelled in three different ways in English, the different fonts used in children's picture books, the fact that people lie to one another all the time, why it is that bullying thrives, our daily acceptance of malice. Living with Ben is like wearing an extra pair of glasses: I begin to see and understand things a little differently. I begin to inhabit new territory.

On Sunday I followed a maze and got lost. I lost my pen! Then I went to a park and I swung so high on a swing. The wind blew into my mouth! All day I carried an easterly wind in my mouth.

THE AUTOBIOGRAPHICAL STORY

"Mum, am I intelligent or muscular?" asks Ben, wandering into the kitchen with a pen in his hand.

"Oh, why do you ask?"

"I'm writing a biography, like we did in school."

"Oh, I see. Well, which do you think you are?" I ask.

"Intelligent?" says Ben, with a slight question in his voice.

"Yes, I think so too." (No one would argue that Ben is muscular.) "What else is in this biography?"

"No sisters or brothers. No pets. Abhors eggs. Abhors is another word for hates, mum. Likes—what do I like?" he asks.

"Well, you have to answer that. What do you like?"

"Likes spelling. Now I'll write it down." And he walks back to his room. I can't help thinking that a choice between intelligent and muscular is very limiting, but now is probably not the time to have a conversation about that. After a few minutes he comes back in and says, "Mum, what sort of freak am I?"

"Freak?! What do you mean, Ben?" I'm ready to demolish anybody who's called Ben a freak, but I try to sound calm so that he will tell me who has said this to him.

"Well," he says, "Jamie is a football freak and Bala is a Spiderman freak, and Lucy is a Bratz freak. So what freak am I?"

"Oh!" I say, breathing out with relief. "Well, what do you think? What did you write at school?" I'm expecting him to say numbers freak or swimming pool freak or Mr. Men freak. But instead he says, "I'm a question freak."

And he's right. Ben is a question freak. He is showing me very clearly that he knows himself and that he can write his own story. It strikes me that in spite of our neurological difference and all that it implies, we have many similarities. I, too, have become a question freak, and I, too, write my stories. If we are writing, between us, an "unnatural history," stories of life "lived against the grain of normalcy" (Rapp and Ginsburg 2001, 552), then perhaps we are contributing in a small and very personal way to cultural change and social inclusion. This is my hope. This is why we share our stories.

11

Nurturing the Nurturer

Reflections on an Experience of Breastfeeding,
Disability, and Physical Trauma

HEATHER KUTTAI

10 OCTOBER 2005

For months, I felt that this pregnancy was going so well. However, I have been in the hospital for a week now, subjected to numerous tests to find out why my body is experiencing such severe symptoms that appear to be related to my spinal-cord injury. I hate being away from Patrick. He is only eight, after all, and he needs his mom. I hate being away from Darrell and my home, too. But mostly I hate feeling suspiciously scrutinized, treated as if my disability is solely responsible for my problems and the problems of my family and my unborn baby. Am I imagining things, or is there an unspoken feeling that I should not have become pregnant again in the first place?

12 OCTOBER 2005

We were waiting on the tests to let us know if the pain, elevated heart rate, shortness of breath, and fevers are due to an infection in my back, when an x-ray revealed that the stainless steel rods fused to my spinal column to correct for scoliosis when I was twelve years old have broken and moved apart. I don't know what it all means, but I know it isn't good for me or the baby. But this information helps me understand why my body has been under so much stress.

When Patrick came to visit me after school, he could see I was sad. He wanted to know why, and I felt that he needed to know the truth, so I told him about my broken rods. I told him as honestly and simply as I could. I said, "Honey, the rods in my back have broken. We do not know why. It may have happened even if I was not pregnant. We cannot do surgery to fix the rods while the baby is still inside me, but once she is born, I expect that I will need a big operation."

28 NOVEMBER 2005

It has been a difficult few weeks but I am breastfeeding my brand-new baby daughter, Chelsea, with one arm and writing this with my free hand. She came safely and swiftly, and we are all so grateful.

18 DECEMBER 2005

I am in much more pain than I thought I would be postpartum. I really thought that once Chelsea was born, I would be more comfortable. I am so crooked that I can't see my face in the bathroom mirror anymore. If I did not attach the breastfeeding cushion around my waist and to the back of my wheelchair, I would not be able to sit up. My elbows are already red and sore from leaning on it so I can hold myself up.

20 DECEMBER 2005

Every day that passes, I am a little worse, a little sicker, a bit more crooked. Based on my chest and thoracic x-rays, Dr. L felt I needed a white-cell scan. When they called with my test's time, I asked whether or not it would affect breastfeeding. The answer was that I would have to wait twelve hours after the scan to nurse.

My heart broke. I cried to the point of hysteria. Without breastfeeding, anyone could take care of my daughter, anyone could take my place. I felt disposable, without value, without importance. Well-meaning others say, "You turned out okay without breast milk, didn't you?" This is not the point. Breastfeeding makes me a valuable human being right now when I can do little else to take care of my baby.

28 DECEMBER 2005

Sometimes when I nurse Chelsea she feels like an extension of my body. She is the healthy part.

4 JANUARY 2006

I had my MRI done yesterday. The radiologist who reviewed it was alarmed at all the abnormalities. He communicated with my family doctor, who also became alarmed and who then talked to me about spinal infections, infection in the muscle, the lungs, and possible tumors. She and my rehab doctor talked, and they both advised me to pack my bags because I would certainly be admitted to the hospital soon.

I have spent the better part of the day crying. Not from my body's problems as much as from the anticipated separation. I feel like it would be worse to have my arm ripped out than to be separated from my children. I live in a body that is devalued in so many ways. My body takes on a new value, importance, and even status when it is pregnant, nurturing, and breastfeeding. The threat of having that importance taken away is devastating. People keep telling me, "Lots of babies are not breastfed and they turn out all right." Well, of course they do. I am not stupid. There are women who cannot breastfeed; there are babies who are adopted. Of course not all babies have to have breast milk. This is about *me*. My body's value. Without breastfeeding, I become irrelevant. Anyone can take my place. I become invisible.

13 JANUARY 2006

I had a CT scan today, and the procedure also included a biopsy of the fluid that is building around my spine. The doctor removed 120 cc of dark brown fluid. We don't know what it is yet. I hate entering a hospital and becoming an object instead of a subject. I become medicalized, dehumanized, pathologized . . . far from normalized.

On the other hand, Chelsea is growing fantastically. She is a spectacular baby—at her last doctor's appointment, she had doubled her birth weight.

19 FEBRUARY 2006

Breastfeeding makes me feel healthy. I know I am sick, but I say, almost chant, to myself all day long, "My body is strong." When I do this, I visualize nursing Chelsea. This body function gives me an overall feeling of wellness and strength, productivity and vitality. Amazing. Considering my body is falling apart. I am falling apart.

21 FEBRUARY 2006

I have to have a bone scan in a few minutes, and I am waiting at the coffee shop in the hospital until it begins. Chelsea is with me. She is sleeping right now, and I cannot help but splash big tears on her little face and hands. I will nurse her in a few minutes because depending on what the test reveals, it may be the last time I ever do that.

25 FEBRUARY 2006

I am lying down to write this. Once again, I am having a lot of discomfort. It occurred to me that most of my body is, has become, completely unfamiliar to me: the way I look, how my clothes (don't) fit, the way the skin now hangs off my newly atrophied legs, how my bladder and bowels no longer signal any fullness, how my feet don't settle on the footrest of my wheelchair, and of course, how obscenely crooked I am, how my left hip bone grinds against my ribs on the right side, how laborious it is to take a deep breath, how pushed up and over my intestines are, how they push food back up my esophagus, causing vomit to come in my throat. And the pain. And the sweating and the unrelenting effort it takes to hold myself up all the time when I am in my chair, making it so hard to dress and change Chelsea because I have to hold myself up with my elbows, yet somehow I do this and more.

The one familiar thing is breastfeeding. My breasts still work. No wonder I am so attached to it. So many people (well-meaning) continue to encourage me to give nursing up because they want me to have less stress. But they do not understand that I need to breastfeed because, despite everything else, I can still feel a little bit healthy, useful, female, whole, human. My cells cannot be so sick if I am nourishing Chelsea's healthy and strong cells. And sometimes I look at Patrick, doing his karate or practicing his guitar, and I think about how strong and amazing all his cells are and how I once nourished them, too. It is this idea that is keeping me alive.

29 MARCH 2006

Before he went to sleep tonight Patrick told me, "It doesn't matter how your back turns out, Mom. I need you and I love you."

10 JULY 2006

My surgery is tomorrow morning, and I am currently in my hospital bed, unable to sleep. I have listened to all my "strong" songs, and then I went through my scrapbook that holds pictures and memories of the people I love best.

I did not nurse too much the last few days. I want Chelsea to have the chance to learn to like the bottle. So far, as long as I am around, she just swats the bottle away. When I said good-bye to her, I kissed her about a hundred times and made her laugh before I passed her off to Darrell and his mom. Patrick crawled into bed beside me and we talked about how we are always together whether we are in the same house or not. I asked him to think happy thoughts.

It is just hours away. Soon it will be minutes. Soon it will be over. All my cells are well. I am healthy, strong, and well. I am resilient. I know how to heal. My cells choose life.

11 JULY 2006

I am in Observation; the surgery is over. Darrell writes this for me since holding a pen is difficult. I may be lucid, but I look awful. I was prone for the whole twelve hours, and my forehead, chin, and breasts are swollen, bruised and have lacerations. I am bruised up and down my arms and neck. The pain is intense. I am just trying to focus on breathing.

Later . . . Darrell brought Chelsea to me tonight. I did not imagine I would nurse her when she came—with all the pain, it did not really occur to me. However, she took one look at my bruised and swollen face, smiled, and held out her arms. I took her and although it was brutally hard, I nursed her on the left side since my right is viciously bruised.

14 JULY 2006

I have nursed Chelsea about two times a day, and she is not as desperate as she once was. Sometimes she is just happy to sit with me and eat Cheerios.

24 JULY 2006

I had all of my staples removed today. There were over sixty but we lost count. I am having so much pain, though. Something does not feel right. Everyone wants and expects me to not have any more pain. They cannot understand why I am still saying that I have pain. I want to kill all of those people.

20 AUGUST 2006

I am having a fever every day and profuse sweats at night. I am in a lot of pain. My orthopedic surgeon is concerned and wants to rule out an infection. He found during surgery that my spinal cord was severely damaged; there were gaps where there was no spinal fluid flowing at all, so some strange body reactions might be expected. I cannot shake the feeling that something is terribly wrong. When the chills come and when the pain is at its worst, I lose all my hope and imagination. The only thing that gives me any faith that my body is going to be okay is knowing that my breasts still work and that their milk is nourishing a beautiful baby.

7 SEPTEMBER 2006

How could I have gone from being crooked to morbidly crooked to straight to crooked again? The idea of another surgery makes me want to die.

14 SEPTEMBER 2006

"Tell me about your day," I said to him as I picked him up from school. "It was good. We watched a movie about honesty." "What did you learn?" "That it is important to be honest, even when it is hard."

Deep breath. "Patrick, I have to be honest with you now, and it is going to be hard. I saw the doctor today and the top half of my back is not healing. The new hardware is coming apart and away from my spine and I need another surgery." He closed his eyes. "Oh no. This is terrible, Mom. Is this why you have so much pain?"

"Yes. There is more that you have to hear, though." "Okay." "I will have to be in bed for several weeks afterward. And the doctor insists this has to happen at the hospital so we make sure my back heals this time."

His brown eyes. So warm. So much love and concern. "I will do anything to help you, Mom. I believe you can do anything."

15 SEPTEMBER 2006

Darrell kissed me tonight like we were both seventeen years old again. He tells me I am beautiful. I told him today that I am never going to get tired of hearing that.

25 SEPTEMBER 2006

I have to wean Chelsea because my surgery is in five days. I hardly touched her at all today. I already miss her little warm body, how her body used to need my body. I already miss being able to give her something special and how nursing proved I was her mama and that I deserved to be her mama.

1 OCTOBER 2006

Tonight as I nursed my baby for the last time, I whispered to her all the reasons that nursing has meant so much to me. I told her that I continued to nurse her despite how nearly everyone discouraged me and thought I was irrational for doing so.

28 NOVEMBER 2006

I have been discharged today after my second twelve-hour surgery, installation of two titanium rods, twenty titanium screws, active bone cells to promote healing, and several liters of donated blood followed by an eight-week hospitalization where I could only raise my bed to an angle of thirty degrees. I am home.

Today is also Chelsea's first birthday. After we celebrated with dinner and cake, I was even able to help her get ready for bed. Darrell tied my breastfeeding cushion on to the back of my wheelchair and I held Chelsea close. She seemed really uncomfortable, though, squirming and twisting in my arms. She kept trying to put her hand in my armpit and then I realized what she needed. I slipped off my T-shirt and dropped it on the floor next to my wheelchair. She rested her warm cheek against my chest, sighed, and fell asleep.

12

Vulnerable Subjects

*Motherhood and Disability
in Nancy Mairs and Cherríe Moraga*

SUZANNE BOST

Motherhood is idealized in modern American culture (as in most cultures), but being a mother deviates from the ideal modern American subject. Motherhood is not conducive to individual integrity, self-reliance, or reason. Pregnancy, birth, and breastfeeding are boundary violations that emphasize our permeability as bodies and as subjects. Parenting involves connection and emotion more than rational objectivity (as when my spine tingles every time my baby cries). In short, motherhood revolves around qualities that have been demonized since the Enlightenment. *As what* are mothers celebrated, then? As pitiful dependent creatures? As ex-centric and mystical beings? As heroes battling challenges to their integrity?

As the presence of reserved "stork parking" in major shopping malls attests, mothers are given accommodations alongside people with disabilities. Pulling up next to a "disabled parking" slot to take advantage of the much-needed extra space—or, alternately, refusing the stork parking because I want to defy the assumption that I'm incapable of pushing my baby across a snowy parking lot—I am engaging in questions about self-reliance relevant to both mothers and people with disabilities. How does modern American subjectivity incorporate people who need "special" assistance? Must equality revolve around individual independence? I am interested in the alternatives to self-reliance posed by both motherhood and disability as well as the pressures these identities put upon American cultural ideals. Measuring Nancy Mairs's autobiographical narrative on living with multiple sclerosis, *Waist-High in the World: A Life among the Non-Disabled* (1996), against Cherríe Moraga's autobiographical narrative about motherhood and illness, *Waiting in the Wings: Portrait of a Queer Motherhood* (1997), reveals the cultural contingencies of our corporeal ideals and enables us to imagine "other" viable ways of being.

The material and social structures in which we live often assume English speakers with heterosexual families who are able to open doors, climb stairs, and read signs. They also assume independence, vigor, and health as shared ideals. These cultural biases are masked by the pretense that medicine, law, and the built environment are culturally neutral and objective—a pretense that marks all difference as "deviance" rather than "different but equal." Yet viewing the world from a wheelchair, as Mairs does, or identifying with a culture whose values differ radically from the dominant one, as Moraga does, makes visible the narrow limits of any ideal. Mairs's experience of mothering, as a white heterosexual woman with a visible disability, certainly differs from Moraga's, a Chicana lesbian who is not herself disabled. Yet both narratives represent motherhood as an exercise in vulnerability, and both writers seemingly abandon self-reliance to embrace the interdependence that their personal experience mandated. Mairs turns to Catholicism, and Moraga to Mesoamerican cultures, as they search for worldviews within which they can experience vulnerability as a positive attribute.

"The mark of self-reliance, for me," Mairs writes, "is not whether or not I open a door for myself but whether I accept the burden of my limitations" (1996, 105). Cultural expectations create "burdens" that are as real as the limits of one's body. In the "fitness"-obsessed contemporary United States, Mairs's use of a wheelchair is considered pathetic, "depressing," "shameful and at least a little suspect" (100, 206).[1] Although "health," itself,

1. I put terms like "fitness" and "health" in quotation marks because they are cultural constructs with prejudicial regulatory functions. "Fitness," as a metaphor, highlights this fact since it implies that bodies must be made to "fit" a certain size or shape dictated by religion, fashion, political exigency, cultural taboos, etc.

is a temporary condition that involves an unnerving degree of corporeal fluctuation (from our regular digestive processes to aging) and permeability (from our porous skin to our dependence upon pills or lotions), American popular culture defies this vulnerability by celebrating athletes and exercise, assuming anesthesia as the proper response to pain, and marketing products that promise to seal off our bodies from germs (like the foreign policies that promise to protect our nation from alien intrusions). In this context, disability presents an unwanted reminder of the vulnerability of the human condition. From her wheelchair, Mairs will never embody the ideal celebrated in popular culture ("a lithe erect form in motion"), and her body and identity are therefore considered "spoiled" (47–48). Americans shun people with disabilities in order to defend the illusion of self-reliance, "as though obliterating all signs of frailty will protect them from the falls and fractures to which each year makes them more vulnerable" (101).

> Illness and deformity, instead of being thought of as human variants . . . have invariably been portrayed as deviations from the fully human condition. . . . The afflicted body is never simply that—a creature that suffers, as all creatures suffer from time to time. Rather it is thought to be "broken," and thus to have lost its original usefulness; or "embattled," and thus in need of militaristic response, its own or someone else's, to whip it back into shape; or "spoiled," and thus a potential menace to the bodies around it. (47–48)

In order to defend the obsession with human vigor, disabled bodies are perceived as deviations in kind, rather than examples of human variety, and vulnerability is thereby purged from what it means to be human.

Because she cannot escape her own dependence upon others for assistance like opening doors, reaching for items on high shelves, or even simply cleaning herself, Mairs searches for a way to accept care without being an object of pity. Rather than meekly begging for assistance or risking injury by attempting self-reliance, "I must discipline myself, then, to turn my body over to strangers under conditions less offensive to my sensibilities" (82). Her "discipline" is not about physical exercise but, rather, exercising her mental willingness to embody demonized qualities. Rather than viewing her body as "bulk to be raised from the bed," "monitored for signs of decubiti," and transported from place to place by others, "I must imagine my body to be something other than problematic: a vehicle for enmeshing the life I have been given into the lives of others. Easy enough to say. But to do? Who will have me? And on what terms?" (56). She finds, in Catholicism, a mind-set through which her vulnerability is valued rather than shunned.[2] Premodern and mystical, rather than "Enlightened" and rational, Catholicism embraces qualities purged from the self-reliant, secular subject.[3] The Lives of Saints, for instance, focus on bodies that are penetrated by stigmata, disabled by religious raptures, overcome by visions, and committed to suffering as Jesus did. Catholicism values different sorts of bodies than the "fit," muscular, sexy icons of American popular culture. The corporal works of mercy endorsed by the Catholic Church, in Mairs's view, discipline "the part of the human psyche that transcends self-interest" and celebrate caregiving as an intersubjective activity (78–79). If caregiving is reciprocal, then receiving care is not passive or useless but, rather, an active way to help others: "Permitting myself to be taken care of is, in fact, one of the ways I can take care of others" (83). Dependence is an asset in the economy of reciprocal caregiving. Mairs also argues that Catholicism is "extraordinarily tolerant of multiplicity, on the theory that it takes all kinds of parts to form a body" (63). Disability, in this light, serves a crucial function in the human body and enriches the lives of the nondisabled.

This rhetoric celebrates the disabled body as an ennobling reminder of the variability of the human condition and an occasion for giving and receiving care. But what of disabled mothers? Although motherhood disables all women's bodies in many ways, there is still an expectation that

---

2. See Mairs's *Ordinary Time: Cycles in Marriage, Faith, Renewal* (1993) for a more extended view of her "disability theology."

3. As a Catholic, myself, I am well aware that modern Catholicism is not often practiced in the liberal and mystical fashion that Mairs embraces, as Catholicism, too, has been changed by the individualistic rationalism in "the West" today. (Here, the connotation and denotation of "West" clearly diverge, as cultures to the south of the United States are more likely to maintain a mystical or communal Catholicism.)

mothers must protect their children, filling in the gaps that make children vulnerable and giving care unconditionally. Mairs struggles with a sense of guilt that, in need of care herself, she cannot always be a pillar to her own children (34–35). *Waist-High* captures this sense of guilt with the recurring image of the wheelchair: numerous times the narrative describes the children pushing their mother's wheelchair, a seemingly constant uphill battle—"pushing, titling, swerving, pushing, pushing, pushing" (186)—that involves relinquishing control to the children, who must labor to provide their mother's mobility. Many of these incidents occur on family hiking and camping trips, highlighting how the mother's disability gets in the way of the children's pleasure and thwarts the entire family's desire to retreat from the world of machines to experience "nature." She writes that her daughter tried to "punish me for my illness and dependency," and for disabling the family's full access to the Carlsbad Caverns on a trip to New Mexico, by "whip[ping] the wheelchair along at breakneck speed" (186). This language reflects the mother's anxiety that her disability has made her family relations unnatural and has given the daughter power to injure the disabled mother (by pushing her at "breakneck speed").

In the context of Mairs's discussion of corporal works of mercy, mothers should allow their children to share in the work of giving care, and the mother's disability should provide the occasion for enjoying this reciprocal vulnerability that Western ideals suppress. It is ironic, then, that Mairs worries about needing care from her children—a performance of motherly concern inconsistent with her earlier-stated theory. Yet it is also Mairs who quells this anxiety by quoting her children in her own narrative and putting words of acceptance in their mouths (or quotation marks). When she elaborates on her relationship with her daughter, she quotes her daughter in terms that deny any perversity in the mother's dependence: "'because this change in our roles was so gradual, it seemed natural to me'" (34). The narrative thus embodies ambivalence, expressing both maternal guilt and pleasure in relinquishing maternal control. Indeed, as Mairs herself represents it, both of her children argue that having a disabled mother is "normal," from their perspective, demonstrating the contextual relativism that contradicts any one ideal.

The relative ease with which Mairs creates a viable, even celebrated, life out of MS has much to do with privilege: the class privilege that enables her to purchase a Quickie P100 joystick-powered wheelchair, the familial privilege that supplies her with willing caregivers (husband, sister, children), and cultural privilege, living in a city with elevators and accessible public transportation as well as being exempt from racism and xenophobic exclusion as a white woman whose family "has lived in New England for some fourteen generations" (173). She demonstrates over and over how insurance, reliable caregivers, supportive communities, and education are central to experiencing disability as more than a tragic burden (76, 97, 109). Since contemporary American society is still generally designed for the nondisabled, integrating people with disabilities requires money and effort.

> [I]n a society where the rearing of even a healthy child is not viewed as a community undertaking, where much touted "family values" are always ascribed to the nuclear and not the human family, the parents of a disabled child will find themselves pretty much on their own. If they are lucky enough to have health insurance, the insurer, whose goal is to maximize shareholders' profits rather than the well-being of patients, is not about to spring for a $7,000 power wheelchair that would enable a child with muscular dystrophy to mingle on an almost equal "footing," though it might provide $425 for a manual wheelchair to be pushed by an attendant (which it would not pay for). A school system, underfunded by screaming taxpayers, is not likely to procure a Kurtzweil machine that would permit its blind students to "read" their own textbooks. Unless they are wealthy, Mom and Dad do the pushing, the reading, and whatever other extra duties are required on top of their jobs and their care for any other children in the family. (110–11)

Modern American society is not truly committed to incorporating its citizens with disabilities as equal participants in civic life, as evidenced by reluctance to support the structural modifications and job equity mandated by the Americans with Disabilities Act. So people with disabilities are pushed to the margins figuratively, as the nation purges the "unfit" from its sanitized self-image, and literally, as most people with disabilities find themselves stuck on the wrong side of heavy doors, tall curbs, or stairways at some point or other. Enjoying race, class, and heterosexual privilege puts Mairs on the "right" side of many barriers, but she is nonetheless marginalized by a society that defines "fitness" based on the ability to stand up and walk unassisted.

Although her race and her sexuality subject her to more overt marginalization in her dealings with medical and legal institutions, Moraga's Mexicanness and her queerness ultimately help her to embrace embodiments that are demonized in the modern United States. *Waiting in the Wings: Portrait of a Queer Motherhood* is divided into three sections—about lesbian insemination and pregnancy, about Rafael Angel's premature birth and three months in the neonatal intensive care unit, and about his co-mothers' unraveling relationship during his first year of life—establishing a parallelism between the three periods based on crisis and transformation. Throughout each of these stages, Moraga describes the tension she experiences between her politically oppositional identity and the conventional narrative of pregnancy, birth, and motherhood. She adamantly does all three as a butch Chicana dyke, defying dominant culture patterns of conception (getting pregnant with her lesbian lover and a syringe), beauty (embracing her growing size and wishing for a dark-skinned baby), birth (describing giving birth as "an animal pleasure"), hospitalization (resisting its objectivist repression of culture, faith, and feeling), and motherhood (resenting the "white male pediatrician-types with their nurse-wives and seven kids 'bonding' their way into my Mexican psyche" with their ideas about family and child-rearing (Moraga 1997, 53, 87).

Moraga is not explicitly disabled herself, but her narrative is a meditation on identities deemed "unfit," and her motherhood is "queer" in many ways. The hospital setting disables Moraga as a mother because she cannot care for her baby without the mediation and assistance of medical staff and machines and because she must submit his body (and her own) to the regimen created by the hospital. Her breast milk is looped into the network of machines that feeds her baby, her mothering occurs through the walls of his incubator, and she and her partner start to incorporate the scent of hospital detergents pressed into their own clothes and skin (66). The co-mothers face harassment from a homophobic hospital security guard who questions their right to access in the middle of the night (75–76), and Moraga repeatedly finds her Chicana feminist values challenged by the Eurocentric, patriarchal medical institution that treats all patients as objects to be "repaired" according to one standard of "health." She combats the institutionalization of her son by infusing multiple cultures and faiths into the "science" of his caregiving, surrounding his incubator with healing stones, arrowheads, dolls, and prayer cards, gifts that represent his expansive *familia* of queers, Native Americans, and Chicana/os (81).

From the beginning of the narrative, Moraga poses her own identity as ex-centric to conventional motherhood: "We make babies with strangers in one-night stands or on the doctor's insemination table. . . . We cannot make babies with one another" (15). Lesbians must depend upon others (doctors, male donors, medical technology) in order to become mothers. By describing this relationship as both illicit ("with strangers in one-night stands") and unnatural ("on the doctor's insemination table"), she deflates the purity of motherhood and embraces it in a "queer" way. To become a mother, she must re-create the role as well as her own self: "Having babies was something 'real' women did—not butches, not girls who knew they were queer since grade school" (20). If women are assumed to be constitutionally permeable and dependent, then they are "naturally" suited for motherhood. But butch dykes, who are supposed to possess the hard, stoic qualities of the self-reliant, are not supposed to be "mother material." It is, however, through her sexuality that Moraga recognizes her own capacity to mother. She realizes that, as a lesbian, she "had nursed dozens of hungry women" and that the caregiving and self-surrender involved in this loving had prepared her for motherhood (22). As a mother, she is both subject and object of an erotic corporeal give-and-take. When she gives birth, she feels "thoroughly entered" and is "temblando like the best of sex," and she describes the intimacy of nursing as "a kiss that lasted" (53, 99).

A parallel thread in the narrative is the aging of Moraga's own parents. In the section right after the one detailing the insemination, and right before the one detailing her positive pregnancy test, she gets "flashbacks, mental glimpses of [her] parents waiting for [her] at the Hollywood/Burbank airport. With each visit, they seem a bit smaller physically, a bit older, slightly more vulnerable" (26). As the embryo takes hold inside her and her new identity as mother begins to form, she witnesses the waning of her own mother, feels "this family slipping away," and "grow[s] to comprehend, somewhere inside [her] heart, how transitory this physical life is" (26). Creating a family and creating a life means creating something that is susceptible to death and disintegration. Accepting motherhood, for Moraga, is about accepting human vulnerability. The image of the aging mother redefines motherhood based on vulnerability rather than on strength.

This "transitory" hold on "physical life" comes to define Moraga's own experience of mothering and family-making. Rather than mourning the loss of control that comes with having delivered her baby at just twenty-seven weeks of gestation and turning his body over to the medical professionals in the NICU, she expands her sense of family to include all of the bodies and machines that vulnerable bodies depend on. Although the image of the mother pressing her "milk-hard-breasted body" against the incubator is initially tragic, she comes to think of the machine as her baby's "apartment," a home that is saturated with steam from his breath and icons of his queer family's faith (57, 70, 81). She recognizes that the clinical labor of the hospital employees who "watched [Rafael] throughout the night while we slept" is also a form of mothering. "Some of them have even come to love Rafa, thinking of him as 'their baby'" (78). At first she is afraid of her dependence on these women, but, in later reflection, "it is not our dependence on the nurses that I fear, so much as the loss of the connection. These women have become our family" (78). Moraga and her partner ultimately incorporate the nurses' mothering by taking their guidebooks and gifts home with them in the car.

Rafael's extended illness becomes the occasion for recognizing the illnesses intertwined with all of our lives, and Moraga's narrative of her son's birth incorporates the deaths and illnesses of the artists and activists that form her political and spiritual family: the death of César Chavez, memories of Audre Lorde's cancer and funeral, the deaths of Chicanadyke Myrtha Quintanales's mother and father, poets Ronnie Burke and Tede Matthew's deaths from AIDS, the deaths of Moraga's uncle and the birth father's father, her partner's mother's gradual "crippling" from Parkinson's disease, and Moraga's own seemingly constant battles with pain, depression, anxiety, colds, flu, and allergies (ironically caused by the "seeds of life," "pregnancy happening everywhere" around her in the springtime [38]). These multiple illnesses unsettle the boundaries of the "portrait of queer motherhood" in this narrative, making it about communal vulnerability more than birthing a new life.

Even after Rafaelito has been released from the hospital, his life is defined by its tenuousness: "He is so tiny, so vulnerable." In Moraga's dreams, he is "always on the verge of disappearing, melting away, dissolving in water" (79). Initially, she is "afraid to be so vulnerable to the fragile life of another human being" (90), and the journal entries from her baby's first months at home focus on how her own sense of self is turned upside down as she adapts her body to his cycles of sleeping and eating. As Rafaelito fights cold after cold and infection after infection, his mother's temperature, too, rises and falls (106). Her body falls into a "haze of prolonged and private illness, an acute exhaustion, a longing for respite, finding none" (105). Ultimately, rather than fighting vulnerability, Moraga accepts it as an alternate ideal, embracing "that endless circle of birth/death/rebirth that we Mexicans have always bemoaned and celebrated, dancing drunk with life around the lip of the grave" (85). It is important that she represents this intertwinement of life and death as something particularly Mexican, distancing her sense of life from the obsession with maintaining "health" and fighting death in the contemporary United States.

Moraga conceived two plays during the period of her pregnancy and new motherhood. *The Hungry Woman: A Mexican Medea* (2001) investigates maternal ambivalence through figures of murderous mothering (Euripides's Medea and the Mexican wailing woman, La Llorona, both of whom are mythologized for killing their own children) and the Aztec fertility goddess, Coatlicue, who embodies both creation and destruction. *Heart of the Earth: A Popul Vuh Story* (2001) retells, with contemporary Chicano allusions, the Quiché Maya stories of the initial failed and dismembered creations that ultimately formed the human race. Both plays adopt Mexican indigenous cosmologies that conceive death and dismemberment as part of the creation of new life, allowing us to view Moraga's medical journey as a recovery of ancient corporeal sensibilities. She writes of turning to her daily readings of "Maya ritual bloodletting" after being rushed to the emergency room during her pregnancy for "heavy bleeding due to polyps sloughing from the cervix" (Moraga 1997, 39). I would argue that she found, in the Aztec and Mayan traditions she invokes in her plays, a way to view human vulnerability as not simply "other" to health (the perception of modern Western medicine) but as a vehicle for understanding humans' place in a larger (epistemically Mexican) cosmological context.

In his study of Mesoamerican corporeal ideology, Alfredo López Austin (1988, 360) claims that "physical defects were considered signs identifying men as individuals with supernatural powers," because people who were chosen by the gods were often marked in some visible way. It was believed by the Aztecs and the Maya—and, to a degree, by many of their descendants today—that illness was a sign of disequilibrium between man and the elements of the universe; health was therefore a matter of finding balance within and between bodies rather than simply a matter of keeping alien germs out and reinforcing an individual's bodily boundaries (255). Fertility and decay were part of a balanced life cycle, and blood, bones, and shed skin were viewed as having regenerative powers. Much of what we know about Aztec and Maya sacred practices centers on the permeability of the human body, in particular the rituals involving human sacrifice, auto-sacrifice, and the sharing of blood and flayed skin. Religious ceremony was enacted with dancing, bleeding, and costumed bodies in order to invoke divine forces. Most of these ceremonies were public displays to which the entire community bore witness, and performing these ceremonies in sacred places like the pyramids demonstrated the intention of reaching from this world up to the gods with the bodies of the performers. Incisions of the skin, like tattooing, piercing, and bleeding, were prized—perhaps because they visibly indicate the thin boundary between human life and death as well as between the corporeal and the spiritual realms. Bodies must signify differently in a culture that values community, permeability, and divine intervention more than self-reliant individuals. Moraga's focus on the processes of giving life to Rafael Angel presents a vivid example of this possibility: incorporating another being and then physically dividing, removing pieces of body in surgery, and linking bodies to networks of machines and caregivers.

Perhaps her investment in Mesoamerican cosmology enabled her to feel these processes as sacred rather than abject.

Moraga forges her own *mestizo* faith from Aztec and Mexican Catholic roots: "My Catholicism—its Mexican symbols, its indianism—is such a private prayer that it no longer even resembles the religion. I *am* a heretic, not because I am faithless but because I am a believer—of something else, not here" (Moraga 1997, 107). Belief is heresy in a society that worships secular rationalism and that locks its religion into institutional formulae. Moraga's religion is about letting go of, rather than propping up, the self, and it enables her to have faith in things beyond reason: "I believe in an emptiness that can be filled with selflessness. I don't know how to arrive there. I don't know how to even find the path, but I will clamber toward it in the dark with my son by my hand. Until it is time to let go" (107). This embrace of vulnerability coincides with the upheavals of motherhood and illness. As with Mairs's embrace of Catholic caregiving, Moraga's faith remakes her experience of "disability" into a path to the divine, though Moraga's faith lacks the certainty and guidance of institutional religions like Catholicism.

Moraga's experience in the hospital required her to open herself to medical technologies and hospital staff rather then shoring up her Chicana-dyke boundaries. Is this open-bordered selfhood a transcultural phenomenon experienced by all who become sick? Or is it easier for Moraga to accept this alternate way of being because of her racial and sexual identity? It is convenient for Moraga that research into her Mesoamerican cultural past provided her with a model for a more permeable sense of selfhood, and she (somewhat problematically) identifies with ancient Mexico in opposition to the racism, classism, and homophobia of the contemporary United States.[4] It might seem that her appeal to ancient cultural

---

4. Moraga explains her journey back to her roots as having begun in contemporary Mexico, where she encountered her own "cultural outsiderhood" as a Chicana lesbian, leading her back beyond the reach of living cultures to the pre-Columbian temples, where it was not the peoples or their visible legacy but "the natural landscape in which those templos were placed" and "the buried history" contained within them "that brought a shudder of recognition to the surface of [her] skin" (Moraga 2001, x). This is a past emptied of

sensibilities keeps the openness she writes about at the margins of the modern world, and Moraga's writing has indeed long been invested in ex-centricity to the dominant culture.[5] But in the hospital where her baby shares the NICU with Alex, who has sleeping limbs; Simone, who is blind; Freddy, who has "Downs," and other "one- and two- and three-pound human animals with swollen brains and strokes and weak hearts and drug addictions and troubled families . . . mirroring Rafa's own embattled state" (69), vulnerability and interconnections are the norm, shared across cultures. Although Moraga reaches this realization as a Chicana lesbian, this queer sort of mothering ultimately crosses beyond the boundaries of any identity.

Illness shifts our thinking about bodies and identities. Any body, as revealed through sonograms, blood tests, and microscopes, is a locus of constant fluctuations; it is also positioned as matter in need of care, vulnerable. In their essay "Bodies Together: Touch, Ethics, and Disability," feminist disability scholars Janet Price and Margrit Shildrick (2002, 72) note how people are led to reflect on the fluidity of embodiment when they care for the disabled: "[W]hat was uncovered during that acute period of Janet's illness [multiple sclerosis] was that, through the mutuality and reversibility of touch, we are in a continual process of mutual reconstitution of our embodied selves. Moreover, the instability of the disabled body is but an extreme instance of the instability of all bodies." Whether experienced personally or indirectly, illness and disability force us to think about bodies beyond their personal boundaries. As MS causes

---

people—people who would inevitably judge, exclude, or resist a Chicana feminist understanding of indigenous Mexico—and *felt* through an organic or mystical connection, free from the constraints of history. The connection Moraga feels to ancient Mexico is an ideal, rooted in ideas and cosmology, not a realist genealogy.

5. Mairs's understanding of Catholicism is equally resistant to hierarchy and oppression. In *Ordinary Time*, Mairs argues that "the Community of God" translates into "just distribution of all goods" and "a *new* world order—a wholly fresh way of conceiving relatedness as inclusive and egalitarian rather than exclusive and hierarchical" (1993, 188, 190). Mairs argues this as a "Catholic worker," but she suggests that any spiritual path (God, Allah, Mother Earth, chaos) can lead to this conclusion (8).

fluctuations in her motor skills, Mairs's sense of self is reconstituted at the intersection of her weakening legs, her wheelchair, the efforts of the children she depends upon for mobility, and the quality of the terrain through which she moves. When she becomes a mother, Moraga's sense of self is reconstituted at the intersection of her body, the baby she nurses, the machines she nurses through, and the nurses who maintain the machines. Since bodies are intertwined with the world beyond their skin, they are also unstable, subject to continual transformation. Selfhood is thus not a matter of individual integrity but of contextual interaction. Like Price and Shildrick, Mairs and Moraga challenge the modern assumption that "separation rather than contact figures the adult self" (Price and Shildrick 2002, 71) and share their vulnerable bodies with children, with parents, with professional caregivers, and even with anonymous readers. I do not mean to romanticize illness or disability as alternate ideals. Rather, experiencing these deviations from normative identities and idealized embodiments points out the limits of such norms and ideals. While deviation leads some to cling to norms all the more tenaciously, Mairs and Moraga learned to relinquish the boundaries they could no longer practically maintain. This relinquishing has truly revolutionary potential.

Waist-High in the World and *Waiting in the Wings* are not just personal narratives; they incarnate a critique of modern American subjectivity. "Medical consumerism" has turned bodies into sites for capitalist exploitation, manipulation, and standardization. (The language of health "management" reflects medical corporations' control over individuals' bodies.) David Morris (2001, 59–60), whose work focuses on the cultural dimensions of pain and illness, notes, "Health (or an appearance of health) has become a prized commodity, as proudly displayed as a new SUV, while illness is an evil warded off with multivitamins and gym memberships." Given current levels of medical and pharmaceutical intervention in the United States, the vulnerable body represents a breakdown in defense for the medical engines; it is unruly, unstandardized, traitorous. Rather than submitting docilely to militaristic body mythology, the bodies of the newly born, the disabled, and the aging expand our thinking about how bodies should look and act. Their permeability and interdependence challenge the logic of policed boundaries. If the bodies of its people reflect the security and prosperity of the nation, pointing out our constitutional vulnerability presents an affront to the self-reliant self-image of the United States. Ideally, this affront will lead us to rethink the human subject around which we conceive medicine, architecture, and government policies. If we were to restructure public spaces and to rewrite the public policies that privilege self-reliance, Americans with disabilities might no longer be relegated to the psychic margins of the national imagination. We might then learn to value vulnerability and attachments to others as ideal ways of being in the world.

PART FOUR

Reimagining Activism

A Politics of Disability and Mothering

Parental activism is one of the most fraught aspects of the disability-rights movement, and this is not a new phenomenon. Several generations ago, parents of the disabled were expected to let go of their children and hand them over to institutions, an act for which they were later castigated. Today's parents may receive blame for their overzealousness in seeking cures, or for infantilizing their children by keeping them perpetually in their care. Rather than reading mother activism in such simplistic, binary terms, the essayists in part 4 illuminate the complexities of the middle ground in the work of activism. These accounts detail the mixed nature of activist practices and the coming-to-awareness of a situated politics, as mothers learn how to advocate for social change, get better care for loved ones, or increase awareness of the lives of those with disability. These nuanced descriptions of committed action—whether breaking a silence, negotiating the labyrinthine world of institutional care, working with or against governmental agencies, or providing care and treatment for members of their families—enlarge our understanding of the possible scope for, tensions in, and history of activism.

In "From Surrender to Activism: The Transformation of Disability and Mothering at Kew Cottages, Australia," Corinne Manning creates a space in traditional historic accounts of institutional living for the voices of mothers and caretakers, voices that have often been missing or silenced in these accounts. This rich history covers the years between 1953 and 2008 at

Kew Cottages, an Australian institution established in 1887 for people with intellectual disability. Manning foregrounds the words and acts of the women, highlighting their continued work of "mothering" alongside their emergent roles as activists and agents for change within the then-rigid world of state or governmental care.

In "History Examined: One Woman's Story of Disability and Advocacy," Marilyn Dolmage shares the story of her own evolution, over the last fifty years in Canada, to become actively engaged in fighting the inequalities suffered by people with disabilities and their families. In a narrative that spans a lifetime, including childhood memories of a brother with Down syndrome, who was institutionalized at a young age, and her later experiences parenting her own son with disabilities, Dolmage reveals strategies, struggles, and victories as she advocates for inclusion and equality.

"My Mother's Mental Illness," presents a reversal of the traditional mother-daughter relationship as Whitney Jones-Garcia engages in the difficult decision to hospitalize her mother. Framing the piece with then-recent newspaper clippings of psychiatric patients in the United States who died of neglect at similar institutions, Jones-Garcia identifies the challenges and fears in making such a decision and the difficulties of not doing so, as she details the realities of caring for her mother herself over a period of days.

"A Schizo-ly Situated Daughter: A Mother's Labor" provides another snapshot of a mother-daughter relationship of committed care. Elizabeth Metcalf articulates the multiple forms of labor in which her mother engaged during Metcalf's fifteen years as a psychiatric patient. Like many parents of children with disabilities who lack formal education or training, Metcalf's mother had to become an activist, a case manager, a counselor, a physical therapist, and a security guard, in order to care for her daughter when this work was not or could not be performed by others.

In "Motherhood and Activism in the Dis/Enabling Context of War: The Case of Cindy Sheehan," Abby Dubisar argues that the experiences of mothering, applied to disability and war, enable as well as constrain rhetorical strategies for US women's peace activism. Focusing on activist Cindy Sheehan, Dubisar outlines a tradition of mothers' peace activism and illuminates its relationship to the contemporary collective activism of veterans. Dubisar concludes that Sheehan's activism emerged from two strategic identifications she makes: like a war veteran, a figure with whom Sheehan identifies, the war "disabled" her by killing her beloved son and, like other mother-activists, her role as mother allows her to claim authority and agency to seek change.

From Surrender to Activism

The Transformation of Disability and
Mothering at Kew Cottages, Australia

CORINNE MANNING

This oral history of mothering at Kew Cottages, Australia,[1] provides an understanding of the ways in which mothering roles evolved and changed over time as attitudes toward parental involvement in the lives of institutionalized children altered. While the experiences of mothers has often been absent from previous historical accounts of institutional living, I have foregrounded their testimony as well as the voices of women staff as active agents. That silence reflected the once widely held belief that once children were committed to state care mothering ceased. Women's

---

1. This chapter comes from a larger oral history project documenting the history of Kew Cottages in living memory (Manning 2008). Primary evidence emanates from over one hundred hours of oral history interviews and written accounts obtained from a range of people associated with the institution, including families, staff, residents, and volunteers. Research methodology incorporates techniques pioneered by academics in the field of oral history and inclusive intellectual disability research from the United States and United Kingdom (Atkinson 2004; Atkinson, Jackson, and Walmsley 1997b; Atkinson et al. 2000; Atkinson et al. 2005; Bogdan and Taylor 1976; Perks and Thomson 2006; Walmsley 2006; Walmsley and Johnson 2003). Theories emerging from research areas on mothering, gender, disability, and oral history have formed the basis of qualitative analysis (Barnes and Mercer 2003; Cocks et al. 1996; Coleborne and MacKinnon 2003; Goggin and Newell 2005; Johnson and Traustadóttir 2005; Longmore and Umanski 2001; Rapley 2004; Read 2000; Shakespeare, Gillespie-Sells, and Davies 1996).

voices in this study counter this misconception and provide an emotional and raw insight into disability and mothering.

Established in 1887, Kew Cottages was Australia's oldest and largest specialized institution for people with intellectual disability. The history of mothers' activism at the institution reveals that a radical transformation in the perception of disability and mothering occurred across the period 1953–2008. For most of Kew's existence, mothers were not encouraged to be active in their children's care—this was believed to be the responsibility of staff and female working residents. Mothers were frequently told to surrender their children into state facilities and simply to "forget" about them. However, from the 1950s on, reforms in Australia's mental-health service resulted in the emergence of formalized avenues of parental activism within the Cottages, and a significant shift in mothering began, with mothers acting as agents of change, as they increasingly adopted roles as advocates, volunteers, and lobbyists and worked alongside staff to raise the standard of care for residents.

Australia's first purpose-built institution for people diagnosed with what is now referred to as intellectual disability, Kew was regarded as a world-leading facility when it opened in 1887. It offered both residential care and educational opportunities at a site isolated on a hillside in a leafy suburb, approximately eight kilometers from the city of Melbourne, in the state of Victoria. Although Kew Cottages was established as a children's institution, from the outset adults also resided there. In its first year of operation, 40 males and 17 females lived in the new facility with 40 percent of residents being aged 15 years or above. By 1968, when the population peaked at 948, Kew Cottages had grown to be Australia's largest institution for people with intellectual disability.

Kew Cottages was constructed adjacent to Kew Lunatic Asylum—an infamous institution for people experiencing mental illness. Until 1962, residents were committed to the Cottages under government legislation that applied to both people experiencing mental illness and people with intellectual disability. This system required two doctors to certify an individual as being of "unsound mind" and in need of custodial state care. For many mothers, committing an adult into such a notorious institution was difficult enough; surrendering a child proved almost unbearable. The trauma experienced by many mothers was intensified by the regulation that their children be certified "insane" before their placement at Kew. In 1959, the Mental Health Act streamlined two distinct processes regarding the provision of state care for people with intellectual disability and those experiencing mental illness. According to Kew's psychiatrist superintendent, Wilfrid Brady (1963, 345), when this legislation became operative and residents could be voluntarily admitted, parents and doctors, finding it abhorrent to declare a baby or young child "insane," welcomed this change.

From 1887 thousands of mothers sent their children to live at Kew Cottages. Undoubtedly, some mothers rejected their children because of their disability and looked upon the Cottages as a welcome "solution" to their perceived "problem." Interviewees who held this viewpoint or who had severed their relationship with their children upon placing them at Kew did not volunteer to record their recollections for this history; their story therefore remains hidden. The majority of mothers interviewed identified home pressures and/or a lack of medical expertise as central to their decision to place their children at Kew.

Some mothers, such as Hilda Logan, were forced to relinquish their children into state care by circumstances beyond their control. In 1956, when this photo (fig. 1) was taken of proud parents Hilda and Bob with newborn son, Andrew, they were unaware that he was intellectually disabled. As a toddler Andrew's development stopped; years later he was diagnosed with autism. For twelve years Hilda resisted institutional care for her son. Home life was tough, as Andrew was an active child who slept little and was prone to escaping:

Our house was like a fortress. I always had a key to the front door in my pocket as we had to deadlock it to stop him opening it. All of the fences were taken up an extra two feet and we had cyclone gates across the back of the drive. If he got over those, his father had made a magic eye that went over the drive and a hooter sounded in the house as he ran through the beam. When the hooter sounded I would start *running*. . . . He sure could run!

13.1. Hilda Logan, Bob Campbell, and their baby son, Andrew, 1956. Courtesy of Hilda Logan.

When Andrew was eleven years old his father died. Soon after, Hilda was diagnosed with suspected cancer requiring major surgery. With inadequate access to family, community, and government support, Hilda was forced to send Andrew to Kew Cottages, "I couldn't leap fences as I had done in the past and run after Andrew." Tears of sorrow and pain trickled down Hilda's cheeks and her voice quavered as she described the loss of her son into state care, "You never, ever get over it—ever." The lack of agency, which Hilda experienced, was common among many women who felt compelled to place their children in institutions.

Often shocked and confused when their children were diagnosed as intellectually disabled, many mothers called upon the guidance of medical practitioners when considering care options. Parents were often forced into a dependent relationship with doctors who offered specialist knowledge about disability and Victoria's health system. The social conditions in Australia up until the 1970s, particularly the lack of disability support services, made life extremely difficult for parents who chose to look after their children at home. Many medical experts believed that institutional care was not only in the best interests of the children, but also of their families. Until the late twentieth century, medical professionals frequently advocated that the specialized medical services and developmental programs at the Cottages offered children a brighter future than staying at home. Overwhelmingly, mothers' testified that they were advised by doctors to relinquish their children into institutional care.

Although the majority of interviewees believed that Kew Cottages benefited their children, a great many lived with an enduring sense of guilt and shame at being unable to care for their sons or daughters at home. The women's grief and sense of failure as mothers was often reflected in their faces when they spoke about "giving up" their children. As Rosalie Trower declared, "I felt like a latter-day Judas, that I had *betrayed* my son, I had betrayed my *son;* he'd gone to an institution." Even decades after her son's admission to Kew, Rose Miller felt saddened about extinguishing her legal parental rights: "Now when something comes on the TV and they show these parents with a severely retarded child at home trying to battle through it, you think to yourself: 'Oh, I should have done that!'"

The high level of influence that doctors wielded, and parents' dependence upon them when making informed decisions, was highlighted by the experience of Joan Jones. In 1962, Joan and her husband were faced with the difficult decision about the future care of their newborn son, Richard, who was diagnosed with Down syndrome. Joan recalled:

> He was our second child. . . . No two parents could have been less prepared for this event. Neither of us had any personal experience with

a seriously disabled person. And so the question of what was the best thing to do for our baby seemed overwhelming. We turned to our doctors who we then believed were experts in these matters. My obstetrician, when asked what was the potential of our child would only say, "Well, he'll never make a prime minister." The pediatrician, on the other hand, assured me that this child would never have the emotional development for us to be able to do anything for him and strongly advised placing him in care and concentrating our lives on our seven-year-old daughter . . . at the time we believed this advice to be sound.

Following the pediatrician's advice, Richard was sent directly from the maternity hospital to a small private infant hospital. Joan was happy with the care that Richard received but was critical of the hospital's attitude toward family inclusion. When the matron of the hospital was on duty she refused to allow young siblings into the building. Joan's daughter was forced to wait in the car outside, sometimes peering through a window in order to catch a glimpse of her baby brother. It was clear that Joan was unhappy about the exclusion of her daughter but felt powerless to override the matron's rules. When alternate accommodation was made available at Kew Cottages, Joan took advantage of this opportunity.

When Richard was six weeks old, a bassinette became available in the nursery ward at Kew Cottages and was offered to the Jones family. Joan remembered Richard's admission:

> I shall always remember that day, when having had two doctors certify our infant son . . . we committed him to an institution, for as we thought, the rest of his life. We had been to the Cottages earlier to talk to Irena Higgins, the senior social worker at that time, and told ourselves that, with very few alternatives, this was the best thing to do.

Joan recalled that Richard's transfer to Kew was a positive experience: "The family was welcomed as a whole and assured that we were all welcome to visit as often as we wished and to regard our baby's new home as our home too." This inclusive and caring attitude lessened the guilt and sadness Joan felt at committing her child into permanent state care.

Elsie Welchman's experience starkly contrasts with Joan's and reveals the struggle that many women endured when considering what constituted "good" mothering. On 20 December 1963, Elsie and her husband, Geoff, drove their seven-year-old son, David, to Kew for permanent admission. Previously, David had gone to Kew for a fortnight's respite care. This stay was extended to three months when he contracted shigella, a severe form of diarrhea rampant at the Cottages. David became severely ill and was transferred to the institution's hospital ward where he nearly died. It was not surprising that Elsie was reluctant to place her son permanently at Kew. But as her health began to fail because of the pressures of caring for David and his three siblings, Kew Cottages appeared to be her only option.

Elsie's story of placing her son at Kew reveals that notions of "failure" for some extended into the realm of their identity as medical professionals. Elsie spoke about looking after David at home; her experience was difficult yet rewarding because she fulfilled her maternal responsibilities in the face of adversity. Although she acknowledged that the decision to place David at Kew was in the "best interests" of her family, Elsie's testimony clearly revealed that she also felt a sense of failure as a mother and as a nurse:

> I felt I should have been able to cope with it because I was a trained nurse. I should have been able to look after him, his needs and the others as well, I'd been efficient in my job and I felt I should be efficient in my parenting as well. . . . It was the hardest thing we ever did, we felt he'd been thrown to the lions . . . the nurse came to get him to take him down to the units, and said: "Is that David?" and I said: "Yes" and she said: "He can't come to our unit, he's too small, it's a school ward. He'll get his teeth knocked down his throat."

Elsie and Geoff were unwilling to leave their son in a potentially violent situation, and they took him home. Within hours the superintendent of the Cottages phoned demanding David's immediate return to the facility, as he had been officially signed over as a ward of the state. The Welchmans acquiesced after they were assured that their son would be placed in more suitable accommodation.

Beryl Power was also critical of her early experiences at Kew when in February 1965 her six-year-old son, Geoff, was admitted. He was blind and required support to complete everyday tasks such as bathing, dressing, and eating. Beryl was dismayed by her early observations. She remembered being told not to come and see him for a month to give him a chance to settle in:

> but I could come and look at him through one-way glass if I wanted to! Which I did and was appalled by the sight of children sitting on the floor of a big day room with no furniture or toys, and one staff sitting on a stool knitting with a can of air freshener at hand. Another staff was also on duty out of sight whose job it was to clean anyone up who had been incontinent. Otherwise, nobody rated any attention other than just being watched.

Beryl felt that the maternal love and support she offered Geoff at home was absent at the Cottages.

This publicity photograph (fig. 2), which was taken in the 1960s, promoted Kew Cottages as a place that offered high levels of care. However, many mothers, like Elsie and Beryl, discovered that the reality of life at Kew was vastly different from the media spin. Over its lifetime, the type of care offered at the Cottages was mechanical and devoid of meaningful interpersonal relationships. Staff shortages often resulted in a focus on completion of rudimentary duties such as cleaning, feeding, and bathing residents. This viewpoint was supported by Kew's first pediatrician, David Pitt (1999, 149), who noted that state institutions such as Kew continually suffered from inadequate staffing and resources. Generally, facilities and living accommodations were substandard and overcrowded. The staff-to-resident ratio varied over time, but it was not unusual for one staff member to be responsible for up to forty residents, during the day, and up to eighty to one hundred residents at night. With persistent overcrowding, the individual attention that children received while living at home could not be replicated at the Cottages. In recognition of the institution's failings, in the 1950s a small group of staff and parents mobilized to demand more humane conditions for residents at Kew.

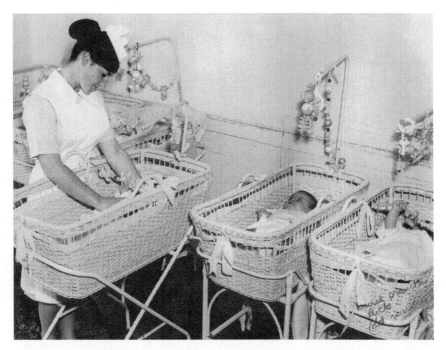

13.2. Nursery ward at Kew Cottages, ca. 1960. Courtesy of Kew Residential Services, Department of Human Services, Victoria, Australia.

In 1953, Austra Kurzeme commenced work as a ward assistant and was horrified at the conditions. As she walked through the ward, Austra noticed her charges "huddling in a heap on the floor, cold, half naked and half of them already smeared with feces, and the smell!" She observed that staff failed to interact with residents in a meaningful way, particularly during work details. In his study of asylums, Erving Goffman ([1963] 1986) argued that residents in institutions were often objectified by staff as "work," which created a tension between providing standards of humane care and ensuring institutional efficiency (74, 78). That was certainly the case at Kew. Austra was critical of the speed at which nurses' bathed residents: "I saw some nurses just pull the child through the water, make the hair wet, the face wet, the bottom clean, and dry and put some powder on, and then the child appeared to be bathed." She explained that there "just wasn't time" to administer a thorough clean because so many residents needed to be washed within strict time periods. Some mothers were aware of inadequate personal hygiene standards and confronted staff about the issue. Elsie described one such occasion: "David came home and he was absolutely filthy. . . . I sat down and I wrote this letter [stating] that he often came home in this *disgraceful* manner and I couldn't take it any more." The letter was given to the manager of Kew Cottages, and the charge nurse responsible for the ward was reprimanded. After this episode, the charge nurse refused to speak with Elsie for over two years. The nurse's response was most likely intended as a form of punishment for Elsie's criticism of staff at Kew. This highlighted the potential negative reactions faced by some mothers who dared to challenge institutional practices.

Despite the prevalence of impersonal care, efforts were made by a small group of female staff to create a more intimate and homey environment in their ward—the nursery. This task was easier in the nursery than other wards because the staff-to-resident ratio was frequently lower than elsewhere—one staff member to twenty residents. Color-coded ribbons were affixed to bassinettes, as featured in the previous photo, which reflected a baby's gender, pink for girls and blue for boys. Kew social worker Fran van Brummelen noted that the atmosphere in Kew's wards "was *very* dull. Except for the Nursery. . . . The staff knitted all their clothing . . . [the babies] were always dressed beautifully." Fran recalled that many nursery staff considered themselves surrogate mothers; one charge nurse referred to the residents as "her babies." She added that this particular nurse constantly demanded that "her babies . . . receive what a 'normal' baby had, or even better." Clearly some of these female staff assumed a maternal role. The nursery staff's adoption of a "motherly" persona may have accounted for Joan's positive account of her baby's admission, as opposed to Beryl and Elsie's negative experiences when their older children were sent to the schoolboys' ward.

To offset staffing shortages, an elite group of female residents was used as unpaid labor in the nursery. This type of employment proved to be empowering for a few female residents, who were able to experience mothering roles that were unavailable to most women with disabilities. More important, women's testimonies reveal that a rewarding reciprocal relationship existed between this group of "resident workers" and children. Female residents who were assigned to the nursery, predominantly in their forties to sixties, were categorized as "high functioning." Although this type of unpaid labor was in many ways exploitative, residents such as Katie Collins, Dolly Stainer, and Lorna White relished their time in the ward and formed loving relationships through working with young residents. "Resident workers" were responsible for cleaning, feeding, and bathing children assigned to their care. Katie often referred to her charges as "possum," while Dolly Stainer simply called them "my babies." The roles that Katie, Dolly, and Lorna filled were highly valued, particularly by parents who visited Kew. Joan recalled, "One day when I arrived I was met with a lovely sight. Dolly and Katy [sic] were sitting in the sun outside the Cottage and there on Dolly's knee (see fig. 3) was my little Richie, happy as Larry to be having a cuddle." Mutual affection was often exchanged, a prize highly valued in an institutional world where residents were habitually starved of meaningful relationships.

The possibility for maternal engagement between staff and residents lessened when residents were transferred from the nursery to wards that housed people of similar age. Until the early 1960s, all residents less than twelve years old were cared for by women in the female division. In their biography of resident Dolly Stainer, Cliff Judge and Fran van Brummelen argued that the female division had a more maternal environment than the male division. Their opinion appeared to be based on the gendered assumption that women were "naturally" maternal, a supposition proven false on many occasions. For example, in an interview, Fran van Brummelen indicated that female staff were sometimes aggressive toward residents. She claimed about one charge nurse that "If she didn't like a child, well the child had a hard time of it . . . emotionally she could be quite, a bit, abusive. . . . She *hated* these children who came in for respite." Some female staff were not averse to using physical violence to control their wards. As resident Clare Turner testified, during the 1960s and 1970s she was often struck by female staff members for refusing to eat her porridge.

Once a male resident reached the age of twelve, he was transferred to the male division. Prior to the 1960s, the majority of male staff showed little compassion for residents and frequently used aggressive physical and psychological control mechanisms. One reason for the introduction

13.3. Dolly Stainer, holding Richard Jones, and Katie Collins. Courtesy of Kew Cottages Historical Society.

of female staff into male wards was to curb this type of behavior. Staff member John Wakefield was pleased with this institutional change:

> [It] just changed the whole attitude, particularly the male attitudes. I know I had a couple of very remarkable ladies . . . who came in and softened up the unit. They were the "mothers." They were usually older women with experience with their own kids. . . . They took away that blokey military approach.

Fran supported John's claims: "Just having female staff in a male unit changed the climate completely . . . there'd be much less aggressive behaviour." When official practices of gender segregation were abolished in the 1960s, some male and female staff members were assigned to work together. The belief was that through mixing staff a more balanced approach to care for residents would be achieved. But the benevolent, "maternal" care present in the nursery was not replicated in other wards at the Cottages, where the staff-to-resident ratio was far higher and the children were more active and/or required a complex and high level of support needs.

Although nursing staff in the majority of wards were unable to provide quality personal care, sometimes they prevented vulnerable children from being placed in wards where their welfare was threatened. This was clearly evident in Elsie Welchman's earlier testimony concerning her son's admission to the schoolboys' ward. The charge nurse fervently opposed this placement, and her opinion was validated by the superintendent's decision to admit David to a more suitable ward. This episode illustrated the willingness of some staff members to challenge the institutional hierarchy as a means of ensuring the safety of children in their care. However, it could also be interpreted as staff ensuring that their wards ran efficiently without unnecessary violent disruption.

The existence of violence at Kew Cottages was distressing for many mothers who witnessed their children's abuse and/or attended to their wounds. Rosalie Trower's son, Stephen, was admitted to Kew in 1982 at the age of thirty. On weekends, Rosalie often took Stephen home and was perturbed to find bruises and scratches all over his body. She discovered that he was being regularly attacked by a fellow resident. One Monday Rosalie returned Stephen to the Cottages after a home visit. She parked her car and was about to open the door when they were seized upon:

> there was a fellow . . . who was set to kill Steve . . . this fellow appeared, out of the blue, made a dive at Steve's side, I banged the buttons down so he couldn't open the doors, he then threw himself on the bonnet, shouted and screamed, there was *nobody* around. . . . As I locked the doors, I thought: "There's only one way out of this, just drive out, get out of the place," so I did.

Rosalie drove to the central administration building and met with Kew's chief executive officer, Max Jackson, and social worker, Fran van Brummelen. Rosalie demanded that Stephen be moved immediately to another unit. The only available alternative was a unit that was terribly overcrowded, but Rosalie agreed to the transfer in order to protect her son.

She was angry that she had to resolve the situation: "he was safe there [in his new unit], of course, [but] I *had* to do that." Stephen was fortunate that his mother recognized the abuse and demanded action. Many other residents endured continual abuse as they had little or no family contact or advocates who were willing or able to assist them.

Mothers such as Rosalie who took an active interest in their children's welfare at Kew spoke about the conflicting emotions brought about through visitation. Mothers expressed their joy at fulfilling their "mothering role" through taking their children home for periods of time. Anna Davison explained that when her daughter went to live at Kew in 1958 at the age of five, she "looked forward to visiting on the weekend. . . . I used to think to myself: 'Well she has one very happy day.'" Similarly, Elsie spoke about her pleasure when she brought David home for visits: "he just loved being home . . . he'd lie on the floor and rub the carpet with his fingers. . . . His life out there was so different from what it was at home." However, David's anguish when returning to Kew made home visits bittersweet:

> He hung onto me, he wouldn't let me go and he cried and I had to say: "Well I can't take this." So for a while, no even to this day, I can't go down there unless we're taking him out. If I go down he grabs hold of me and pushes me towards the door, he wants to come home . . . he won't get out of the car when we get back with him . . . he clings to me and makes me feel, guilty.

Family visits to Kew Cottages were also traumatic for some mothers and residents. When Patty Rodgers was admitted to the Cottages at the age of seven, her mother caught two trains and a tram to visit her daughter each week. Patty's sister, Margaret, recalled the turmoil of visiting her sister at the institution: "just going to see Patty used to be terrible because she'd scream when we left, this went on for years and years." Patty agreed with her sister, stating, "that's right!" The presence of mothers visiting at Kew was also painful for many residents who had no familial contact. Abandoned as a baby, resident Ted Rowe never knew his mother. However, he yearned for her to come and visit him at Kew: "When I'd see the others I'd start to cry and say, 'I wish I had my mummy . . . coming to see me.'" Visitation was a complex issue which brought to the fore the raw emotion of mother-child separation.

Despite the potential emotional distress of visitation, some few mothers regularly volunteered to supplement the care given their children. For example, Beryl was unhappy with the dental hygiene standards: "Geoff's teeth were never cleaned because the staff said they didn't have enough time. So I said well you won't mind if I clean them when I come. So at every visit—about three times a week at that time, I would duly come equipped and do the job myself." Beryl was able to maintain Geoff's oral health, while many other residents suffered ill-health from poor dental hygiene. Beryl also helped to feed her son whenever possible. During her time in the ward she witnessed systematic rough treatment of residents. On one occasion her own son was physically chastised by staff despite her presence:

> Not long after Geoff had been admitted . . . I brought him back from a home visit at mealtime. They had two large stainless steel cylinders, one with gravy into which they tipped mashed potato and coarse chunks of meat, then sloshed it half cold onto residents' plates. I had stayed on to help Geoff eat because he needed coactive assistance. But it looked so disgusting, I broke down when Geoff refused to eat it and he was literally taken "by the collar" by the ward doctor who happened to be there at the time to see Dr. Brady [the Cottages superintendent].

Such experiences contributed to Beryl's feeling powerless as a mother and revealed the extent to which parents were "invisible" within the institution. In order to remedy this situation, Beryl sought avenues of activism to raise the standard of care within the institution.

In 1951, Dr. Eric Cunningham Dax, an English psychiatrist, was appointed the inaugural chairman of Victoria's newly formed Mental Hygiene Authority. Renowned for his progressive ideas, Dax (1961) introduced multidisciplinary care at the Cottages and encouraged people in the general community to become involved with the institution as volunteers and visitors.[2] An increased presence of mothers at Kew resulted from these reforms and also led to the establishment of the Kew Cottages Parents' Association (KCPA) in 1957.

A few progressive staff at Kew, particularly female social workers, also advocated for changes to institutional culture, believing that parental involvement at the Cottages would result in improved standards of care for residents. The formation of KCPA was instigated by Kew Cottages' first social worker, Irena Higgins. KCPA, which grew to be an influential advocacy group at Kew, encouraged parents to maintain an interest in their children's welfare after their placement into institutional care. It also assisted parents who were considering admitting their children to an institution or were on a waiting list for placement. Although men were active in the organization, women dominated in numbers and in its activities, enabling mothers to develop a critical new role in institutional life and disability in general. Historian Arthur Lloyd (1987, 105–11) wrote that KCPA members used a variety of means—regular meetings, information sessions, visits to peoples' homes, and publications—to keep parents informed and connected with others in their situation. Rose Miller was grateful for this help:

> Immediately after [Sean] was put onto the waiting list of the Kew Cottages, I got their newsletters. There was a fellow called Mac Brazier who was the editor of the newsletter. He made you feel you're not the only one in this position. . . . I was getting these newsletters which sort of cheered me up in my hours of horror.

KCPA enabled a small group of mothers to negotiate a place for themselves within the context of the institution. The organization, which started with 70 members, quickly grew to over 560 families by 1966 (Godwin and Wade 2007, 4). Members represented a variety of parents from many walks of life. Celebrated pianist June Epstein (fig. 4) was elected as

---

2. This philosophy of care was also expounded by influential Scottish psychiatrist Maxwell Jones (1953).

13.4. First president of the Kew Cottages Parents' Association, June Epstein, with Dr. Eric Cunningham Dax. Courtesy of Kew Residential Services, Department of Human Services, Victoria, Australia.

its first president, with Jack Camp as secretary. For over fifty years KCPA mothers were effective activists who served as a driving force behind improvements and reforms at Kew Cottages. This group of women was successful in making the transition from surrendering their children into state care to engaging actively with institutional authorities and staff.

One of the primary goals of mothers' activism at Kew was improving the physical landscape and daily care of residents. Most residents were exposed to continual deprivation: food was regularly recycled and clothes were often substandard. In recognition of poor living conditions, fundraising became a significant activity conducted by mothers belonging to KCPA. Anna was a KCPA member who joined committees and working groups to raise money for the Cottages. She recalled working for years on the "Towel Project": "We all got together on those towels and it was a wonderful project. .[We sold] many thousands. . . . We sort of wondered what people *did* with our towels because we sold so many!" Other fundraising activities included selling cards for special occasions, approaching philanthropic and commercial bodies for donations, and hosting an annual fete at the Cottages. The fete, which ran from 1961 to 2001, drew thousands of people to the institution and raised substantial funds. As noted by Louise Godwin and Catherine Wade (2007, 22–28) in their history of KCPA, fundraising activities resulted in improvements to the fabric of the institution. Many women felt that their involvement in these activities created new, meaningful relationships between themselves and their institutionalized children. As Hilda noted, "we [KCPA] used to have somebody who visited each of the units and liaised with the charge nurse, as they were called in those days, about what small things we could provide to help our children have more pleasant lives." As a consequence of mothers' activism, institutional life was improved.

In 1961, a formalization of volunteerism at Kew resulted in the formation of the Visiting Services of Auxiliaries. This development emerged from the government's reform agenda which resulted in greater community engagement with people who lived in state mental-health facilities. In its heyday, in the 1970s and 1980s, there were over five hundred volunteers who assisted staff and residents at Kew. Mothers constituted an important group within this cohort. Women interviewed for the history often explained that being volunteers allowed them to feel as if they were fulfilling their maternal roles not only for their children but for others who did not have familial contact. Olive Earl remarked that she enjoyed working in the swimming program at Kew, where she supported many female residents in hydrotherapy. She explained that her daughter Lorraine "didn't know us as her mother and father . . . but going swimming with her and the other children made us happy." Olive often felt saddened that Lorraine was unable to reciprocate her expression of maternal love, but through her work with other residents she overcame this feeling of loss.

The institutional system, however, also disempowered mothers by limiting their voice and often framing their activism as "troublesome meddling." Hilda recalled that in the early years of KCPA, many staff were suspicious of parents and openly confronted them about their activism. Beryl described such antagonism: "parents were expected to be denied access beyond the entrance room [in each ward]. But I was a rebel and made it clear that there was no door behind which I would not enter where Geoff was living. So I made myself very unpopular." Although a small group of mothers openly challenged staff actions and institutional procedures, the majority felt that they had no right to question those caring for their children. As Rose stated, "I've always said to myself: 'Well *you* couldn't look after him, how can you criticize any people who are there!'" Other mothers feared potential negative repercussions for themselves and their children if they were seen to be "making trouble."

As staff recognized the potential benefits of mothers' involvement in daily life at Kew, a change in attitude permeated the institution. This shift occurred over several years as parents and volunteers increasingly became an integral part of the Cottages. Because of her forthright manner, Beryl stated that her relationship with the charge nurse responsible for her son's ward was often volatile. However, when Beryl became the liaison officer for KCPA, this relationship altered. The charge nurse wanted KCPA to pay for the repair of a blender that was used to blend food in the ward. She knew that Beryl was in a position to negotiate payment for this service from KCPA funds, and thus her attitude shifted. According to Beryl the "frightful confrontations" ceased and a more amicable relationship ensued. This episode illustrated the benefits of mutual alliances between mothers and staff in improving the working and living conditions of people at Kew. Fran argued that some staff took advantage of these relationships and women's maternal love for their children. She witnessed one staff member not only encouraging mothers to provide ongoing voluntary work, but convincing them to lobby management on her behalf. Fran stated that if mothers "were cooperative, well then she [charge nurse] sort of *exploited* them." Staff such as this charge nurse played upon the maternal guilt that many mothers felt for placing their children at Kew. However, the positive aspects of mothers' activism far outweighed the negative ramifications. Mothers created a powerful force for change not only for their children but for other residents at Kew.

Reforms introduced in the 1950s resulted in a transformation of mothering at Kew Cottages. From this era, policies were introduced to encourage family and community involvement with mental health institutions across Victoria. Because of these changes, increasing numbers of mothers adopted roles such as volunteers and activists at the institution. Initially, mothers' involvement was supported by a small group of staff at Kew, while the majority questioned their motives. Gradually, staff members were able to recognize the benefits of utilizing mothers in easing their workload, providing additional resources, and lobbying management on their behalf. Mothers' activism served as a powerful mechanism for women to reclaim their status as mothers within the institutional regime.

14

History Examined

One Woman's Story of Disability and Advocacy

M A R I L Y N   D O L M A G E

T hrough my own story and the story of my family, I map the struggle for equality for people with disabilities. This narrative timeline charts the ways that disability has shaped my life and identity and also reflects attitudes and connects approaches to disability and mothering since 1952 in North America.

The door opened; my mother was home from the hospital. I was four and ran downstairs to meet her asking: "Where's the baby?" A horrible hush fell, broken moments later by my mother's sobbing. It felt like my fault; I had been warned not to ask. I had been told that the baby had been "born wrong" and would not be coming home. (Maybe I hoped my mother would tell me where he had actually gone and who was looking after my baby brother, since I had planned to help.) I learned in that moment that I must not ask such questions.

I did know his name was Robert Bruce. At first, it seemed easier to believe that he had died, even though a girl who lived down the street once told neighborhood children that I had killed him. Later, I found a letter in which a physician at a government institution informed my parents they need not bother to send him gifts. When I happened to visit the town in which that institution was located, I secretly looked up its phone number, imagining the possibilities. Every time I was ill as a child, I had the same eerie nightmare: I was riding smoothly in a big bus even though the road was very rough, past a lawn that seemed perfect although it was full of noxious weeds, with an infant who seemed beautiful even though I was told he was very deformed. All during childhood, I stared at people whose disabilities seemed apparent, my curiosity rooted in my own loss. Once, my father's business involved our family in a charity activity for "crippled children," where I felt mortified to win the magician's rabbit meant for one of those other kids—less lucky than me—who had been "born wrong."

It feels as if I have always been searching for Robert, even though the only time I ever saw him was in a casket. I will not forget his tiny, lifeless eight-year-old body, but I saw no family resemblance then, only what I thought seemed "wrong" about him.

Still wanting answers, I majored in psychology at university and found a summer job in another government institution. Its uniformed staff marched children—like little soldiers—around the grounds; I loved taking them to the fields to play out of sight of the buildings. Most days, we were required to lock them into basement "playrooms" and conduct toilet training and behavior-management programs, and I concluded that I was too impatient for what was called "front-line work." I watched visiting families, identified with their pain of separation, and decided to change my career path, knowing how much families like mine needed help.

I found a position as a social worker at the institution where Robert had died. On my second day there, I read his file, trying to reconcile the facts and my memories, wanting those questions answered: What could be so "wrong" about a baby that his parents would abandon him at birth and for whom society would develop and maintain such segregated systems? I learned that Robert was diagnosed at birth as having Down syndrome (long before chromosome testing). I knew my parents were proud that they could afford a specialist who had such expertise. They accepted professional advice that he would never return their love (as if that was his job) and that his presence (not his absence) would harm my older brother and I. My grandfather paid for a private nursing home at first and then took Robert at the age of three to the institution. I have only one photograph of Robert, taken then, in which he looks as big as he did when he died. (I now see family resemblances in that picture, and the twinkle in his bright eyes prompts me to worry about how the institution would have treated him in the subsequent five years.) Robert never developed much strength or mobility (and so I wonder if he spent all his time restrained in one of the institution's "cage cots," cribs topped with bars). My parents' only role in Robert's life may have been to lobby politically to get him that institution "bed," which was fully government funded. I learned that an institution doctor discouraged a plan they once had to visit him there (and my work experience showed me that staff seemed more careful with children whose parents visited). How ironic that this institution was called a "hospital school," since Robert never attended school and died of pneumonia, having not been given penicillin. (My parents had been told he would get all he needed there but seemed relieved when he died.)

During the five years I worked at the institution, my job was to encourage connections with families and to open institution doors to the community. I even recruited my mother as a volunteer visitor and took her on one of our facility tours, which too often felt like "freak" shows, although they were intended to raise consciousness about the need for reform.

Before we began our own family, my husband, Jim, and I were careful to undergo and clear all the genetic and other tests available. As fate would have it, our first child was born with life-threatening disabilities. Coming out of anesthetic, I heard the words "spina bifida." He was rushed away for immediate surgery to repair his spinal cord before I saw him, and I knew that he might never walk. Before I was fully awake, before Jim and I had talked, I decided we could not call him Timothy, as planned. I understood charity stereotypes about "crippled children," and I didn't want our son to be named "Timmy"—an Easter Seal icon. Thus his name would be Matthew—our second choice—which I subsequently learned meant "gift of God."

I did not see Matthew until he was ten days old. Noticing further problems no one had mentioned, I remembered a phrase I had read in institution files, "multiple congenital anomalies." I felt like running away and was ashamed that I had judged other parents for doing so. But I did stay; we learned to care for our baby and adjusted our assumptions. As I was rocking Matthew one day in the hospital, while the nurses' radio played "Mother and Child Reunion," I stopped a team of doctors from examining and disturbing him. That was the moment when I learned that

Matthew had a heart defect, but also that I had become his advocate. I had grown up dreaming of being a mother who loved unconditionally; Matthew would receive the love Robert had missed. I was now surely on "the front lines" as a parent.

I always understood that Matt's life would be much harder if he had intellectual disabilities as well as physical. He was constantly assessed. It was difficult enough to see that our baby couldn't do what other children his age were doing, but professionals also compared his development unfavorably to other children with spina bifida, no matter that he faced more complex medical challenges. A neurosurgeon seemed horrified that Matt's head was too small (what did that mean?); therapists said he was not "ready" for the specialized equipment they prescribed for other children (so who would help him?). Everyone seemed so pessimistic about Matthew's future that we surreptitiously looked through his hospital file to see if they knew something we didn't. I learned to introduce my child to anesthetists the night before his many surgeries, by describing his "anomalies": head to toe, or toe to head, so much that was "wrong."

People we met in the multidisciplinary clinics shared our joy when our daughter, Leah, was born when Matt was almost two. Then they told me this was when they usually suggested "placement" for kids like Matthew. Now that we had a healthy (perfect?) baby, we could send Matthew away to be with other kids "just like him," where he would get "just what he needed." I was labeled "hysterical" when I quite calmly responded: "Oh? Where is that place? I didn't know it existed." By that time, my social-work colleagues were sending the most disabled people to private, for-profit nursing homes, a common practice to downsize government institutions.

I concluded that, if something happened to us, Matt would have better options only if he became less disabled, and so we put more pressure on him to gain skills. A tragic lesson finally made us realize that therapy should no longer be our priority. Although Matthew had learned to walk with crutches, he would often drop to the floor and cry, causing quite a scene. Behavior therapists taught us to ignore this behavior, and Matt did become more compliant. It was months later when we realized that pressure on his spinal cord was causing him great pain. He had learned, all right, that we would not respond to his only way to communicate his pain.

After all, he had been assessed as being not "ready" for communication system assistance, especially because he did not follow visual cues. The pediatric ophthalmologist he saw every year because of congenital "malformations" said Matthew was "a bit short-sighted, but don't worry about it." It was not until Matt was seven that we happened to find a new doctor who prescribed glasses. Immediately, Matthew's development improved; his world opened up, and I learned to demand change in this all-too-often abusive system—and to stop pressuring my son.

We were an especially busy family after our son Jay was born when Matthew was three and a half. We welcomed the help Matt received first at a nursery school for children with disabilities in another town. However, we wanted him to be part of our own small community and always knew that his greatest progress happened when he was with other children, especially his sister and brother. As a parent volunteer, I established extra resource help so that children with disabilities could be included in our local, parent-run nursery school. Matthew was welcome and thrived there, but greater struggles came when he started school. The new special education experts at the school board persuaded us to send him to a school for students with disabilities. The intensive speech therapy promised there never happened; we soon saw that Matt was regressing. He was powerless to assert his rights and prove his potential, and so were we. Collaboration with parents was discouraged, and our questions were unwelcome.

His brother and sister challenged us: Why was Matthew "segregated"? Did it mean they should now be ashamed of their brother, whose life was increasingly different from theirs? Shouldn't he attend a school like theirs, with a library and gymnasium, alongside other kids who could help him read and who would love learning sign language, too? Our challenge to find better education for Matt led us through legal battles and moved us to another community, but also connected us to allies among whom we learned more about advocacy and inclusive education. This personal experience informs the work I continue to do—professionally and politically—to support families and schools and promote change in education policies and practices. (I coordinate research, policy analysis, and community and professional development projects for a coalition of disability-rights groups across Ontario, Canada). So much has come to be understood about rights and pedagogy in the last twenty years, but too many families are still struggling.

Our family's advocacy for community support has always been part of the larger struggle for systemic change. It was a battle to ensure our children attended school together, and to assist Matt to have the education, medical treatment, employment, and community life he wanted. But it was worth it, not only to improve his life but to improve the lives of his brother and sister, too, and other children of all abilities. Our family benefited from an innovative direct-funding arrangement, meant to save the government money by keeping children like Matt out of institutions. Matt could avoid segregated programs because he could hire support people to help him participate in scouting, YMCA, and other community recreation programs. Although he faced more medical crises during his high school years, he attended regular classes of his choice, felt that he belonged, drove his power wheelchair expertly, mastered literacy for computer communication, and became a piano keyboard virtuoso. When he finished high school, we fought to ensure Matt got enough individualized funding to maintain an active life. He still lived at home, but he contributed as a volunteer and found a job, providing office support at an employment center, helping other people looking for work.

Matt's sudden death just weeks before his thirtieth birthday devastated our family. In my grief, there is bitterness about so many struggles and lost opportunities, but I feel so proud of Matthew. We have wonderful family memories. After all we have been through, Matt remains our hero. So many people, to whom his life connected, joined us to mourn his loss; I wish he could have heard my tribute to his beauty, brilliance, courage, and confidence.

A discussion about mothering needs to consider fathers, too. My hospitalization after Matthew's birth allowed Jim to be more involved from the very start than many fathers typically are. The school board we challenged legally over Matt's education was Jim's employer throughout his thirty-one years as a high school teacher. During the crises, we experienced our closest partnership as a couple. Matt relied on his dad's strength during difficult medical treatment. Jim particularly encouraged and supported the many family travels and adventures that enriched all our lives.

The institution in which my brother died has finally closed, but other forms of segregation persist. Science seems to strive for a world without disability; euthanasia threatens the lives I work to improve. For over forty years now, I have worked alongside people with disabilities and their families to create new supports and relationships. Inclusion remains very elusive but I have lived its beauty and know it is so worth the struggle. I thank my children and their partners for insights gained along the way, and for hope about the future.

I try to keep both Robert's and Matthew's stories alive, in the hope that history, examined, will stop repeating itself.

15

My Mother's Mental Illness

WHITNEY JONES-GARCIA

18 JULY 2008

My mother has run away from home.[1] She is hiding in a bathroom stall in a department store basement. "How did you manage to call me?" she asks. "My phone doesn't work. It's in emergency mode." She talks quickly, breathlessly, stringing her words together so quickly that I can barely keep up. She was ordered to leave her apartment by her neighbors—criminal pieces of garbage—who live two floors below. They set up a sound system so that my mother can hear them and so that they can hear her. They have a hellhole under their bathroom floor where they torture and kill people, but sometimes they say "kill with kindness," which means they drug people instead of killing them. My brother, or his twin, is there now, and if she didn't leave when they told her to, he would be killed, but maybe they meant something else, like kill with kindness. Criminal pieces of shit.

Someone is knocking on the stall door. It's 10:00 p.m. The store is closing.

I call my brother Dylan for help. Almost twenty years ago, my brother asked me, "Do I have a twin?" Our mother says so many things. Some things are true, some things are related to the truth, and some things are

---

1. Whitney Jones-Garcia is the pseudonym of an associate professor in the humanities at a university in the northeast. Her essay records her experiences of actual events. With the exception of Esmin Green, Steven Sabock, and Millie and Susan Smiley, all names and place names have been changed to protect the privacy of the individuals involved.

true only to her. I showed my brother his birth certificate, and the solid check mark beside "single birth," and the familiar loops of our mother's signature. "They forced me to sign that," she would insist later.

My brother leaves work early—he has a new job bartending—to look for our mother. She won't tell us exactly where she is. Her calls are being monitored. She shouldn't even be talking to us on the phone. "I was told that bad things would happen to Dylan or Zack if I called," she says. Zack, the twin, seems to move in and out of her consciousness. Years have gone by without any mention of him, but right now he is a fixture. I wish he did exist. We could use the backup.

This is the first time in over three years that our mother has left her apartment by herself. My brother Dylan takes her to the grocery store every week. Occasionally my brother Tom visits her. But he lives on the opposite side of the city, in an adult-care home, and shares my mother's diagnosis: paranoid schizophrenia. Planning and executing a trip to see her can be difficult for him, and lately she tells him that he cannot visit. She is worried that he will be kidnapped by her neighbors. I live hundreds of miles away, but I visit usually once a month and stay with her for several days. I take her out shopping, to lunch, to dinner, and to meet the manager of the rental property she inherited—her only source of income. Under other circumstances ("normal" circumstances?), I would be thrilled that she left the apartment by herself. But she left tonight not only out of fear, but also because the voices she heard ordered her to leave. She followed a command. I am used to her having delusions and hearing voices. I am even used to her talking back to the voices she hears sometimes. But this time is very different. She is doing what the voices tell her to do. This feels dangerous.

My brother easily finds my mother. She's at least somewhat predictable, and it's late. There's only a short list of places she might be and he finds her at his first stop. Her phone really is in "emergency mode"—she had called 911 earlier in the day, which enabled the GPS tracking on her cell phone. Explaining this to her, of course, only reinforces her other beliefs that her calls are monitored. Dylan takes her back to his apartment, where she stands by his front door the whole night, listening to his neighbors talk about her.

24 JULY 2008

I've been in town for two nights so far, staying with my mother, and things are not going well. I'm exhausted from the previous day, from driving aimlessly around town trying to escape the voices. Her interactions with me are fitful and sporadic. A half an hour can go by without her speaking to me or even seeming to notice that I am with her, then suddenly there will be a crisis—a clear threat from the voices—we have to leave wherever we are quickly, in a panic. At night she shakes me awake so that she can see my face and make sure I am still breathing.

My mother cannot tell me when she last slept, and it is clear that she hasn't been eating or bathing. Her mismatched clothes are hanging loosely off of her. She has lost ten pounds in two weeks, she tells me proudly. Her left forearm is scrawled with ink—a jumble of letters and numbers from car license plates. Her neighbors are holding children hostage next door, and this is part of the evidence she is accumulating against them. When a number she has written on her arm starts to fade, she rewrites it carefully again in blue pen.

I spend the morning on the phone, trying to coordinate a visit from a mobile crisis team. I'm in the apartment with my mother; Dylan is across town initiating the call to the Southern Crisis Hotline, a toll-free one-stop shopping for behavioral health issues. I've called several times before and have prepped him on how to get past the operator, directly to a counselor, and how to get the counselor to start the process for a mobile crisis team visit. Everything seems to be clicking into place. But we quickly hit a snag. There is only one social worker today, who is still on his first call and has two more before us. It's not yet noon, but we are too late to make today's list. Take her to an emergency room, the counselor tells us.

By the end of the day, I do take her to the emergency room, but I have spent the majority of the day trying to engage her and trying to work up to this step. Talking to her is difficult. I have to compete with her hallucinations. She often hushes me so that she can hear the sound system better. As I drive up to the hospital emergency entrance that night, my mother puts her hand on my shoulder, looks me in the eye, and asks, "Are you awake?" She has been in deep discussions with voices from the sound system for the past hour. She has not noticed much else.

"Why are we here?"

"I think you need to see a doctor."

We have a standoff. I try to get her to come into the hospital. She refuses. My mother will not walk into the emergency room. I use the opportunity to make a small negotiation nevertheless. I will get back in the car and take her to the store to buy a cold drink. In return, she will allow us to go back to the apartment so that I can sleep. I am very, very tired. On the way home, I see a police car ahead and contemplate causing an accident. If I hit them, then maybe we could both go to the emergency room. The irony of this is not lost on me. I am the one who is dangerous to myself and to others now.

"If you really want to help me," she says, "you'll take me to see my children." The request is not completely unreasonable, but Dylan is at work and it's past the visiting hours at the home where Tom lives. And something about this sounds strange: "my children." Eventually I realize that she doesn't know exactly who I am. When I leave town days later, she asks me where I am going. When I tell her I am going home, her eyes widen. "Do you have an apartment in this complex?" No, Mom, I live in New York, remember? "Oh, I'm really confused now. I thought you were the other one." I now have a duplicate. Even when she wished me a happy birthday yesterday, she was not speaking to me.

31 JULY 2008

Two days ago, the voices in the sound system told my mother that they had killed Zack and Dylan. My mother called the coroner, but they wouldn't come. My mother called the police, but they couldn't help. And she finally called the Southern Crisis Hotline. An ambulance took her away.

I drive up to the same emergency room where we had our standoff, and I walk down to the secure unit. Dylan is sitting in a chair. My mother is pacing the floor, demanding to leave. She realizes now that the guard at the door is not there to keep people out. He is there to keep her in.

"Mrs. Jones, put those bags down, please. You need to get back in bed." The guard has already dialed the charge nurse, who comes huffing around the corner followed by five other nurses, residents, interns, a female guard, anyone she can get to follow her.

Lately I tend to think of my mother as timid and fearful. She is, after all, paranoid, and even the slightest wayward look from a passerby or a sound as common as a car starting can give her cause for alarm. But as she stands there surrounded by strangers in scrubs, I can't help but be impressed and simultaneously dismayed by her courage and her stubbornness. She has somehow managed to get a pen from the guard and is now insisting that the charge nurse tell her the phone number for the hospital administration. She wants to report all of them for their illegal, criminal activities against her. Unfortunately, my mother's stubbornness is equally matched by the charge nurse's frustration ("I have other patients!"), and as my mother aims the pen at her forearm in an attempt to write down the telephone number, the army of scrubs intervenes, taking the pen, pushing her into bed, rolling her onto her side, and injecting her with 10 mg of Geodon.

Geodon (zyprasidone) is one of many new generation antipsychotics, used to treat symptoms of schizophrenia and bipolar disorder. In the injectable form, it is used to treat "acute agitation" in patients with schizophrenia. One might think of Geodon as a newer, improved version of Haldol, the old psychiatric emergency standby drug of the *One Flew Over the Cuckoo's Nest* generation. But this is not an analogy I want to push too far. This is not a fictional novel about thwarted masculinity. Our charge nurse is no Miss Ratched. She is Jennifer, a young white woman in blue scrubs and rubber clogs. She looks tired, and her curly hair is messy. And although very much in charge, she also seems slightly overwhelmed by responsibility. Afterwards, the female guard shook her head: "It ain't right to do that. Not in front of the family. That's a shame, that is."

1 AUGUST 2008

When I wake up, I know I'm sick. After the shot of Geodon kicked in, my mother slept for hours. I snuck away from the hospital and back to

my mother's apartment, where I took advantage of her absence by cleaning ruthlessly. I attacked the refrigerator. At first I started throwing out
the things that were undeniably rotten: bags of apple slices fermenting in
their juices, grapes turned into raisins, toxic takeout boxes from my previous visits, six dozen eggs. I filled bag after bag. Then I threw out the things
that would soon be rotten: milk, deli peach tea, mayonnaise. I pulled out
every shelf and bin, and waged chemical warfare in the kitchen at large.

In the bathroom, a large heavy bag sat hidden in the corner. About
a year ago, my mother became convinced that her downstairs neighbors
had rigged her toilet and were collecting the contents of it whenever she
flushed. She believed her toilet emptied into the hellhole where her children were being tortured. The bag in the bathroom held her feces from
the past week.

I wake up to a clean apartment, but I am sick. I am feverish and alone,
and the sounds of the apartment are unsettling, almost frightening. I
seem to be turning into my mother.

By the time I return to the emergency room, my mother is gone. They
have finally transferred her to Southern Regional. I call Dylan to tell him.
He spent fourteen hours in the emergency room yesterday, and I feel
guilty for leaving him there so long especially because he has to work a
twelve-hour shift today. Dylan asks me if I have seen today's paper. No,
but I pick up a copy. The headline reads: "Mental Patients in Jeopardy."
The story is about Southern Regional; according to the report, negligence
and abuse at the hospital have contributed to the deaths of at least 136
patients from 2002 through late 2007.

I call admissions at the hospital at least every half hour. On some calls,
I let the phone ring only five times. Sometimes I count to twenty. Eventually someone answers. The woman I talk to will not confirm that my
mother is a patient; medical privacy laws prevent staff from giving out
any information. After some minor sparring, she tells me that I can come
to admissions to see her. When I arrive, a very cordial man unlocks the
door to let me in and leads me through several locked corridors to a "family waiting room." After almost an hour, someone comes to see me. She
apologizes for my wait, but tells me that it is against policy for patients in
admissions to have visitors. "It is too upsetting and disruptive." She also

tells me that my mother has been admitted, but there are no open beds. They will transfer her today to one of two private hospitals that the state contracts with: one is near the airport, one is near her apartment.

They do not transfer her that day. My mother and eight other patients spend the night sleeping in chairs in admissions. They give her a blanket, a baloney sandwich, a small container of liquid soap, and access to a shower.

When I hear of her night at Southern Regional, I think of Esmin Green, the woman who died in admissions waiting for psychiatric care at Kings County Hospital, Brooklyn, this past June (Marzuli 2008). The well-known and widely distributed video images of Green falling to the floor are ingrained in my head, as are the words of her daughter. I also think of Steven Sabock, who died after sitting neglected, slumped in a chair, for over twenty-two hours in a psychiatric hospital day room in Goldsboro, North Carolina, in April (Bonner 2008). Like my mother, he had not eaten regularly for days. Video of Sabock shows him sitting in a chair overnight and being nudged in the shoulder with a breakfast tray the next morning, by a staff member who moves on when Sabock is unresponsive. Sabock sat in the same chair for twenty-two hours, until he finally left the day room in a stretcher, too late.

13 AUGUST 2008

Appleford, a private behavioral and mental health hospital just fifteen minutes from my mother's apartment, is a stark contrast from Southern Regional, and not just because the television works in the waiting room. Most of the patients have addictions, bipolar disorder, or both, and most, unlike my mother, have insurance. The waiting room is crowded with family members and pamphlets for Abilify. At Southern Regional, visitors are so rare that in the past I have been consistently mistaken for a social worker. But at Appleford, I am always a daughter.

In order to get discharged, my mother has agreed to attend a seven-day outpatient program and to take medication for two months. As we leave, she insists on going immediately to the drug store to get her medication. I am amazed and happy. But as I pay for the medication, my mother grabs my wallet. "I'm sorry, but I need evidence." She stares at my credit cards, at my driver's license. She stares at me. And then she tells me about my twin. She heard the nurses talking about us the day we were born. "You met her in the 80s, but you probably don't remember because those criminal pieces of shit brainwashed you. Her name is Olivia Jones." My mother's name. She pauses dramatically, expecting an appropriate reaction from me. Shock and awe. Righteous indignation. Anger that my twin was stolen and that I was cheated out of a sister. But I disappoint her once again. I say nothing. My grief over Olivia Jones, who lives within this illness, my sister and my mother, is a chronic and familiar silence.

In *Out of the Shadow,* a documentary about her mother's mental illness, Susan Smiley (2006) asks, "Can I be the parent to Millie that she has never been to me?" After a childhood of abuse and neglect, this is a question that Smiley considers "a moral battle" and a "true crisis" of conscience. But in the context of a public health care system that is woefully inadequate in meeting the needs of people with severe mental illness—people like Esmin Green, Steven Sabock, Millie Smiley, and my mother—the responsibility for caring rests increasingly with family members, whether we are up for the task or not. Perhaps in some sense I am an eponymous twin of my mother—a mothering born out of and into schizophrenia.

16

A Schizo-ly Situated Daughter

A Mother's Labor

ELIZABETH METCALF

At one time I agreed with the theory on "schizophrenogenic moth-ers," insisting I had one to all who would listen to my expertise about the etiology of my creative brain. Prior to that, I thought "Munchausen by proxy" caused my psychiatric disability and that I was my mother's proxy. (Munchausen by proxy runs in the gene pool I call family. I have a cousin who breeds new and imaginative ailments in her elderly mother each year: two years ago it was Alzheimer's, which miraculously cleared up by the following Christmas . . . go figure.) Someone had to be blamed for the wiring in my brain, and my mother was an easy target, being my sole familial caregiver. I have seen more than my share of in-patient units, and discourses rich with mother-blame abound, as moms can never reach the pinnacle of selfless perfection that some of us desire, no matter how hard they may try.

Like most, Mom and I had our share of difference in my upbring-ing, but she made up for all previous shortcomings when, at age twenty-seven, after a harrowing graduate program, I could no longer care for myself in any responsible way. I moved back under her roof. She is a tough, stoic woman but her voice broke when she said, "You will always have a home here, Elizabeth." I was not exactly thrilled with the arrange-ment, as my peers were entertaining ideas of new jobs and relationships and the highlight of my year was getting SSDI, which at the time signaled to me defeat, a notion I have since given up because the aid served its purpose when I needed it.

218

Mom only worked outside the house occasionally; caring for me was a full-time job. I think she would have liked actual paid labor, as she always talked about going back to work one day. But my fear was so out of control I could not go anywhere alone, so even grocery shopping was done in tandem. We had an agreement: I would buy her tuna fish if she would pay for my tampons as my food stamps would cover only what you could eat. We figured that those who constructed the program must have been men.

Mom has no formal education past high school but quickly became an expert social worker. She wore many and diverse hats in varied vocations throughout my fifteen-year career as a psychiatric patient:

Case manager. My mother's training in bookkeeping made navigating the Medicaid spend-down process a cinch; the endless forms involving computations gave her a project to showcase her math wizardry.

Motivational counselor. I took a three-year sabbatical on the couch in her living room, my depression so debilitating I would only get up to buy cigarettes every day as she refused to enable the addiction and knew it was the sole reason I ventured out of the house; she was always volunteering ideas for me, chanting, "You must do something with your time!"

Physical therapist. The side effects of the medicines would cause my muscles to get rigid and stuck in excruciatingly painful positions in the middle of the night. It would take me an hour to get one arm free to ring the cowbell next to my bed. . . . The sound was her cue to get up and begin to soothe the muscles on the contorted body that lay screeching in agony. (The doctors told me this does not happen on the particular cocktail. . . . They lied.)

Security guard. At times I could not close my eyes to go to sleep for fear that the reaper in my depressive hallucinations would hurt me. Mom read her books outside my door until I fell asleep and promised to slay the reaper if he came too close.

Julie, my cruise director. Life in the hospital was a monotonous series of the following events: eat, sleep, smoke, and entertain the residents. When I was locked up locally, Mom brought the Scrabble game every night, at times breaking the rules of visiting hours until she got caught and ushered out by nurses who took their jobs a bit too seriously. Once she stressed out the nurses by bringing my chocolate Lab, who loped through the unit hallway, frantically trying to greet me. How she was able to smuggle a ninety-five-pound dog into the locked unit is beyond my understanding.

Senior attending physician. During an in-patient stay to reintroduce a drug that had previously caused toxicity, my fever spiked into extremely dangerous territory. I was in the ICU, where mom stood guard. When the nursing staff had neglected me for four hours, not noticing that mom had stayed well past visiting hours, she lost her cool and began teaching the basics: "A temperature does not get much higher than one-hundred-five-point-two; she is delusional and it is not because of her psychiatric issues. I want you to do your job and get some water to cool her off." They threatened to call security if she did not leave, but all of a sudden people were attending to my febrile state.

I could go on with her list of career accomplishments. I have healed significantly since those days, and though I still have momentary lapses outside the realm of normalcy, most of my time is spent in relative lucidity inside the more favorable institution of academe rather than the mental hospital. I am always asked my diagnosis for whatever reason people want to know, and because it falls into the mundane, "not otherwise specified," category, I simply say "Schizo-ly situated," my own made-up psychiatric label.

I have often looked back at those days and wondered whether or not I could, like my mother, give myself so selflessly if handed the same circumstances. This question will always remain unanswered, as I have chosen not to have children, but I frankly do not think I have it in me. I have spoken to many mothers of children with disabilities, and they tell me I would surprise myself.

Even though this literal question will never occur, something struck me as similar last year in the middle of paper deadlines and a planned trip out of town with friends. My mother called with the unfortunate news that she had breast cancer and would be having a lumpectomy. She asked if I had time to travel home to take her to and from the hospital. I canceled my trip and headed to her house immediately without question. I was thinking on the drive that it was so very strange that I was put in the able-bodied caretaker role in our relationship for the first time in thirty-nine years. Many of us get to this point with our aging parents, but I had a difficult time navigating the role reversal, as she had never admitted to having any needs before. Mom is not yet comfortable with her needs being the focus of our relationship, either, because old habits do not disappear so simply. Adjustment to our new roles are slow, but we are learning to negotiate our futures with care and respect—we will let the rest fall into place as it always has.

17

Motherhood and Activism in the Dis/Enabling Context of War

The Case of Cindy Sheehan

ABBY M. DUBISAR

Us peace activist and mother Cindy Sheehan built her authority as a peace activist by yoking her antiwar mission to her role as a mother of a dead soldier son. In a statement addressed to Donald Rumsfeld, secretary of defense during the war on Iraq, Sheehan (2005, 45) wrote: "I wish I could convey to you in person the pain and devastation your reckless policies have brought to my life. The grief is so profound and primal that it can't be described by the written word. You can't see my red, swollen eyes or my grief-etched face. Your policies have created a hole in my heart." As an activist strategy that made her a household name and, as some would say, galvanized the United States peace movement of the early-twenty-first century, Sheehan concretized her emotional pain as a physical disability and then used this metaphor of disability to speak out against the war. What are the benefits and costs of such a rhetorical strategy?

This chapter[1] takes as its starting point the belief that the experiences of disability, here applied to mothering and war, enable as well as constrain rhetorical strategies for US women's peace activism. Disability studies

---

1. I would like to thank the editors for their insightful and compelling comments on this essay, as well as Rebecca Dingo, Denise Landrum, and Kate Ronald for offering perceptive and engaged readings of revisions of this piece.

scholars Jay Dolmage (2005), David T. Mitchell (2002), and Amy Vidali (2010) all analyze the implications of disability and metaphor, examining language that appropriates disabilities and the implications of disability metaphor. For example, writers who use disability metaphors in literary narratives, Mitchell argues, employ such language to provide a "shock feature of characterization" and use it as an "opportunistic metaphoric device" (2002, 15). Dolmage furthers this analysis of metaphors and invites his audience to understand that metaphors are "more than words" and powerfully form our social world. For example, "When bodily experience is written about, metaphors do the work: they explain how we understand and live in the world, and then, in a way, they dictate how we will experience it in the future" (2005, 111). Without metaphors, communicating about bodily experiences would be nearly impossible. Uncovering the entailments of metaphors and the effects of their deployment helps us understand not only the power of language, but also the long-lasting effects made possible by constructions of embodied experiences that rely on normative/nonnormative characterizations. Vidali (2010, 34) gives her audience a framework to apply when analyzing metaphors of disability, one that more fully engages their diversity. She encourages an approach that "refrains from policing metaphor; encourages transgression; . . . and invites creative and historic reinterpretations of metaphor." Taking into account such approaches to better understanding metaphors of disability, this chapter works to understand the relationship between disability metaphors and antiwar activism, specifically in the context of Sheehan's rhetorical choices.

What are the consequences, for Sheehan, of using disability metaphors? In what ways are such metaphors effective for some audiences but not others? This analysis of Sheehan's rhetorical strategies considers possible critiques of her application of disability metaphors, while also engaging the benefits of her alignment with the disability community, connecting the embodied experience of mothering to the embodied and disabling experience of war. Sheehan's stance as a mother (also fraught with metaphors) is both a plea for audiences to believe her and locate "truth" in her experience and a means to build *ethos* or credibility, to balance her personae both as an "average American mom" and as an expert on US foreign policy and militarism.

Further, focusing on Sheehan in the larger context of an extended conversation on mothering and disability engages a contemporary understanding of the tradition of mothers' peace activism and illuminates its relationship to the contemporary collective activism of veterans. Those interested in peace activism and disability may be familiar with the tradition of a disabled veteran using her or his position as a hero and sometimes displaying the disabled body to argue against war. In contrast, the tradition of mothers advocating for peace includes in its history women around the world speaking from their own mothering experience, arguing for peace as the main method of preserving life in all contexts. Studying Sheehan is important to a current understanding of activist strategies open to mothers because she combines disability and mothering roles for activist purposes. In addressing her US audience she claims both roles: like a veteran, war has disabled her by killing her beloved son, and, like other mother activists, she uses her role as mother to claim authority and agency to seek change.

MOTHERS FOR PEACE: COLLECTIVE IDENTIFICATION AND STRATEGIC ESSENTIALISM

Even though Sheehan does not cite the influence of other women or mother activists in her work for peace, many have come before her. In fact, women's peace activism, defined as women identifying their gender as the motivator for their activist stance and as a site of authority from which to speak against war, began in the context of classical rhetoric. In 42 BCE, Hortensia argued against civil war. According to Cheryl Glenn (1997, 68–70), Hortensia is the only classical woman rhetor whose actual words are recorded by history. With her speech Hortensia represented many Roman women when she decried a ruling that Roman women who owned property be forced to pay extra taxes to support a civil war. In Hortensia's terms, such war deprives women of their sons, fathers, husbands, and brothers, and therefore has negative outcomes uniquely affecting women, who were already politically marginalized. The exigency of war that motivated Hortensia to force her way into the Forum and speak marks the recorded beginning of women's peace activism, understood in gendered terms.

From the time of Hortensia, women have set themselves apart and relied on their own collective experience to build rhetorical arguments for a vast collection of activist causes, including arguing for peace. The history of women's gendered peace activism in the United States is long and rich, and even a mere glossing of it would far exceed the confines of this essay. Sharing a few brief examples gives an understanding of how connecting motherhood specifically to peace activism has been a reliable and ongoing strategy for women, in the United States and beyond. In 1870 Julia Ward Howe publicized mothers' abilities to make political change when she penned the Mother's Day Proclamation as a pacifist reaction to the Civil War. She issued a call for action and hoped to speak for all US mothers when she wrote, "Our sons shall not be taken from us to unlearn / All that we have been able to teach them of charity, mercy and patience. / We, the women of one country, will be too tender of those of another country / To allow our sons to be trained to injure theirs" (qtd. in Benjamin and Evans 2005, 82). Not only did Howe's words bear importance in her time and help to establish the official observance of Mother's Day; her proclamation has been used more recently by contemporary peace organizations like CODEPINK, who host annual Mother's Day rallies and incorporate Howe's words into their own gendered peace work.

Generations later the Women Strike for Peace (WSP) movement during the 1960s in North America comprised women who yoked their activism to their roles as mothers and to the goal of preserving the world for future generations. As Amy Swerdlow (1993, 187) writes, the Toronto Pledge of the WSP declared, "Women may be able to do what no government can do, pave the way to peace through the love and protection of their children." However, during this same period, younger women against the Vietnam War were beginning to interpret their antiwar stances, not in mothering, but in feminist terms. Harriet Alonso (1993, 193) notes that by 1965 female student activists were frustrated with the way women and women's issues were being treated in organizations like the Student Nonviolent Coordinating Committee and Students for a Democratic Society, and they began connecting the second wave of feminism to peace activism.

This movement led by younger women shook up the motherhood argument and problematized how US women's peace organizations recruited younger members, represented themselves as women *or* mothers or both, and defined how their activism was gendered. One poignant example relates to the WSP. In 1968 the Jeanette Rankin Brigade (JRB) protest occurred, which Alice Echols (1992, 175) names the first all-women's antiwar action. The JRB was made up of WSP members, and its organizers were "older, liberal women with experience in peace organizations and church groups" (175). They approached the younger women of the Women's Liberation Movement (WLM) about participating in the protest, an interaction that proved explosive. Echols writes, "Women's liberationists rejected as sexist all culturally received notions about women, and they found the Brigade's equation of femaleness with maternal selflessness especially repugnant" (176). New York members of the WLM went so far as to organize a separate demonstration. They conducted a funeral processional and burial of "Traditional Womanhood" in Arlington Cemetery. During the procession they chanted, urging women to stop "acquiescing to an order that indulges peaceful plea / And writes them off as female logic / Saying peace is womanly" (176–77). This example shows a feminist critique of the mother-activist argument, which seemed—to a new generation of activist women—antiquated and offensive and an enemy of feminist progress.

Despite turmoil within and between women's organizations on the sexism in, and the danger of, essentializing women by using the figure of mothers for the mission of peace, some activists continued to utilize, on their own terms, the motherhood argument. In 1981 the Canadian organization Women's Action for Nuclear Disarmament (WAND) began to attract US organizers. The group maintained the association of its mission to motherhood in spite of the establishment of many other feminist women's peace organizations. These new organizations defined themselves by working for peace and women's rights, but WAND's mission stayed focused solely on the nuclear arms race, and its original founding statement affirmed the connection between motherhood and peace by stating, "The first priority of women . . . is the survival of our offspring . . . endangered by the present militaristic policies of those in power" (Alonso 1993, 240). WAND members thus maintained a collective identification as mother activists.

MOTHERS WITHOUT BORDERS: UNDERSTANDING MOTHER
ACTIVISM FOR PEACE IN DIVERSE CONTEMPORARY CONTEXTS

In the twenty-first century some women activists like Sheehan continue to
define their peace advocacy in terms of an ethic of mothering. US military
mom Susan Galleymore collected more than thirty mothers' stories in her
2009 book *Long Time Passing: Mothers Speak about War and Terror.* She established the organization MotherSpeak in 2004 and started the project of
collecting mothers' stories after having visited her enlisted son in Iraq in
order to try and convince him to stop fighting. MotherSpeak "encourages
the voices of the apparently voiceless, especially mothers who can teach
us about war and terror and how it affects their communities." The stories from mothers in Iraq, Israel, the Occupied West Bank, Lebanon, Syria,
Afghanistan, and the United States emblematize MotherSpeak's mission
of peace.

Even though US women like Sheehan and Galleymore may collapse
diverse experiences of mothering into a universalizing stance that runs
the risk of colonizing the very different experiences of women and mothers around the globe, claiming an activist voice on the basis of being a
woman and mother historically has served as a galvanizing strategy for
women in contexts beyond the United States. It is worth noting, however,
that the stance of motherhood can and has also been deployed for the purposes of justifying war. In fact, many have argued that the tropes of traditional motherhood promote war more than they promote peace, or that
valorizing mothers as peacemakers limits women's potential for power
and agency.

SHEEHAN'S CONSTRUCTION OF PEACE MOM:
EMBODIED SUFFERING FOR ACTION

Sheehan's activist stance fits into a long, complex, and ongoing history of
women peace activists who have built their activist authority around their
roles as mothers. Because she layers more meaning on her activist stance
by highlighting her position as a military mother of a dead soldier son, her
position can be further historicized. Analyzing Sheehan in light of *mater*

dolorosa (the Mother of Sorrows, or suffering mother) highlights an additional lineage of activist mothers. Some women's groups, most notably Mothers of the Disappeared, have used this icon to connect to women's suffering, both through public mourning and in the context of war.

Sara Ruddick (1998, 215) explains that the *mater dolorosa* is "the most deeply rooted [female identity] within war stories. . . . [She] not only mourns war's suffering, she also holds lives together despite pain, bitterness and deprivation." Audiences who experience Sheehan's embodied sorrow and public grief may be familiar with this role, as it appears in popular culture and religious iconography, among other contexts. In several ways, Sheehan recontextualizes *mater dolorosa* because what she does with her sorrow and grief is quite different from its more traditional nurturing emphasis. Sheehan utilizes her suffering position for action. The central tension of Sheehan's activist work, a tension that enables her antiwar argument, is her combination of the rhetorical tradition of mother activism and disabling grief, situated in the iconic *mater dolorosa*. Refiguring this icon, she comes to embody the atrocity of war and to (re)write herself as a veteran. Instead of nursing or rebuilding, Sheehan takes a different path of action for her sorrow and pain. From the start she became a fierce and very outgoing activist for change. Instead of defining the peace mother as nurturing or caretaking, she rebelled from those traditionally female attendant roles to question the war head-on, to camp out at the president's Texas ranch, disrupting his vacation to make the point that grieving mothers cannot take a vacation from their anguish. She demanded that her grief—situated in her embodied presence—be addressed.

This extremely active and forthright stance made all the difference for Sheehan. In order to explain her motivation for activism and to help her audience understand her experience, Sheehan described how the war affected her life and how she herself was a victim of its atrocity. Her physical descriptions of her suffering grounded her activism in tropes of disability. Analyzing her rhetorical stance necessitates theorizing pain's relation to change and disability's relation to an implied healthy body politic.

Ultimately though, her strategies for peace activism risk reinforcing ableism. By blaming war for her pain-filled grief and by communicating this embodied pain as the most destructive and horrific experience imaginable, Sheehan builds an argument that writes pain and disability as perverse, to be avoided under all circumstances. Because Sheehan is arguing for peace and against war, and doing so with embodied discourses of pain, eradicating war means eradicating pain and disability. Despite the fact that Sheehan is creating a counterdiscourse to hegemonic narratives that war deaths are heroic and meaningful, speaking out against a US political culture she understands as murderous and imperialistic, and having the best intentions for creating peace and justice, her rhetorical strategies are at times troubling. She risks sentimentalizing women and mothers; upholding an ideal of a body free of suffering, pain, or "disfigurement"; and potentially obscuring the political and social importance of providing support for people living with disability, most specifically war veterans. Analyzing Sheehan's metaphors of disability leads us to a richer portrait of Sheehan that considers not only the ways in which she critiques disability, but also refuses to let the powerful and mainstream discourse creators (such as then president George W. Bush, then secretary of defense Donald Rumsfeld, and others) control the meaning of her experience. That combination makes Sheehan's rhetorical choices both potentially negative and positive. Such dual implications may affect the disability community, activist mothers, and audiences more broadly conceived. Dolmage (2005, 112) writes, "Largely, those who define disability are not those who experience it . . . those who develop the definitions are not those who would identify themselves as experiencing disability—they therefore may have a vested interest in marking out the other as 'not me.'" Sheehan makes blurry Dolmage's clear distinctions because she both follows the pattern of wresting definitions by claiming that those who call for war, define war, and mark war's disabilities as heroic do not experience it, yet she also constructs war-based disabilities in order to call for their cessation. What audiences must decide is whether Sheehan's position is one of power or not. The history of women's mother-based peace activism shows a long lineage of women pleading for a position at the podium, and Sheehan must also actively pursue an engaged audience, finding all available means of persuasion. Dolmage further reminds us that "the normate assumptions inherent to dominant discourse will not easily be dislodged . . . discourse that comes from a privileged position in our cultural hierarchy (like biomedicine) is granted a sort of naturalization and truth, regardless of its veracity" (112). Whether audiences interpret Sheehan as a privileged, able-bodied, white woman who knows nothing about war or disability, or an authoritative mother who experienced firsthand war's disabling pain depends on their receptiveness to her metaphors and such metaphors' ability to persuade.

DEPLOYING THE PEACE MOM: WRITING AND SPEAKING PAIN AND GRIEF

Since 2004, when she started her advocacy, Sheehan has defined her activism in very physical terms, describing the effects of the war on her life in terms of bodily injury and pain. In order to understand Sheehan's rhetorical strategies, I am relying on three books that collect Sheehan's writing and speeches from a wide variety of contexts including blog entries, letters, and interviews, covering her most prolific years of peace activism. In her memoir *Peace Mom: A Mother's Journey Through Heartache to Activism* (2006b), and her collections *Not One More Mother's Child* (2005) and *Dear President Bush* (2006a), Sheehan heavily relies on constructing her own narrative of disability through the experience of child death and her refusal to recuperate from the wounds war has inflicted upon her.

The catalyst for Sheehan's activism came on 4 April 2004, when her son Casey was killed in combat in Baghdad. Shortly after he died, his sister wrote a poem about the family's grief. Hearing this poem is the moment Sheehan cites as her epiphany, jolting her from complacency and energizing her activism in the midst of her "pain-soaked existence." She writes, "I was transformed from a private mother into a public peace mom. I was transformed from a shy and horrible public speaker into a brave and powerful orator. I was transformed from a nonwriter into an able author on fire for the truth" (2006b, 59–60). This conversion sparked her career as an activist, one that she has continually defined as marked by disabling pain and sorrow, conditions that are paradoxically also enabling, since she has utilized that position for action—suffering has enabled her to speak and write loudly and clearly for peace.

On 9 January 2005, Sheehan wrote Donald Rumsfeld a letter, which is reprinted in *Not One More* (2005, 43–46). Sheehan was responding to Rumsfeld's statement that he "felt the loss" experienced by family members of dead US soldiers and that he shared their grief "at his core" (43 and 45). Sheehan refuses to let Rumsfeld make use of her grief for his own purposes, writing,

> My nights are full of grief and my days are full of pain. . . . I wish I could convey to you in person the pain and devastation your reckless policies have brought to my life. The grief is so profound and primal that it can't easily be described by the written word. You can't see my red, swollen eyes or my grief-etched face. . . . You have created a hole in my heart and in our family that can never be filled. Never. (2005, 45–46)

Not only does Sheehan not permit Rumsfeld to impose his own meaning on the deaths of US soldiers, but she also emphasizes and reclaims her own ongoing grief. The foundation of her rhetorical strategy is to use a mother's inconsolable grief as the motive for peace activism, translating her son's death into change. By publishing this letter and addressing the misuse of grief, she keeps a mother's grief central and claims its proper use as her motivating force.

Noteworthy also is the cover image of the 2005 volume of Sheehan's writings. It shows Sheehan holding an Iraqi Veterans Against the War (IVAW) sign and standing next to several young men. Several pages of photos are featured in *Not One More*. One image centers around a young man in a wheelchair, Tomas Young, who is situated behind a microphone and next to Sheehan, surrounded by IVAW soldiers (91). The photo's caption notes that Young was wounded in Iraq on the same day that Sheehan's son was killed. By including such information, Sheehan aligns herself as closely as possible with the experience of disabled veterans like Young. The documentary *Body of War* (2007) also featured Young, and in an interview featured on the film's website Young articulates his own activist position following his military service and the film's ability to communicate his "reality" by stating, "Everybody enlists in the military with the full knowledge that they might die in combat. But nobody joins the military imagining they will end up paralyzed, in a wheel chair. I hope this film makes people think long and hard before they agree to sign that enlistment contract. *Body of War* will provide more accurate information about the reality of war for them to consider" (Young 2007). Here Young's message resonates with Sheehan's. To the question, "As the war continues, more young Americans will come home severely wounded. How will both this film and your political activism help these returning veterans?" Young responds, "Perhaps when they see *Body of War*, injured veterans will realize that they have a valid voice in the anti-war discussion. Silence is not patriotic, at least not in my book. I hope the film will inspire more of them to speak out." Here Young aligns himself with Sheehan and the peace movement by using the rhetorical strategy of the threat of disability.

Through such imagery as the photograph with Young, Sheehan likewise aligns herself with the disabled soldiers of the war, framing herself and her peace work as being wholly connected to their activism and bodies. She needs them and their support because they offer credibility to her peace mission, showing that she is connected to those who have experienced war firsthand. The iconic nature of the disabled veteran's body is a powerful cultural symbol, one that audiences recognize as representative of the reality of war's outcomes and an ongoing, visible memory of war's battles. For example, US movies critiquing the Vietnam War, such as *Born on the Fourth of July* (1989) and *Coming Home* (1978), feature the disabled veteran speaking with increased authority, embodying authentic knowledge about the war experience and building veteran positions, as icons who translate "foreign" combat experiences to a domestic civilian audience.[2] In sum, Sheehan gains rhetorical power by identifying herself with physically disabled veterans, but there is danger in this association as well, as she too simply claims to understand veterans' experiences, both their past embodied knowledge of war and the present physical and mental consequences of their service. In this identification, she also appears to endorse

---

2. Those interested in the history of disabled veterans and their representations should consult David Gerber's edited collection (2000).

an unstated warrant that living with disability is a horrendous outcome of war. That said, as far as I am aware, no critique of Sheehan from disability activists or veteran activists has been launched against her based solely on her disability metaphors or her associations with disabled veterans.

Identifying herself with veterans is also relevant for understanding Sheehan's 2006 volume of writings, *Dear President Bush*. Hart Viges, an Iraq war veteran, wrote the foreword to the book, offering testimony to the significance of Sheehan's advocacy. Viges describes his war experience: it left him contemplating suicide after his deployment ended, and he eventually became active in Veterans for Peace. He went to Crawford, met Sheehan, and began to speak out against the war. He compares Sheehan to Rosa Parks, describing her as a "spark" for the peace movement (2006a, xxx). He is moved by her ability to use grief and sorrow rhetorically to communicate her message, stating that she "is bringing her pain out to bear, letting everyone know that there are thousands of other mothers going through what she is going through . . . showing the country how war destroys the family" (xxx). He persuades readers to believe that she has been successful to a degree, able to take the pain she is experiencing and use it to effect change. Reciprocity can be noted here as well, as in 2006 Sheehan wrote the foreword to Veteran for Peace activist Mike Ferner's book *Inside the Red Zone: A Veteran for Peace Reports from Iraq*, in which Sheehan credits soldiers as being the real heroes (2006, x).

Sheehan's memoir, *Peace Mom* (2006b), perhaps most fully exhibits Sheehan's rhetorical use of grief, sorrow, and physical and emotional pain. As she chronicles her history as a mother, the experience of suffering Casey's death, and the reflections she has to offer on her activist life thus far, the *mater dolorosa* persona comes to life through her descriptions of the grieving experience. Sheehan writes, "After Casey was killed in Iraq, I walked through my days in a state of pain that was and still is both physical and emotional" (69). The effects of her son's death are bearing on her body and mind, in the most literal sense. Later in the book Sheehan writes, "I had horrible back and neck spasms, and I discovered that a broken heart wasn't just an expression: it was a literal pain that hurt worse than any broken toe or finger I had ever suffered. Women always talk about how painful childbirth is. Child death is far more painful; it's like having a vital part of oneself amputated without anesthesia" (87). Because the parental disability of child death is hidden, since its visible physical and mental manifestations are few, the position of pain and suffering must continually be reinscribed to remind audiences of the grief-stricken condition. In offering these descriptions and metaphors Sheehan believes that her audience is invested in a condition of normalcy—that is, shares a desire to eradicate pain and disability and to protect mothers. She is constructing herself as a "normal" mom who does not "deserve" to have her son killed and, in the process, reaffirming the ideology of normalcy more than directly attacking the politics of war making.

The reference to amputation in the previous quotation is especially dramatic and problematic. The visual image Sheehan conjures by describing her son's death as her own un-anesthetized amputation exemplifies the intensity of her pain and, moreover, aligns her experience once again with that of a war veteran, for example, one missing a limb whose body is permanently refigured. Such a comparison is risky, as her imagined identification of being like a veteran, through the dead limb/son equation, appropriates a significant outcome of modern warfare, which she has not experienced. Likewise, ableist cultural understandings of amputees often focus on how veterans have "overcome" the difficulty of living in an amputated body or how prostheses facilitate a return to normalcy. For example, coverage in the *New York Times* of Iraq veterans with amputations portray such individuals as forever-changed persons who express concern over their now-freakish bodies; as heroes able to overcome their circumstances and surpass others' expectations that amputation would leave them depressed, inactive, and immobile; and as bionic, elite athletes competing in the Paralympics with impressive prosthetic limbs and record-breaking abilities. Such depictions work to reassure readers that amputees are rehabilitating and will lead "normal" lives; at the same time they freakify the veterans with photographic portrayals of their changed bodies. These discourses and images contribute to a widespread belief that being disabled is a grotesque horror.

At the same time, however, the outcome of Sheehan's claim of being disabled by Casey's death is much more than merely rhetorical. Soon after his death she lost her job because of panic attacks (2006b, 90). Panic attacks are a form of invisible disability, often discounted by ableist culture. While Sheehan tries to harness all available ways to make her disability argument persuasive—in convincing her audience that her disabilities are both physical and emotional—relying on this range of pained embodied experiences is fraught with its own problematic elements. Her overall argument implies that through the cessation of warfare emotional and physical disability can and should be prevented and eradicated.

IMPLICATIONS FOR PERSONS WITH DISABILITIES AND ACTIVIST MOTHERING

As any rhetorician does, Sheehan accepts risks and drawbacks to the position she has developed as a speaker and activist. While she may be enacting a transgressive practice of disability metaphor that exemplifies Vidali's vision, one that, "actively mines our own stories and artful re-renderings that play on the diversity of ways that we come to see and know" (2010, 34), Sheehan's attempts to collect all available means of persuasion that layer emotional arguments in the positions of disabled, grieving mother, may be potentially problematic for some audiences. Her work has implications for others, including persons with disabilities and activist mothers, who may see Sheehan adopting roles that undermine their own subject positions, whether or not they support her antiwar stance.

Tobin Siebers (2001, 178) warns that "pain is not a friend to humanity. It is not a secret resource for political change. . . . Theories that encourage these interpretations are not only unrealistic about pain; they contribute to an ideology of ability that marginalizes people with disabilities and makes their stories of suffering and victimization both politically impotent and difficult to believe." Siebers goes on to note that "there are only a few images of pain acceptable on the current scene, and none of them is realistic from the standpoint of people who suffer pain daily" (743). Perhaps the pain that Sheehan exhibits in making public her sadness is one of the few culturally acceptable types of pain, a mother's grief. Sorrowful mothers are at times a protected group, given permission to grieve longer and more fiercely than others who suffer the death of a loved one. Siebers, however, might not classify the type of pain Sheehan is suffering with that of individuals who suffer physical pain daily, as she wishes. He notes that physical pain is neglected by current body theorists, who regularly align their understanding of pain with psychic or emotional pain, often caused by societal influences (744). But Sheehan has no interest in body theory or its critiques. She might be crossing an important line between emotional disabilities caused by intense sadness and embodied pain, such as when she references amputation to discuss the palpable absence she feels from the death of her son. However, to her, her pain is as real as the most intense physical pain, and thus she does not imagine distinguishing between these types of disabling experiences.

Her rhetorical moves and metaphorical constructions yield a range of effects on her audiences, some of whom criticize her as being too melo-dramatic or even exploitive. In May 2007, Sheehan announced her retire-ment from the peace movement by writing a blog entry entitled "Good Riddance Attention Whore," sharing negative critiques launched her way over her three years of activism, accusations that she advocated on behalf of her own self-interests and desire for the media spotlight. In the end, many audiences failed to find Sheehan persuasive, and she left the movement convinced that her son died for nothing. Whether audiences were less convinced by her public form of embodied grieving, unwilling to see a mom as an authority on matters of war and peace, or resistant to any antiwar message, her counterdiscourse was not successful, in her own terms.

By using suffering and pain as rhetorical forces, she may have incurred additional risks of alienation from her audience. Ruddick notes, "displays of suffering are notoriously unpredictable. . . . People who wit-ness suffering may respond with sympathy and help, but they also may turn away out of indifference, fear, disgust, or worse, be strangely excited by the spectacle" (1998, 216). Elaine Scarry (1985, 5) further theorizes how problematic and unstable communicating pain can be, specifically because of its ability to evade language. Physical pain has no referential content, so it is not of or for anything. Pain takes no object and thus resists objectification in language. Sheehan's positioning of her embodied grief may not be the best example for mother activists to follow because of its instability and subjectivity. Both Scarry's theorization of pain as slippery, never sufficiently communicable, and Ruddick's observations about outsiders' reactions to suffering bring to light the risks Sheehan takes when building her arguments in the context of embodied mother-pain. Furthermore, Sheehan and other activists, relying on turning pain into action, may endure audience reactions similar to the very real lived experience of persons with disabilities, who are ignored and misunderstood on a daily basis, not only because truly comprehending another persons' embodied experience, whether pained or not, is nearly impossible, but also because people without disabilities often interpret disability as related to pain. People associate pain with mortality and death and turn away from pain, just as cultural attitudes of normativity and ableism motivate people to distance themselves from the disabled.

Despite these risks, many are invested in translating pain into power and action. Feminists like Audre Lorde, writing about her experience of breast cancer, encourage women to find power in the shared experience of pain that is part of embodiment. We are all only temporarily "abled," and Lorde implores us to make use of experiences of illness, pain, and disability by attempting to "integrate this crisis into useful strengths for change" (1995, 421). Sheehan's work answers Lorde's call: Sheehan speaks from her own experience, makes political meaning of her own personal situation, and moves her suffering from a private and hidden experience to a shared argument that war creates grief-stricken mothers, investing herself in communicating that experience to bring about action and change.

Sheehan's particular activist strategies have further implications for mother activists. Related to Sheehan's appropriation of disability, her position as *mater dolorosa* runs the risk of sentimentalizing her experience and the experience of other mothers. Using the role of mother to ground an activist stance has been critiqued by second- and third-wave feminists and others as reaffirming traditional women's roles of caretaker and nurturer, as essentializing women and limiting their individuality by portraying them as relational rather than autonomous.

Sheehan's combination of the dis/enabling power of grief with the tradition of mother activism does lead to other risky implications, such as begging the question of whether mothers must have to suffer the death of a child or some other dramatic event in order to be activists. Also, when

Sheehan positions herself as an "über mother," and tries to engage all US women through their potential for motherhood, she interprets the experience of mothering in a limiting way, yoking it to biological connections and sentimentalizing the role of mother as the only true and pure voice for peace. Similarly, Sheehan hopes her activism will have positive consequences for potential victims of war around the globe, yet she never situates her work in the context of contemporary mother activists for peace around the world. Instead she assumes the universal applicability of her own understanding of what is necessary to end war.

On the other hand, Sheehan has shown that the role of mother is one that still attracts attention and holds authority. In 2005 *Time* magazine ran a feature on Sheehan during her "occupation" of Crawford, Texas. One particular bit of analysis speaks to the power of Sheehan's being a mother and emphasizes that role. Because she is a mother, the US administration does not have protocol for dealing with her. The *Time* reporter mentions a TV ad running in Crawford that featured Sheehan's plea to Bush. Using ads on TV, however, is not something a mother does but is a rhetorical move of a politician. Analyzing the potential significance of occupying such rhetorical spaces, the article stated, "Once Sheehan starts acting like a politician . . . she will become just another voice in the debate—easy, in other words, to neutralize. But until then, Bush's team cannot fire back hard, as it usually does when it is criticized. Sheehan must be handled, as an adviser to the President put it, 'very carefully'" (Ripley 2005, 25). This understanding of Sheehan's persona is particularly important when measuring the implications of her work to other activist mothers, showing how the rhetorical positioning Sheehan developed enabled her to occupy multiple spaces of authority and move between rhetorical situations—gaining a political audience, garnering support from veterans and others against the war, critiquing the president and other members of the administration from the "innocuous" position of mother, and claiming as her most powerful voice the experience of a mother whose son was killed in war.

The idea of diversity must remain at the center of our future discussions of the intersections of feminism, activism, war, and disability. Vidali's discussion of metaphor seems the most productive and inclusive because of her emphasis on diversity. She writes, "A disability approach to metaphor attends to how diverse bodies impact metaphor acquisition and use, which shifts [concern about] disability away from something only 'used' or 'represented' by metaphor. [The approach] must engage the full range of disability; resist the desire to simply 'police' or remove disability metaphors; actively transgress disability metaphors by employing a diverse vocabulary; and artistically create and historically reinterpret metaphors of disability" (2010, 42). Sheehan's "body" of work shows the complexity of using disability and mothering metaphors to both activate a political persona and push the limits of what diverse audiences find persuasive.

Sheehan's activist career was in some ways short-lived but in other ways very prolific. It is impossible and perhaps too soon to determine definitively what lasting effect her work will have on our understanding of the dis/enabling power of pain and disability or the rhetorical power that mother activists will continue to have in the twenty-first century. What we do know is that she was able to gain notoriety and have her voice heard. For now she remains one of the United States's loudest, clearest, and most uncompromising voices against war, a voice articulated out of a place of dis/enabling grief and mothering.

PART FIVE

Multiple Identities, Overlapping Borders

The essays of part 5 highlight the problematic concept of identity. In both disability studies and feminist theory, identity is a contested concept. While a singular group identity can be claimed for political purposes—for example, under the banner of "women's rights" or "disability rights"—a group named *woman* or *the disabled* is obviously heterogeneous, not unified. There can easily be many important differences among the members of such a group, and the familiar terms of "race," "class," "nation," or "gender" are only starting points for naming some of these categories of difference. Current theories of identity formation, whether primarily sociocultural, phenomenological, or postmodern, recognize that identities are multiple, with both overlaps and gaps. The many identities that individuals claim or are named by thus produce contradictions and tensions. These chapters explore the problematics of identity always already present at the intersections of disability and mothering. By ending the book with this section, we hope to expand the many threads connecting mothering and disability and also remind readers of the dangers of considering only one relation among many.

Julie Maybee's "The Political Is Personal: Mothering at the Intersection of Acquired Disability, Gender, and Race," begins this work of expansion. As a feminist, and a partner in an interracial marriage, Maybee recounts events in her life that made her aware of the sociocultural constructs of gender and race. When her daughter experiences a disability, Maybee is quickly able to see the social construction of disability as well. As a feminist intent on raising an independent-minded daughter, Maybee describes how she must negotiate these various cultural attitudes about disability, race, and gender, revealing the ways that social meanings in categories of identity affect the personal experiences of mothering a disabled child—that is, how the social and political become personal.

In "'You Gotta Make Aztlán Any Way You Can:' Disability in Cherríe Moraga's *Heroes and Saints*," Julie Minich rereads Moraga's play through a disability studies lens. She argues that the play not only critiques heteronormativity, but also revisions nationalism through the disabled body. Moraga's play shows how "a deep commitment to a revolutionary, queer Chicana/o cultural nationalism (a nationalism that Moraga later terms 'queer Aztlán') and a profound unease with the ideology of body normativity . . . haunts the concept of the nation." Although the play does not fully "realize" a new basis for nationalism, Minich concludes, "the play's ending elucidates both the ethical importance and the ethical problems of predicating nationalist claims on a disabled body politic."

In "Intersecting the Postcolonial Mother and Disability: A Narrative of an Antiguan Mother and Her Son," Denise Cordella Hughes-Tafen examines the history of and attitudes toward disability on the Caribbean island of Antigua as she recounts the experiences of her own mother's mothering of her autistic brother. Hughes-Tafen notes both how mothering a child with autism affects a woman's position in this society, and how a woman's position in turn impacts her mothering choices. Her mother comes to the United States to access education for her son, and Hughes-Tafen traces the difficulties of noncitizen residents in getting services. In her account, she emphasizes the intersections of race, gender, class, and nation as she describes her mother's efforts to advocate for her son in both a developing country and in the United States.

Shawn Cassiman's chapter, "Mothering, Disability, and Poverty: Straddling Borders, Shifting Boundaries, and Everyday Resistance," uses data from in-depth interviews with disabled single mothers living in poverty to reveal their resistance to dominant social constructions of themselves as "bad" mothers. Their everyday resistance stories emphasize the limited support for mothers in the United States following welfare reform, the impact and stigma associated with disability, and the selfless dedication demanded of all women who choose to mother in such an environment.

18

The Political Is Personal

Mothering at the Intersection of Acquired Disability, Gender, and Race

JULIE E. MAYBEE

The social model of disability urges us to define disability as a category of identity that is socially constructed. In the classic version that was developed by the Union of the Physically Impaired Against Segregation (UPIAS and Disability Alliance 1976), an organization founded in the mid-1970s, people are not disabled by their bodies or impairments, but by the societies in which they live. Impairments do not disable people; society's prejudice, discrimination, and oppression disable people with impairments. This social model was intended to replace the medical model of disability, which defined disability in terms of the physical and/or mental impairments of an individual. The social model suggests that *the political is personal*. Social and political institutions and attitudes disable individuals and thereby construct the personal experiences of impaired individuals *as disabled.*[1]

Research on the mothers of disabled children has been dominated by the medical model of disability and a focus on the personal and psychological aspects of being the mother of a disabled child (Ryan and Runswick-Cole 2008). As Sara Eleanor Green (2007, 151) writes, it has focused on the supposedly "individual, emotional burdens of having a child with a

---

1. An excellent summary and history of the social model can be found in Thomas 2004.

disability rather than on the burdens imposed by negative public attitudes toward disability and inadequate support." The literature on mothers of disabled children has emphasized issues such as denial, acceptance, grief, stress, depression, or what Green calls the "Subjective Burden," while de-emphasizing if not completely ignoring the "Objective," sociostructural constraints and benefits of being the parent of a disabled child (151).

With the goal of contributing to the "corrective literature" (Ryan and Runswick-Cole 2008, 202), I draw on the social model to examine how personal experiences of mothering and disability can be constructed by social categories and expectations. Although I offer the story of only one mother, like other qualitative data, mine is a narrative that can point toward "broader themes in the social, cultural and political" understanding of parenting and disability (C. Rogers 2007, 137). The rehabilitation process we experienced as a family after our daughter Leyna's aneurysm largely reflected the dominance of the medical model. In contrast to this medical approach, I analyze how the social meanings in categories of identity affect the personal experiences of mothering a disabled child—how the social and political become personal. As Monica Dowling and Linda Dolan (2001, 22) point out, seeing the experiences of families and mothers of children with disabilities as socially constructed removes the sense of inevitability that is often attached to those experiences. Socially constructed experiences can be *changed:* society can be reconstructed in a way that produces different experiences.

My experiences may be particularly helpful for mapping an inter-sectional understanding of multiple, devalued identities. In addition to facing the new category of disability identity after Leyna's brain injury, my experiences were complicated by two other social categories. First, my mothering relationship with Leyna and experience of Leyna's disability are complicated by gender. Having defined myself as a feminist commit-ted to the empowerment and independence of women, I raised my daugh-ter to be an independent-minded young woman. This fact has complicated the ways in which I have experienced and negotiated Leyna's continuing dependence after brain injury. Second, my mothering of Leyna is compli-cated by race. I am a white, Canadian woman who is married to an Afri-can American and has two black/interracial children. Although disability and race are similar insofar as they engender negative responses in the larger society, being prepared to be the mother of a black/interracial daughter did not mean that I was prepared to be the mother of a disabled black/ interracial daughter. My story is of a mother who, having learned to welcome two socially spurned categories of identity into my life (gender and race), has had much to learn about welcoming a third. Ryan and Runswick-Cole urge researchers to "incorporate factors such as gender, ethnicity, age, and social class" into experiences of "disablism"—the socially oppressive effects of the negative treatment and attitudes toward disabled people (2008, 207). To that end, I explore how my experience of mothering Leyna has been shaped not only by socially constructed aspects of disability, but also by socially imposed aspects of gender and race.

Leyna's aneurysm left her comatose and completely dependent for nearly two months. She woke up very slowly after that and continues to make small improvements six years after her injury. Her pattern of recovery did not follow the usual trajectory, we were told, according to which the early weeks or months after brain injury are characterized by a rapid improvement that generally slows down and may plateau later on. I lived at the hospital with Leyna (except on weekends) for nearly six months— although toward the end of her time as an in-patient, I began to go home to sleep at night. I wheeled her to her therapy sessions, waited outside or stayed with her during her sessions (depending on the situation), and assisted therapists and nurses whenever necessary. The nurses came to regard me as a fixture at the institutions, which granted me certain privileges—free access to the linen room, for instance. Later, I accompanied Leyna to her cognitive rehabilitation program at least once a week; we did not have enough nursing services to cover all of the hours, yet her need for help with many of her activities of daily living meant that she had to have an attendant or nurse at all times. I worked hard to get Leyna all of the therapies that she could get, buying into the medical establishment's emphasis on "fixing" patients in rehabilitation. As disability studies scholars have pointed out, this emphasis is ethically problematic because it feeds a culture that devalues the lives of disabled people (by implying that they need to be fixed) and, like assimilation models of racial and ethnic relations, reinforces the larger society's problematic demands for everyone to be the same or "normal" (G. Williams 2001, 136; Asch 2001, 300–302). However, since the effects of brain injury can be mitigated by getting people up, moving, and engaged in activity as soon as possible, to the degree that rehabilitation is aimed at improving people's future opportunities, I believe its overall purpose can be justified. Still, I embraced the rehabilitation process with too much gusto. I was going to fix Leyna as best as I could, come hell or high water, to keep as many doors of opportunity open as I could for her future, in light of her changed situation. At first I saw that as my job as her mother. Although Leyna has achieved more independence with her mobility and activities of daily living than some clinicians thought she would, she is still emotionally, physically, and cognitively more dependent than is considered typical for her age.

As part of Leyna's rehabilitation process at the various institutions, I was asked to meet alone with her psychologists. The stated purpose of these meetings was to discuss Leyna's treatment goals and programs, but they had another purpose as well. During an appeal against our health insurance company, we obtained billing documents from the rehabilitation facilities. These meetings were billed as "family counseling." Apparently, I was not meeting with the psychologists about Leyna; I was meeting with the psychologists about *me*. When I (rather than Leyna) was the topic of conversation during these sessions, I am sure the psychologists' thoughts were full of typical emotional and psychological terminology found in the literature on parents of children with disabilities: denial, grief, loss, mourning, fear of the future, adjustment issues, and anger, for instance. Anger, especially, was my overriding principle. We talked a lot about anger. I was advised that I needed to get past my anger and move on to acceptance. I insisted that I was not willing to give up my anger— that the day I gave up my anger was the day I gave up on Leyna and on fighting for Leyna. Anger was my source of energy and motivation, and without it, I was likely to crash altogether. Tellingly, as I will explain later, I also insisted that to accept things meant belonging to a club of which I did not want to be a member.

This account of my responses to Leyna's impairments reflects the traditional, emotional/psychological understanding of mothers and parents of disabled children that is rightly criticized by Ryan and Runswick-Cole (2008), Green (2007), C. Rogers (2007), and Dowling and Dolan (2001). But my responses were as much social and political as they were personal/emotional/psychological, and I wish to interrogate the assumption that my sense of loss and so on could be fully explained by factors internal to Leyna's impairment and my psychology. I had lost something and had a right to be angry, I would like to suggest, but much of the source of my loss and anger had nothing to do with Leyna's impairments. In his book *Two Nations: Black and White, Separate, Hostile, Unequal,* the political scientist Andrew Hacker (1995) describes a parable that has been put to white college students. Imagine, the parable goes, that at midnight tonight you will become black. You will not only have darker skin but will also have other physical features associated with African ancestry. You will be the same inside, in terms of your memory, personality, and so on, but you will be unrecognizable from the outside. Because this change is the result of an error that is not your fault, you will be compensated, and the compensating agency has a lot of money. Since you are a college student, you are likely to live another fifty years or so. How much money would you request? According to Hacker, most white students thought it would be fair to request about $50 million, or approximately $1 million for every year they could expect to live. The students' responses to the parable show, Hacker suggests, that while they may not know exactly what it is like to be black in America, they do know that their white skin has value—that it is a gift to be white in America. The money they requested "would be used, as best it could, to buy protection from the discriminations and dangers white people know they would face once they were perceived to be black" (36). For similar reasons, I embraced rehabilitation and wanted to fix Leyna to make "the problem" go away, and, in my mind, "the problem" was that Leyna was my ticket—nay, sentence—into a social club of which I did not want to be a member. I knew, in other words—though not yet in a conscious way that I could clearly articulate—what "normal" was worth in a society that values the "normal."

It did not take long to learn something about what being the mother of a disabled child would be like. One of the first comments made by a doctor after Leyna's brain surgery to clip the aneurysm, for instance, was that Leyna showed no signs of trauma—a comment indicating that he had determined that the aneurysm was not a result of abuse. I suppose doctors should protect children from abuse, but throughout Leyna's time at the acute-care hospital and at rehabilitation facilities, my own competence as a mother seemed to be constantly under surveillance (Ryan and Runswick-Cole 2008, 204).

Moreover—and ironically—in spite of the presence of so many supposed caregivers in the hospital setting, staffing shortages and poor morale among the employees taught me very quickly that I was largely on my own when it came to caring for my newly disabled child. When Leyna was still very disoriented she would try to undo the supporting straps while standing on the tilt table, a device that allows a person to be strapped on to a table while lying down and then pivoted into a standing position, which forces the brain to make appropriate physiological adjustments—to blood pressure, for instance—and helps to increase wakefulness or awareness. If I was not at the hospital for Leyna's tilt-table sessions, Leyna did not attend those sessions. No staff was willing and/or able to provide the close supervision that was required to ensure that Leyna did not remove the straps and fall off the tilt table. The message that I was on my own with my disabled child was reinforced by the tenuousness of health insurance coverage and financial uncertainties. One day, the social worker came to speak with me. He reminded me that my insurance coverage would be coming to an end soon and asked me, "What are you going to do?" My first thought was that the real question was not what *I* was going to do, but what *they* were going to do when the coverage ran out. I had visions of being cast out by the hospital—of being sent home with a few medical supplies and no help or services.

Dowling and Dolan (2001) argue that having to explain yourself to professionals (sometimes repeatedly) and having difficulty obtaining and paying for needed services are among the ways in which society—rather than a child's impairment—constructs the burden of caring for a disabled child and disables the whole family. These socially constructed burdens also constructed my emotional/psychological/personal responses. I was under surveillance and had lost my independence as a mother in a society that values family independence and autonomy (Bould 1993). In my overriding need to fix Leyna, I was playing out contemporary ideologies according to which Western mothers are required to enhance their children's future prospects, and in which successful mothering is measured by the self-sufficiency and productivity of the adult children (McKeever and Miller 2004, 1182). Moreover, whereas my child had been *entitled* to services from the society before her aneurysm (a free education, for instance), I was now going to have to *fight* for services for her. My sense of loss thus had a basis in reality, and I had a right to be angry. But this loss and anger had their source not in Leyna's impairment, but in the way in which society was responding to her impairment. As Ryan and Runswick-Cole point out, "Parents, too, experience the psycho-emotional aspects of disablism as they begin to 'know their place,' moderate their behavior and learn to internalize the oppression" (2008, 202).

My response to Leyna's brain injury was also complicated by gender in two ways: in relation to social definitions about what it means to be a woman, and in relation to the expectations that society had of me because I was Leyna's mother. First, I had defined myself in a way that rejected traditional definitions of what a woman is supposed to be like. As a child, I had played with cars rather than dolls, climbed trees, played football with the boys; my brother had even taught me to throw like a boy. As a young woman, I made a point of avoiding stereotyped characteristics associated with being a woman. I refused to wear make-up or worry about the latest fashions or hairstyles. I despised gossip. I emphasized my intellectual abilities and avoided traditional duties associated with women, such as cooking and cleaning. In short, I had come to define myself as a "mind/masculine" rather than a "body/feminine." I also valued economic independence. It is therefore not an accident that I grew up to be a professor of philosophy and a working woman. Although I had done the required care-work as a mother—feed and dress the babies, change diapers—I was happy when the children grew up and I had less of this bodily care work to do. I did not spend less time with the children as they got older than I had spent with them when they were younger; I just spent my time doing different things with them. I enjoyed *teaching* them about things and talking to them about *ideas,* and the more I could do these things as they got older, the more I enjoyed being a mother.

Before the aneurysm, I had been working to pass these values on to Leyna. My husband and I had our children when we were still graduate students and had very little money. We were therefore always grateful for whatever gifts we received for the children. We received a number of storybooks about Disney fairy tale movies, such as *Cinderella, Snow White, Sleeping Beauty,* and *Rapunzel.* As a feminist, I was not happy about reading these stories to my daughter—stories in which young, helpless women fall in love with (sometimes instantly!) and are rescued by men. In light of our financial situation, however—and so as not to appear ungrateful—I read these stories to Leyna whenever she wanted (she picked her bedtime stories), critiquing them as we went along. Over time, Leyna became impatient with my critiques, even though it was sometimes clear that my messages were not always being understood in the way I had hoped. "I know, I know," Leyna said once, "you don't just see a guy and fall in love. You meet someone, you get used to him, and then you get married." For a while, Leyna decided she was going to marry her brother because she was used to him. In any case, by the age of twelve, Leyna was an independent-minded young woman who was not afraid to be smart and not overly interested in fashion and other stereotypically feminine concerns. And then she had an aneurysm.

Leyna's aneurysm has left her emotionally clingy and physically and cognitively dependent in ways that rub against both my definitions of myself as a woman and the kind of life I had envisioned for her as a woman. I have had difficulty dealing with her dependence, in part because it returns me to the bodily care work that I had shunned as a young woman and had been happy to leave behind as a mother of older children, and in part because she embodies the image of a woman that I had consciously rejected. Because of my own, resistant gender identity, I am what Todd and Shearn (1996, 393) call a "captive" parent—one who tends to find her prolonged caring role with her disabled child restricting (Ryan and Runswick-Cole 2008, 206). Because I have not valued care work, Leyna's dependence not only undermines my self-image as a successful mother; it also undermines my desire and ability as a feminist mother to resist the dominant definition of femininity imposed on women by society, both for myself and through her.

Moreover, because our society defines women and mothers as the primary caregivers of children, Leyna's dependence after her aneurysm threatened my own future in a way that it did not threaten my husband's. Our society not only *expects* women to be the primary caregivers; it also *constructs* their roles as the primary caregivers through laws and social institutions, such as the wage gap between men and women (Okin 1989; Cudd 1994). During the early stages of Leyna's recovery, questions were raised about what kind of care Leyna would need and who would do it. Because my husband earns more than I do (the wage gap) and because women are expected to be the primary caregivers, it was always assumed that if Leyna's disability forced either my husband or me to give up our jobs, then *I* would be the one to give up my job. I would not have been alone. Structural changes in the health-care system mean that patients are being discharged "sicker and quicker" (Bould 1993, 147), and women have become a "reserve army of nurses" (Dalley 1996, 24), drafted into care-giving services (Leiter et al. 2004, 398). Participation in the workforce by mothers with disabled children is lower compared to mothers of children without disability, and this difference in participation cannot be explained by a lower *desire* to work on the part of mothers of children with disabilities (Gordon, Rosenman, and Cuskelly 2007). Moreover, neither level of education nor economic status affects the mothers' odds of being drafted as the primary providers of care for children with special needs, which suggests that the role is not a discretionary or chosen one. Women with higher levels of education were more likely to stop working altogether, implying that their life choices may be different from the choices faced by women with less educational attainment (Leiter et al. 2004, 398). Few things made me angrier than the thought that I might have to give up my career to care for Leyna full time.

Notice that my anger in this case was constructed by society not only because women are expected and pressured by laws and institutions into being the primary caregivers, but also because society fails to support parents of children with disabilities properly (Dowling and Dolan 2001). My husband or I would have been *forced* to give up our jobs in the first place only because society does not provide enough help to allow both parents with disabled children to work (Lewis, Kagan, and Heaton

2000). The combination of the ideology of family sufficiency and of the duty of mothers to care for children with disabilities meant that I could have faced a choice between giving up my career, which would have violated my resistant gender identity, or failing to live up to dominant beliefs about being a good mother—neither of which is an attractive option. I was angry about the gendered distribution of caregiving duties (McKeever and Miller 2004, 1184) and had legitimate fears about my future. I was not conscious of the social implications of my anger and fear at the time, however, so I interpreted these feelings as responses to Leyna's impairments, rather than as complex responses to the social constructions of disability and gender.

My experiences with the socially constructed meaning of Leyna's disability were also complicated by the category of race. Because I married into blackness as an adult, I can remember the process of learning something about what it is like to be black in America. Of course, I can never experience being black the way that a black person does. When I am not with my family, I am just another white woman, and, even when I am with my family, my being white changes the way in which we are perceived and treated. My husband is a very tall and dark black man—the sort of black man that white women cross the street to avoid having to walk by at night. He tells stories of hearing people lock their car doors as he walks by on the sidewalk while they are waiting at red lights. I like to joke that when my husband and I are together in predominantly white contexts, I make him look legitimate, and he makes me look cool. Nevertheless, my relationships with my husband and family members have provided me with intimate, experiential lessons about race in America to which few whites have access. I have also had to learn what it is like to be a mother of black children—and have sometimes received specific instruction on this topic from black women friends and family members.

In my experience, the category of race highlighted and enhanced many of the negative implications of the socially constructed nature of disability. There is a great deal of pressure on mothers and parents to produce "perfect" children (C. Rogers 2007). Parents of disabled children can be acutely aware of the devalued bodily capital of their children and may feel tainted by the stigma of their parental relationship with their disabled children (Ryan and Runswick-Cole 2008, 200; McKeever and Miller 2004, 1178). After I began reading disability studies literature, I realized that my responses to Leyna's disability were multiplied by my status as a mother of a black/interracial child. Like disabled children, the children of black parents also have devalued bodily capital, and I think black parents sometimes struggle to compensate for this devalued capital in ways similar to the ways in which the parents of disabled children do. Mothers of disabled children who are dependent on medical professionals often negotiate their social situation by both resisting and appeasing those professionals in relation to whom they are socially subordinate (McKeever and Miller 2004, 1183). They also work to improve their children's social capital and hence to encourage others to regard their disabled children as persons worthy of love and care by grooming and dressing their children and thus managing others' perceptions of them. McKeever and Miller found that the mothers of disabled children "invested enormous cost and effort to ensure their children were dressed well and fashionably regardless of each family's class position, ethnocultural background or extent of disability" (McKeever and Miller 2004, 1187). Mothers of black children may express similar attention to dress and presentation as well as patterns of resistance and appeasement in contexts in which they are socially subordinate (see White 1991). My experience of ways in which being the mother of a disabled child added to the effects of being the mother of black children may illustrate how mothers of minority children who are also disabled may face a compounded need to mitigate discrimination by compensating for their children's devalued bodily capital as *both* black and disabled.

We should be wary, however, of what might be called addition models of oppression, according to which experiences of oppression that involve more than one social category can be understood simply by adding together the effects of the different categories—as if black women's experiences could be understood according to the formula "black + woman," or disabled black women's experiences could be understood according to the formula "black + woman + disabled" (King 1988). Some combinations of social categories of oppression may sometimes produce surprising results at the level of experience. While young black men tend to be stereotyped as violent and dangerous, for example, young black men with certain sorts of visible disabilities might avoid this particular stigma. If that is right, then, the combination "black + male + disabled" would turn out to be a more advantageous social position in that one respect than "black + male" would be. It is important not to oversimplify thinking about the ways in which multiple social categories of oppression may be experienced in everyday life.

As the mother of black children, I have felt pressure to compensate for my children's devalued social capital. Because of my disinterest in dress and fashion, in my case, this pressure has not generally been translated into worries about my children's appearance or presentation. My mother complains that she has very few baby pictures in which my daughter is dressed up. Only when we lived in the black neighborhood in one city did I feel pressure to pay special attention to how Leyna was dressed or how her hair was fixed; there, I learned to braid her hair in traditionally African American ways. My own desire to bolster my children's social capital was expressed in ways that highlighted their intellectual talents. This response is not completely surprising, given that I am an academic woman who had compensated for her own devalued bodily and social capital as a woman by proving and pursuing intellectual capabilities. It may also be explained by the fact that I was not raised in the African American culture, in which rituals of home-based hair care, for instance, are a meaningful part of black women's childhood and adolescent social-ization, through which young women learn "important cultural ideals about womanhood and the presentation of self" (Jacobs-Huey 2006, 18; see also Ashe 1995, 591; Gates 1994; hooks 1989, 382). In my family, fixing hair was a socially meaningless, inconvenient distraction.

I also know many other parents of black children who work hard to build their children's social capital through intellectual endeavors, in an attempt to mitigate racist assumptions that blacks are less intelli-gent than whites (Shipler 1998, 293). Of course, the same assumption of intellectual inferiority also attends social definitions of femininity. As a result, I believe that my own need to use intellectual accomplishments to compensate for Leyna's devalued bodily capital as black and as a woman helped to shape my responses to her cognitive impairments. Chrissie

Rogers (2007, 139) has found that parents of disabled children tend to deny the presence of intellectual impairments because of the culture's emphasis on academic excellence. I placed particular importance on Leyna's— rather than my son's—intellectual abilities and accomplishments, I think, because of Leyna's status as a black *woman* and my need to resist not just racist assumptions about blacks' inferior intellectual abilities, but also traditional definitions of femininity, both for myself and through her. This emphasis on Leyna's intellectual abilities fueled my sense of loss over and deep-seated desire to fix her cognitive impairments.

There is another way in which my status as the mother of black children shaped my response to Leyna's impairments. One of the lessons I learned from mothers of black children is that we have to be ready to fight for our children's success against a system designed to ensure their failure. And, indeed, I had been forced to face down various day-care and school authorities over the years for stereotyping and short-changing my children. Parents of disabled children often complain that they have to fight for everything, too (McKeever and Miller 2004, 1189; Dowling and Dolan 2001, 26–27). It did not take long for me to realize that I would have to fight for services and care for Leyna as a disabled child. Because I had married into blackness, racism was a burden that I had willingly and consciously adopted. But I believe my sense of loss and anger about Leyna's impairments was shaped in part by a desire to avoid having to take on another fight. My growing sense that having a disabled child meant that I had another fight on my hands, combined with my experiences of raising black children, helped to make disability a club to which I definitely did not want to belong.

My responses to Leyna's impairment were shaped not only by the social consequences of disability and gender, then, but also by the social consequences of being in an interracial marriage. Married for many years before Leyna had her aneurysm, my husband and I had a developed awareness of ourselves as representatives of the category *interracial marriages.* Many blacks in predominantly white settings see themselves as having to represent all blacks. They have "a sense of always being on display, and of performing a ritual of proof in each encounter" (Shipler 1998, 294). My husband and I had developed a similar social consciousness as an interracial couple in the predominantly white college towns and academic environments in which we functioned. We sometimes joke that the only thing that kept us together during hard times was that we refused to become another statistic—another failed interracial marriage. We have experienced the stares and snide remarks of people who make clear that they do not support racially mixed marriages, and we set out to prove them wrong. I believe this social pressure to have a successful interracial marriage enhanced my feeling that we had to have perfect and successful children as well. When we started to go out in public with our newly disabled daughter, I thought I could feel the disapproving eyes of people thinking to themselves: "you see what can happen when blacks and whites marry and have children."

There is a sense in which our marriage has a devalued bodily capital in a society that generally disapproves of such unions. We are often regarded suspiciously from both sides of the racial divide, black and white. So long as we could present or embody a successful marriage with beautiful and exotic children we could mitigate the costs of our devalued marriage. Leyna's blue-gray eyes made her especially valuable in an attempt to present/embody a successful interracial marriage—I suppose you could say that we "wore" Leyna as a symbol of the value of our relationship.

Now Leyna's status as disabled has undercut our ability to use her to compensate for our devalued bodily capital as an interracial relationship. Of course, it might be suggested that there is a different sense in which she represents a successful interracial relationship. My husband and I are still married, after all, in spite of what happened to Leyna. But I worry that this way of conceiving of our success would reinforce what Chrissie Rogers has called the "tragic" (2007, 137) discourses and negative narratives about disability in the larger culture that feed stigma and pity because it presupposes that it would be understandable for any marriage to fall apart under such supposedly trying circumstances. In any case, the thought that my husband and I are still together does not seem to satisfy my desire to present a successful interracial relationship, perhaps because the success in this case is not readily visible or apparent, but only shows up upon the telling of the story. I have noticed that some friends who accompany Leyna and me in public seem to have an urgent need to tell her story. They report to perfect strangers that Leyna had an aneurysm at the age of twelve and so on. I wonder if their desire to tell the story is fueled by a need to mitigate their devalued bodily capital through their association with Leyna by making her—and hence their—success visible. In the eyes of the larger society, the story of Leyna's progress and of our supposedly heroic perseverance through tragedy makes us look good.

Mothers also sometimes deny that their children are disabled, not necessarily because they have internal psychological problems but because they do not want to associate their children with other disabled children in a disabilist society (C. Rogers 2007, 139). Disability is a club to which they do not wish to belong. Much of my own denial, sense of loss, fear, and anger about the onset of Leyna's impairments had its roots in the socially constructed meanings of disability, gender, and race. Because my feelings were in large part socially constituted, the advice that I should simply accept Leyna's disability was misplaced. Was I supposed to accept the lack of support I was receiving for my child? Was I supposed to accept the added burden of having to fight for a child who is a woman, black, and now disabled as well, in a society that values men, whites, and able-bodied people? Was I supposed to accept the very real (if unjust) loss of prestige and respect I faced as the mother of a black and disabled young woman? Just as we would not ask women or blacks to accept sexism or racism, I should not have been asked to accept the disablism that constructed my responses to Leyna's impairment.

Until we take seriously the ways in which mothers' responses to disability are constructed by social and political forces, we will not only fail to help mothers cope successfully with feelings of denial, loss, anger, and so on, but we will also add to those mothers' social and psychological burdens by denying the justifiable anger that the mothers have toward an inadequately supportive social system (Ferguson 2001, 380). By asking mothers to accept their situations and get past their anger without interrogating what, exactly, they are being asked to accept, we repeat and reinscribe the oppressive systems of gender, race, and disability that mothers and parents of disabled children face.

19

"You Gotta Make Aztlán Any Way You Can"

Disability in Cherríe Moraga's Heroes and Saints

JULIE AVRIL MINICH

Heroes and Saints (first staged in 1989 and later published in 1994) is the most frequently staged play by Chicana feminist writer Cherríe L. Moraga. Moraga's work has long been recognized for its critique of heteronormative family structures, its reformulation of Chicana/o nationalism, and its exploration of relationships between Chicana mothers and daughters, but there is not as yet an account of the role that disability plays in her treatment of these themes. Disability marks a tension that surfaces in *Heroes and Saints* between a deep commitment to a revolutionary, queer Chicana/o cultural nationalism (a nationalism that Moraga later terms "queer Aztlán") and a profound unease with the ideology of body normativity that haunts the concept of nation. This tension, moreover, has remained a central concern in Moraga's work throughout the two decades since *Heroes and Saints* was first performed. I argue that the representation of disability in *Heroes and Saints* is crucial to two aspects of the play: its attempt to radicalize motherhood (and the family in general) and its engagement with nationalism as a basis for activism. By reimagining Chicana motherhood and privileging antinormative Chicana bodies in her vision of Chicana/o social protest, *Heroes and Saints* marks Moraga's first effort to visualize a cultural nationalism predicated on queer and disability politics. The play depicts the splintered Chicana/o family and the disabled Chicana body as the source of Chicana/o political agency and nationalism. Moreover, although Moraga's vision of a new cultural nationalism is not fully realized in *Heroes and Saints* itself, the play's ending elucidates both the ethical importance and the ethical problems of predicating nationalist claims on a disabled body politic.

REFORMULATING CHICANO CULTURAL NATIONALISM: MORAGA'S "QUEER AZTLÁN"

Moraga's relationship to Chicano cultural nationalism is a vexed one. Since her earliest publications, she has employed many of Chicano nationalism's most privileged tropes and themes—labor activism, land, familia, and pre-Columbian cultural practices—yet her work has been marginalized in the Chicana/o literary canon because of its queer content. Her concern with relations between mothers and daughters would seem to place her within a feminist literary tradition, but her critique of racism in the white women's movement has distanced her from many writers associated with that literary tradition. Finally, although Moraga does not identify as disabled, the disability themes in her work have caused her to appear on more disability studies syllabi than many Chicana/o writers with disabilities. Her work, then, belongs to multiple communities (queer communities, Chicana/o communities, feminist communities, disability communities) and is also situated outside of those communities. The sustained engagement with nation in work from a writer who claims a place in and yet is marginalized in so many communities thus raises important questions about nationalism and community. Is the *nation* the best way to create a liberated or decolonized people? What does it mean to imagine a *people* from a queer or disabled perspective? These questions are particularly crucial to an analysis of disability, motherhood, and activism in Moraga's work because of the key role that Chicano cultural nationalism and the notion of Aztlán[1] have played in Chicana/o civil rights struggles since the late 1960s.

Heroes and Saints recounts the activism of a young woman, born with no body, who leads her central California farmworking community in

---

1. Aztlán is the spiritual place of origin for the Mexica (Aztec) people, a paradigm for contemporary Chicano cultural nationalism.

protest against the agribusiness enterprises that are poisoning its land and drinking water. Cerezita Valle, the play's protagonist, resides in the Central Valley town of McLaughlin (based on the real-life town of McFarland), which has experienced a disproportionate number of cancer diagnoses among its residents, especially its children. Cerezita collaborates with local children to hang the lifeless bodies of those killed by cancer on crucifixes in the fields to draw media attention to the agricultural practices, characterized by environmental racism, that are killing McLaughlin's residents. Cerezita's mother, Dolores, who disapproves of political intervention, functions as her primary ideological opposition. Dolores's name (which means "pains" in Spanish) evokes both the stereotype of the long-suffering Mexican mother and Moraga's critique of the institutionalization of that stereotype. Dolores not only resists her daughter's progressive political action but also subscribes to patriarchal, heteronormative views of gender. Meanwhile, although few characters (except the town's children) know what Cerezita is doing until the play's end, her activist work is supported by her neighbor Doña Amparo, her sister, Yolanda, her brother, Mario, and the leftist priest, Juan.

The character of Cerezita is closely tied throughout to the notion of agency, collective and individual (just as Dolores's is tied to a curtailing of agency). In the author's notes to the published version of the play, Moraga writes:

> Mobility and its limits are critical aspects of [Cerezita's] character. For most of the play, CEREZITA is positioned on a rolling, tablelike platform, which will be referred to as her "raite" (ride). It is automated by a button she pushes with her chin. . . . The raite can be disengaged at any time by flipping the hold on each wheel and pushing the chin piece out of her reach. At such times, CEREZITA has no control and can only be moved by someone manually. (1994, 90)

These limits to Cerezita's mobility underscore a central concern of the play: how to act against a social order structured to limit the agency of oppressed people. Cerezita's limited mobility exists alongside multiple social restrictions placed on the residents of her town, drawing attention to the relationships between different forms of oppression. Although Cerezita's disability is not one that exists in the "real" world, it is noteworthy that her *raite* is often replaced by a wheelchair in productions of the play, making an explicit connection between Cerezita's activism and the disability movement. Furthermore, Mario's movement (like Cerezita's) is curtailed, as he is dependent on white, middle-class lovers with cars to travel between McLaughlin and San Francisco. Meanwhile, the citizens of McLaughlin collectively negotiate their struggle with representatives of power: the news media, the growers, the public schools, the Arrowhead water company. At every level, obstacles to the exercise of personal and collective agency are tied to unequal social relations, which are connected to the power that Dolores attempts to enact over Cerezita. Cerezita's mobility is not so much impaired by her physical condition as by Dolores's ideologies of shame, which motivate her to disengage the *raite* in an attempt to prevent Cerezita's political engagement.

With *Heroes and Saints*, Moraga introduces the idea of what she calls (in her essay "Queer Aztlán") a Chicana/o nation "with no freaks, no 'others' to point one's finger at" (1993, 164). Her use of a word associated with the oppression of people with disabilities in this quote—*freak*—underscores her search for a nationalism that is not predicated on body normativity. In this sense, Moraga's critique of the "othering" processes inherent to nation building, and of the demands for physical uniformity that undergird those processes, coincides with Tobin Siebers's assertion that negative attitudes about disability often discursively buttress other forms of oppression. According to Siebers, efforts to "determine who gains membership, and who does not, in the body politic" (2003, 184) often characterize groups excluded from the body politic (people of color, LGBT individuals) as physically or mentally disabled, thereby contributing to the political disenfranchisement of people with disabilities as well as that of other minority groups. The struggle to utilize the political potential in the idea of nation without enforcing a discourse of corporeal homogeneity surfaces in all of Moraga's writings that deal with the concept of Aztlán. It is this struggle that functions as Moraga's most significant point of departure from earlier, often masculinist, versions of Chicano cultural nationalism.

The concern with nationalism in *Heroes and Saints* continues throughout her subsequent work. Nationalist issues are not absent from her early writing; for instance, the 1983 essay "A Long Line of Vendidas," from her first book *Loving in the War Years* ([1983] 2001), positions itself in dialogue with Chicano nationalism in order to claim Moraga's place in the Chicana/o community. However, Moraga's early publications are more firmly located in a woman-of-color coalition than in a notion of Aztlán. *Heroes and Saints* thus represents a crucial moment in Moraga's trajectory, marking as it does the first time that she links her activist commitment to a specifically nationalist consciousness.

MAKING FAMILIA: REWRITING PATRIARCHAL MOTHERHOOD

Heroes and Saints also represents a turning point in Moraga's treatment of motherhood. Much of her early work is concerned with the ways in which the cultural institution of motherhood in Mexican and Chicana/o contexts functions to foment betrayal and distrust among Chicanas. In "Vendidas," Moraga writes:

> Ask, for instance, any Chicana mother about her children and she is quick to tell you that she loves them all the same, but she doesn't. *The boys are different.* Sometimes I sense that she feels this way because she wants to believe that through her mothering, she can develop the kind of male she would have liked to have married, or even have been. That through her son she can get a small taste of male privilege, since without race or class privilege that's all there is to be had. The daughter can never offer the mother such hope, straddled by the same forces that confine the mother. As a result, the daughter must constantly earn the mother's love, prove her fidelity to her. The son—he gets her love for free. (2001, 93–94, emphasis in original)

The character of Dolores exemplifies Moraga's critique of the model of motherhood described above. Dolores resists not only Cerezita's activism but also Mario's queer sexuality; she phrases her objections to Mario's sexuality in terms of his "wasted" male privilege, reminiscent of Moraga's account in "Vendidas." "Why you wannu make yourself como una mujer?" (1994, 123), she asks him, and adds: "God made you a man and you throw it away" (124). Yet throughout *Heroes and Saints,* and unlike in "Vendidas," Moraga also explores new ways to imagine Chicana motherhood. This exploration occurs through the character of Yolanda, who is spurred to political action following her daughter's death, as well as through the character of Amparo, who does not have biological children but who assists in raising children in the community. Finally, and most important, it occurs through the character of Cerezita, who at the end of the play embodies la Virgen de Guadalupe, spiritual mother of the Mexican and Chicana/o people.

In the author's notes for *Heroes and Saints,* Moraga acknowledges two sources for the text. The first is an image from the United Farm Workers documentary video *The Wrath of Grapes:* a child with no arms or legs born to a mother who worked in pesticide-sprayed fields while pregnant. The second is the early Luis Valdez play *The Shrunken Head of Pancho Villa,* in which the central character, Belarmino, is (like Cerezita) a bodiless head. Valdez's play, written at the beginning of the Chicano Movement, uses the disintegration of a Chicano family—symbolized by the birth of sons with no bodies and by another son who returns home from prison with no head—as a metaphor for the political disempowerment of Chicanas/os. Moraga's use of these two sources clearly establishes the play within a Chicana/o cultural nationalist literary tradition, in which Valdez is a central figure and labor activism a central theme. However, Moraga's play differs profoundly from *Pancho Villa.* Notably, while Dolores functions to embody Moraga's critique of the ideal of suffering motherhood, Valdez includes a character almost identical to Dolores (the character of Cruz in *Pancho Villa* is even described in the list of characters as "the madre, long-suffering but loving" [2005, 132]) but does so without critique, offering no alternative images of Chicana motherhood to represent other possibilities for this social role.

Indeed, the trope of the suffering mother appears in numerous Chicano nationalist texts, from the "black-shawled/faithfulwomen" of Rodolfo "Corky" Gonzales's Chicano epic "I Am Joaquín" (1997) to the "Indian mothers . . . so unaware/of courtroom tragicomedies" (1999, 59) in the raúlrsalinas poem "A Trip Through the Mind Jail." The mothers in the raúlrsalinas poem, in particular, demonstrate the politically disempowered form of motherhood to which Moraga responds in *Heroes and Saints:* They watch their sons receive unjust prison sentences with "folded arms across their bosoms/saying 'Sea por Dios'" (1999, 59). In these works by Valdez, Gonzales, and raúlrsalinas, the image of the suffering mother exposes a system that strips oppressed people of their agency but leaves no room for women to contest that system. (The political critique in the work of all three comes from male characters.) By contrast, in *Heroes and Saints,* as Catrióna Rueda Esquibel (2006, 160) has observed, Dolores is juxtaposed with characters like Cerezita, Doña Amparo, and Yolanda in order to comment critically on the notion of the suffering mother as "innocent victim." By placing new forms of motherhood alongside that of the model of motherhood that Dolores represents, then, Moraga makes a claim for Chicanas as active political subjects.

By exploring new forms of Chicana motherhood, Moraga envisions new forms of Chicana/o family and, by extension, new forms of Chicana/o nation. Chicana feminist theorist Rosa Linda Fregoso, following Anne McClintock's famous observation that "[n]ations are frequently figured through the iconography of familial and domestic space" (McClintock, Mufti, and Shohat 1997, 90), develops a theory of what she calls the "Chicano familia romance." Fregoso defines the familia romance as an epic form featuring a patriarchal family that is "designed to stand for the familia of Chicanas and Chicanos" (2003, 71). Because the patriarchal family represents the nation in this way, those who refuse to comply with its norms are positioned as traitors to the nation and to the Chicano Movement. Fregoso argues further that the representation of the mother in the familia romance is particularly damaging, for even when the mother is depicted as the center of the family, "the absence of her narrative agency reinforces gender inequality within the family structure as much as it freezes her in time, within the biologically inscribed role of motherhood" (78). Like Fregoso, Moraga also notes (in "Vendidas") how the apparent privileging of motherhood can coexist with misogyny: "I have never met any kind of mexicano who, although he may have claimed his family was very woman-dominated ('mi mamá made all the real decisions'), did not subscribe to the basic belief that men are better" (2001, 93).

Invoking this notion of the familia romance clarifies the distinction between Moraga's play and the Valdez play that inspired it. Although *Pancho Villa* might not appear to be a classic "familia romance" because it depicts the decline and collapse of a Chicano family, its argument is the same: just as the political agency of the Chicano people is represented through a unified patriarchal family in the familia romance, in *Pancho Villa* the failure of the patriarchal family represents the absence of Chicana/o political agency. *Heroes and Saints*, by contrast, uses a nonpatriarchal family to represent not the failure but the *creation* of the Chicana/o nation. The extended family network privileged in the play's narrative differs significantly from the traditional patriarchal model; it consists of Dolores, a single mother; her children (including Yolanda, also a single mother) and infant granddaughter; and her neighbors Don Gilberto and Doña Amparo, a heterosexual couple without children.

The reformulation of the family is, of course, a hallmark of Moraga's writing. The line "making familia from scratch" (1994, 35), uttered by the character of Marisa at the end of Moraga's first play, *Giving Up the Ghost* (first staged in 1987 and published along with *Heroes and Saints* in 1994), is one of the most frequently cited from her entire body of work. Whereas *Giving Up the Ghost* puts this line in the mouth of a young queer Chicana, however, *Heroes and Saints* places a variation of it in the mouth of an older heterosexual Chicano. Don Gilberto, explaining that he and his wife have informally adopted children from the community after being unable to have children of their own, states: "Pues, sometimes you don't get to choose. But that just teaches you que you gotta make familia any way you can" (1994, 122). By rearticulating the queer concept of "making familia from scratch" through a character *without* an LGBT identity, Moraga insists that a queered model of familia can provide a more liberatory home for all Chicanas/os (queer and straight) than the patriarchal "familia romance."

According to Robert McRuer (2006, 94), a model of family that circumvents the norms of heteropatriarchy is essential to both disability and LGBT activism, both of which oppose "dominant models of domesticity." McRuer says that the independent, nuclear family model privileges the development of independent, autonomous subjects—a conceptualization of subjectivity that denies full personhood to individuals who cannot perform the cultural script of "independence." Furthermore, by reinforcing a norm based on independence, the dominant model of domesticity discourages people who belong to oppressed or marginalized groups from examining how their struggles might depend on the liberation struggles of others—a perspective Don Gilberto rejects when he recognizes his own need, as a heterosexual man, to "make familia any way you can." Indeed, Cerezita's activist project requires interdependence; it is a collaborative effort with the town's children and with Juan that brings together multiple sectors of the community and treats each person's survival as dependent on the liberation of everyone. *Heroes and Saints*, then, helps to illustrate McRuer's argument that an "accessible society, according to the best, critically disabled perspectives, is not simply one with ramps and Braille signs on 'public' buildings, but one in which our ways of relating to, and depending on, each other have been reconfigured" (94).

Moraga herself, in the 1997 memoir *Waiting in the Wings*, also speaks of the need for new domesticities in a way that coincides with McRuer's insights:

> I have never been a strong proponent of lesbian marriages . . . nor particularly passionate about the domestic partnership campaigns for which my white middle-class gay counterparts continue to rigorously fight. No, I've always longed for something else in my relationships—something woman-centered, something cross-generational, something extended, something sensual, something humilde ante la creadora. In short, something Mexican and familial but without all the cultural constraints. (18)

Moraga's rejection of gay marriage here echoes McRuer's sense that new queer and disabled domesticities might offer "much more than the simple incorporation of a privatized couple into a system that guarantees and requires the primacy of the able-bodied and heterosexual family" (2006, 102). Rather than seeking incorporation into a model of family (or nation) that is structured according to a patriarchal logic of able-bodied superiority, Moraga's characters seek to remake the family and, by extension, the nation. By reconfiguring the Chicano familia romance, then, Moraga's redefinition of motherhood and her search for a new paradigm for Aztlán broaden the range of concerns addressed by the Chicana/o Movement and radically expand the Chicana/o cultural family. Furthermore, the play's engagement with disability is not merely auxiliary to this project but central to it; the activist movement imagined in the play depends upon a notion of interdependence that, as in the alternative models of domesticity theorized by McRuer, emerges from disability activism.

THE DISABLED BODY POLITIC OF AZTLÁN

The representation of disability constitutes another point of contrast between *Heroes and Saints* and *Pancho Villa*. Valdez calls for a "cartoon quality" (2005, 132) in the staging of *Pancho Villa*; he also chooses to leave unexplained the bodiless Belarmino's condition, in keeping with the play's refusal of a realist mode of representation. Moraga replaces Valdez's visual satire with an appeal to the pre-Columbian past, describing Cerezita as marked by "dignity of bearing and classical Indian beauty" (1994, 90) and comparing her to the Olmec head figures. These visual references, however, coexist with the largely realist mode of the play, which requires an explanation for Cerezita's physical condition (pesticide poisoning). More important, while for Valdez the emergence of an effective social protest movement is not represented in the play, but is instead postponed for a future when corporeal wholeness is restored by Belarmino's unification with a body, Moraga's Cerezita represents a social protest that emerges from a disabled identity. Moraga thus proposes a political subjectivity grounded in disability and rejects the notion of disability as a metaphor for powerlessness. Following Siebers's observation that "the political unconscious may also regulate aesthetic forms, excluding those suggestive of broken communities and approving those evocative of ideal ones" (2003, 182), this departure from Valdez means that Moraga's treatment of disability has a profound impact on her nationalist vision. While for Valdez the fractured Chicano family and disabled Chicano body represent the failure of Chicano political agency and the lack of a viable Chicano nation, for Moraga the fractured Chicano family and disabled *Chicana* body represent the site from which Chicana/o political agency and nationalism emerge.

Moraga's representation of "the" ideal national body thus parallels her treatment of "the" ideal national family. Just as she sets up the Valle family as an archetypal Chicana/o family, simultaneously undermining the possibility of *one* ideal model for making Chicana/o family, so too does Cerezita become *the* national body in order to undermine the concept of one ideal national body. It is important to note that Cerezita's is not the only nonnormative body in the play. Doña Amparo discusses her body and the way it has been aged by work: "Me 'stoy poniendo vieja. . . . Mira los bunions. . . . You see how the toes all bunch up there on top of each other? . . . Mi viejo usetu tell me I had beautiful feet. Beautiful. Like a movie star. Ya no" (1994, 116). Don Gilberto, meanwhile, speaks frankly about his inability to have children: "Mi madre, she had two of us, see. And my cuate, well it seems he just hogged up all the jugo, if you know what I mean" (121). The biracial priest Juan surprises Dolores by speaking Spanish; the latter doesn't believe he is Mexican until Doña Amparo explains that he is "[h]alf y half" (98). Mario's body, too, changes in the course of the play, as his HIV develops into AIDS. The effect of depicting a range of characters whose bodies do not conform to either US nationalist discourse or Chicano nationalism is to undermine the damage of bodily normativity. Rather than posit disability as a metaphor for a social problem in need of a cure or treat the disabled body as a metaphor for the alienation of a presumed able-bodied audience (as in *Pancho Villa*), Moraga represents Cerezita's body as one kind of body among the many diverse bodies that constitute her idea of Aztlán. Moraga's early concern with coalition among women of color, then, might be seen to resurface in her portrayal of Cerezita, as she raises questions about how queer Chicanas/os and Chicanas/os with disabilities might share an interest in contesting ideologies of body normativity that undergird homophobia, racism, and the oppression of people with disabilities in traditional nationalist formulations.

Heroes and Saints, then, reimagines the Chicana/o nation as predicated on a nonnormative family (with a new model of motherhood) and a nonnormative body. These two projects come together in the play's final scenes, in which Cerezita appears as la Virgen de Guadalupe. This action occurs at a crucial moment in the play: Juan has abandoned the struggle after a brief sexual encounter with Cerezita has caused him to confront too openly his own corporeality, Yolanda's daughter Lina has died, and Mario has left his family rather than tell Dolores of his HIV status. The choice to appear as la Virgen is a strategic one on Cerezita's part, for Dolores has decided that her daughter's political action is too dangerous and, by disengaging her *raite,* has kept her confined to the home. In response, Cerezita asks the town's children to dress her, placing la Virgen's blue, star-printed veil on her head and a white altar cross with her signature roses of Tepeyac imprinted upon it on the *raite,* knowing that Dolores will see this as an apparition of la Virgen and permit her to leave the house. The children dress Cerezita onstage, foreclosing an interpretation (from the audience) of her apparition as la Virgen as a miracle of the Catholic God. However, despite de-emphasizing the power of the Catholic God, the play's use of la Virgen nonetheless reaffirms a commitment to spirituality and the sacred. Indeed, it renders sacred *human* lives and *human* interventions into unjust social relations.

It is as la Virgen, a spiritual mother, that Cerezita appears before the people of the town in their final rally against the agribusiness enterprises. In her speech, she invites them to "[p]ut your hand inside my wound" and states that "[i]nside the valley of my wound, there is a . . . miracle people" (1994, 148). Cerezita's final speech conflates her body and her family (the Valle family) with the land, with the nation itself. It is, she asserts, from her "wounded" body that a new relationship to the land will arise, a movement claiming the land for the miracle people. As she speaks, those who have abandoned Cerezita and her cause return: Juan fulfills his commitment to aid Cerezita in carrying out the final crucifixion (of the body of Cerezita's own infant niece, Lina), and Mario returns to the town and embraces his mother before inciting the people to join him in burning the fields. It is this claim to the land that renders the text's nationalism explicit, for it is at this point that the play's emphasis shifts from contesting environmental racism, ableism, and heteronormativity to linking the play's *people* with the *land.* The reunification of the family at this moment indicates the formation of a decolonized people with a territorial claim. Moreover, Cerezita's appearance as the mother of the people—presiding over both the creation of the nation and the reunification of her family—gives motherhood a radical new role within this reconfigured nationalism. Finally, because this moment represents the culmination of Cerezita's collaborations with many others (the children, Juan, and even Dolores, who finally engages Cerezita's *raite*), it might be read as the invocation of what McRuer calls an "accessible public sphere" (2006, 81), one predicated not on "independence and ability" but instead on "alternative (and interdependent) public cultures" (81).

However, this final moment of national cohesion is not without problems. First, Cerezita's reconstitution of community entails the sacrifice of her own subjectivity and body, as it is hinted in the play that she dies at the end.[2] As Yvonne Yarbro-Bejarano (2001, 79) writes, "Cere's loss of self in the collectivity is at once empowering of that community and deeply troubling, given the traditional teaching that women should sacrifice themselves for others." Moreover, the fact that Cerezita is not simply a woman but a woman with a disability who sacrifices herself in this way magnifies the problem that Yarbro-Bejarano describes.[3] Cerezita's death here thus alludes to but also reproduces the potential violence of the nation-building project, which so often entails the expulsion of bodies and identities that do not conform to the homogenized national ideal. In this sense, the play might be read as pulling back from the possibilities it opens in earlier scenes, depriving Cerezita of the agency and critical perspective afforded her up until the play's conclusion. In such a reading, the disabled character would (once again) be seen as a victim rather than the active subject of an activist movement.

I hope to register the complexity of the play's ending and to suggest a reading that both acknowledges the more disturbing implications of Cerezita's death and interprets this death as an illustration of the problems with using nationalism as a basis for activism. Cerezita's final speech, in

2. This is confirmed in Moraga's sequel to *Heroes and Saints*, a play entitled *Watsonville: Some Place Not Here* (2002).

3. It is worth noting that although Moraga's work often coincides with disability scholarship and activism (as I have noted in this essay), there are moments in which it does not, such as the moment in the memoir *Waiting in the Wings* in which Moraga describes her fear that her son may not be "perfectly normal genetically" (1997, 31).

fact, alludes to these problems as it defines the nation in terms of shared blood: "In this pueblito where the valley people live, the river runs red with blood. . . . It is the same color as the river that runs through their veins, the same color as . . . the pool of liquid they were born into" (1994, 148). The linking of nation and blood here could appear to reproduce the homogenizing impulse behind the most violent aspects of the national-ist project, which erases difference through the eradication of antinorma-tive and minority subjects like Cerezita. Moreover, it is not entirely clear whether Moraga makes the connection between nation and blood to stake a claim to the land based on shared blood *lines* or to stake a claim based on the blood *spilled* by a community working the land under a system of racist, capitalist, and colonialist exploitation. While a case could be made for the very different implications of each—a genealogical birthright ver-sus labor or shared experience—both play a compelling role in resist-ing mainstream US narratives that naturalize inequality by refusing to acknowledge a long history of stolen land and stolen labor.[4] The difficulty of interpreting definitively Moraga's use of the metaphor of blood has resulted in vastly different critical responses to her work. This disagree-ment points to a contradiction that Moraga's work has not been able to resolve: the nation's usefulness as a political tool versus its limitedness as a paradigm for a way of life. I would suggest that rather than attempting to resolve this contradiction, the critic look to *Heroes and Saints* as a work that registers both the activist possibilities of nationalism and its most

4. The difficulty of pinning down exactly how Moraga might intend the metaphor of blood is not resolved by a look at her larger body of work. For example, in a personal essay written nearly a decade after the first performance of *Heroes and Saints,* Moraga links her decision to have a child with the nation-building project of her later writing, thereby seeming to link her nation in a problematic way to blood (and, indeed, motherhood to nation building): "I had a child to make nation, one regenerated from the blood nations Mexicans in this country are forced to abandon. I had an Indian child to counter the loss of my family's working-class mexicanindianism with each succeeding generation" (2003, 94). Sandra K. Soto (2005) has examined Moraga's use of race as a way of thinking through the political salience of her Chicana lesbian identity. Scholars critical of Moraga's writing, meanwhile, have suggested that her work enacts a kind of racial exclusivity in its explora-tion of nation and nationalism.

violent effects. The depiction of Cerezita's death, then, would function as a warning about the problems of basing an activist movement too directly on nationalism. Such a reading does not absolve the play of the problems with its ending, but rather suggests that the play represents both the possibilities and the harms of nationalism.

NATIONALISM, MOTHERHOOD, AND DISABILITY

Moraga's nationalist vision as it emerges in *Heroes and Saints,* then, constitutes a profound reformulation of the notion of Aztlán. By predicating her nationalism on a woman-centered model of family and reimagining the role of motherhood within it, as well as by positing a disabled body politic for Aztlán, she forces her audience to consider how nationalism might be used and understood differently. However, given Cerezita's violent death and apparent self-sacrifice, *Heroes and Saints* also might be read as participating in the problems with nationalism that make it such a controversial and even dangerous tool. There is the possibility of reading Cerezita's death as a way of making visible the harmful effects of nationalism, but there is also the possibility of reading her death as reinforcing those harmful effects. In the end, despite registering her unease with the ideologies of body normativity within nationalism and critiquing the gendered concept of martyred motherhood, Moraga capitulates to these impulses by failing to imagine a different ending for Cerezita. This capitulation, I would argue, is most productively read as an illustration of just how difficult it is to imagine liberation within conditions of oppression. *Heroes and Saints* attempts to envision a liberated nationalist project, but the full realization of such a vision remains impossible in a world still structured by oppressive hierarchies of disability, race, sexuality, and gender.

20

Intersecting Postcolonial Mothering and Disability

A Narrative of an Antiguan Mother and Her Son

DENISE CORDELLA HUGHES-TAFEN

On September 30, 2007, I became a mother. My transition into motherhood has helped me in understanding my own mother and how she has dealt with my brother's disabilities. My mom and I share many qualities, but there are three major identifiers that have shaped our experiences—first, we are both mothers; second, both of us have sons who are US citizens by virtue of their having been born in the United States; and third, we are both immigrant women of African descent. We are both from the Caribbean island of Antigua. What sets up apart is that one of us has a child with a disability. My son has not been identified as having a disability, but my younger brother has been diagnosed with autism.

An examination of disability on this small Caribbean island reveals how mothering a child with autism not only affects a woman's position in this society but also complicates issues of nationhood. My research is best described as a narrative inquiry that includes ongoing biographical interviews with my mother, conversations with Antiguans, and my personal experience as an Antiguan sister and mother. The story of my mother and her journey in caring for her child with autism moves from discovery to seeking solutions and becoming an activist for change. This narrative adds to the growing discourse on postcolonial studies and disability studies by exploring the impact of mothering a disabled child on a postcolonial subject from a developing country and addresses the intersections of race and gender and class. Mainstream feminism has been charged as representing only selected voices—neglecting women

275

of color, working-class women, and women from third-world countries. The feminist movement has been "challenged on the grounds of cultural imperialism, and of short sightedness in defining the meaning of gender in terms of middle class, white experiences and in terms of internal racism, classism, and homophobia (Mohanty, Russo, and Torres 1991, 7). Recently, black feminism (Collins 1998), Africana womanism (Hudson-Weems 1993), and womanism (A. Walker 1983) were added to the list describing various forms of feminism. Outside of the United States, women in postcolonial societies are also engaged in this dialogue. My effort to describe my mother's experience in the Caribbean expands this conversation. Finally, I acknowledge my bias—the subject of my discourse is my own mother and brother, and my interpretation is through my own lens as a Caribbean mother living in the United States coupled with pertinent literature in this area.

CARIBBEAN WOMANHOOD AND MOTHERING

Afro-Caribbean women bring another perspective to the dialogue on womanhood; at the heart of their dialogue is the place of mothers. Although Caribbean women have not given their forms of feminism specific names, Caribbean feminist literature has been engaged in "challenging dominant feminist theories and their inability to adequately engage with definitions of otherness" (Rowley 2001, 39). Because of its colonial anthropological inheritance, the Caribbean has mistakenly been described as a strong matriarchal society. Rowley argues, however, that the Caribbean is a matrifocal society. While both matriarchal and matrifocal concepts imply that women have power, what distinguishes the two is the "impact of women's ability to act at the broader parameters of social, economic, political and ideological order" (Rowley 2001, 23). *Matrifocality* refers to societies where women are central in certain aspects of community life, for example, in their roles as mothers (R. Smith 1996; Rowley 2001; Mohammed 1998; Barrow 1996). On the other hand, matriarchy assumes that women have positions of power not only within the home but also ideologically, socially, and institutionally (Rowley 2001).

It is important to present a discussion of the factors that influence womanhood in the Caribbean in order to understand the impact being a mother with a son who has a disability has on Caribbean womanhood. Overall, this matrifocal nature of the Caribbean tends to inform concepts of womanhood. In her interviews with women from the Caribbean island of Tobago, Rowley noted that there were several factors that influence womanhood in this region. The first is reputation and respectability. Virtue is expected from Caribbean women (Mohammed 1998). There is a social need for acceptance, and in order to gain acceptance the woman has to abide by the societal codes regarding what is considered to be good and acceptable behavior for women. As a result "the construction of the matrifolk therefore begins at a juncture where self is coerced into being marginalized from the experience and immediacy redirected towards a community based sanctioning of shame and reproach" (Rowley 2001, 30). For example, an Antigua woman is expected to be able to cook; this is not a requirement for men. Mothers often make comments that they have to teach their daughters how to cook because they don't want their husbands to return them to their families. A woman not being able to cook is looked on with shame; it is assumed that her mother did not prepare her for the role of womanhood. Failure to comply with the set rules has serious consequences, for example, divorce; hence girls are taught at a young age how to cook and care for their future mates.

A second factor that influences Caribbean womanhood is the expectations governing motherhood and marriage. These are the most pivotal periods in the Caribbean woman's life because it is through motherhood and marriage that women gain their identity as women within their societies. While these are critical experiences for women in the Caribbean, the two are not always connected. Caribbean women often wait until they are much older before engaging in marriage, a way, Rowley suggests, for Caribbean women to affirm their independence. Of the two experiences, mothering seems to play a greater role in determining the identity status of womanhood than marriage. During my own experience living in the Caribbean, it was not uncommon to hear women declare that their children were most important to them. They explained that men can leave you, whereas when you have a child he/she is yours. I also remember that while people were happy for me when I got married, they continuously asked, "So how many children you have now?" It was not until my son was born that I was recognized as a full woman.

A third factor is economics. Caribbean societies are developing societies, and economics play an instrumental role in Caribbean womanhood. Amid the tremendous economic hardships and pressures, there is an overwhelming need for Caribbean women to provide for their children, regardless of the personal sacrifice. The demand sometimes reaches even to the extent of personal levels of exploitation. This personal sacrifice is often misunderstood, resulting in myths of Caribbean women as superwomen (Rowley 2001). These myths assume that Caribbean women can overcome all obstacles. A consequence of this myth is that problems affecting Caribbean women are not considered a priority. Regardless of what comes their way, it is assumed that these women will be able to deal with their own problems without any help.

Compared to their counterparts in the global south, Caribbean women have higher levels of economic autonomy (Momsen 2001). The legacy of slavery, coupled with later male migrations, is responsible for this condition. In the English- and Dutch-speaking Caribbean, women have long had access to land ownership; that is not the case for the Francophone and Spanish islands because their inheritance laws have limited women's access to wealth and property. However, while Caribbean women may own land, women's farms in the English-speaking areas are smaller, less accessible, and are in areas where the soil fertility is low in comparison to the farmland of their their male counterparts. Gender inequality remains. Many women see education as a way of dealing with their economic hardships, so there is a tendency for more women than men to take advantage of education as a path to economic advancement. Many Caribbean universities now have a higher female than male enrollment.

The landscape of the Caribbean has changed politically, socially, and economically since the 1980s, and women from the Caribbean have faced many challenges as wages fell and unemployment, especially for women, increased (Momsen 2001). The global political importance of the region diminished with the end of the cold war, and sources of development aid were reduced. In addition, trade policies—such as the North American Free Trade Agreement (NAFTA) and the establishment of the European Union (EU) trading blocs—left the region out in the cold. The islands are not able to compete effectively at the world market level; many of the islands' economies have taken a beating. Women are left to tackle the results of these economic problems at the family level; in many instances they are the heads of the households. At the family level problems are manifested through an increase in crime activity of family members, drug use, increase in school dropout rates, and teenage pregnancy.

Thus, gender relations in the Caribbean cannot be presented in a simplistic manner; there are many complexities that have to be taken into consideration. Issues of gender in the Caribbean are somewhat of a paradox. Janet Momsen writes:

> Within the Caribbean regional diversity of ethnicity, class, language and religion there is an ideological unit of patriarchy, of female subordination and dependence. Yet there is also a vibrant living tradition of female economic autonomy, of female-headed households and of a family structure in which men are often marginal and absent. So Caribbean gender relations are a double paradox: of patriarchy within a system of matrifocal and matrilocal families; and of domestic and state patriarchy coexisting with the economic independence of women. The roots of this contemporary paradoxical situation lie in colonialism. (2001, 45)

As Momsen (2001) explains, the situation of the Caribbean woman today is rooted in a historical framework of colonialism and slavery. The "double paradox" that exists makes understanding the Caribbean woman a very complicated process. However, another element often missing in descriptions of Caribbean womanhood is the intersecting issue of disability, which further complicates an understanding of Caribbean womanhood. In what follows, I present the interplay of motherhood, which is central to Caribbean womanhood, and disability by recounting my mother's experiences.

MY MOTHER AND BROTHER

In the first year of my brother's life, all seemed normal. He was a very happy baby and met all his development milestones. By his second birthday things seemed to change; he was not talking as much in comparison to other babies his age, but there were signs of speech. He would call my sister as though he was her boss, and he would often participate in the singing of "dish dash dish dash all fall down." However, by his third year, all of that began to diminish. He was no longer able to call my sister, and whereas the "all fall down" before was quite audible, now he would only smile when the song was being sung. My family was concerned, but we were told by his pediatrician not to worry because some kids take longer than others to speak. I was in the United States by this time, and at every call home I inquired about Malcom and his speech acquisition.

Our concerns heightened as time passed. When my brother was four, my mom visited me in the United States so that we could explore solutions. My school had lots of resources on campus, and we decided to take him to visit the speech therapist. After examining him, the therapists told us that they suspected autism and that early intervention and education were essential for him. Without hesitation we contacted the school board, and they sent a team out to observe my brother in the home setting. This process was new to all of us so we did not know what to expect. First came a list of questions: Can he dress himself? Is he potty trained? Can he feed himself?

Although I understood that they were trying to figure out his development milestones, I deemed some of the questions to be more culturally than developmentally meaningful. For example, children in the United States are taught at a very early age how to be independent; that seems to be the goal of parenting. In the case of my own child, I was advised that by two months, at the latest three, my little boy should be sleeping through the night. When he was almost one year, I was asked if he put his legs in his pants when he was being dressed. My son is now a one-year-old, and he does not sleep through the night nor does he put his legs into his pants. I am not the least bit alarmed. What I have learned from my own mother and other mothers in Antigua is to let children develop at their own speed. By eighteen most children in the United States feel the pressure to leave their parents' home, whereas in Antigua children live with their parents for a very long time; there they do not rush to move out.

We were told by the school's assessment team that my brother showed typical signs of autism. His autism, they concluded, was mild, but it probably explained why he was not speaking or making eye contact. However, the school board pointed out that they did not have enough resources in the area schools, so he would only receive limited schooling. My mom and I listened and then decided that this was not adequate, so we began looking for other options. What we did not know at the time was that the schools were obligated to provide services to all students with disabilities. But because of our status as non-US citizens and black women we were not aware of our rights. I now realize that many mothers, particularly those who are from low socioeconomic backgrounds and minority cultures, also face barriers in accessing schooling and therapy for their disabled children. As we did, they encounter developmental tests laden with cultural biases. It is not easy to speak up in the face of these barriers and biases.

With the help of another relative we were able to relocate my mother and brother to another area. This relative lived in a white, middle-class area,[1] and we were able to get Malcom in a school that provided services for disabled students. He thrived at this school. He began learning how to communicate and was also able to maintain eye contact with others. He made friends and loved going to school. His teachers praised his growth and were actively involved in his education. However there was one problem—my mother was not a US citizen. In order to ensure that her son had some form of education and the help he needed, she would enter the United States for months at a time and then would have to leave at the appointed time stamped on her passport. She was very diligent about not staying in the United States longer than the time allowed by law. In 2002, my mom left the United States because the date stamped on her passport

---

1. There is a disparity in funding for schools in the United States. Schools in white middle- and upper-class neighborhoods receive more funding than those in lower socio-economic areas; hence there is more educational success at these schools (Kozol 1991).

was approaching. When she tried to reenter at one of the US-Canadian borders she was denied entry. She begged the immigration officials as only a mother could but was told that only Malcom, a US citizen, could enter. She had done nothing wrong, but because of her status as a non-US citizen and a woman with very little economic means, she was now unable to provide her son with the education and services that would ensure a brighter future for him.

US AND THEM

A discussion in one of my classes brought me a revelation about my mother's experience in the United States. Recently I enrolled in a special education class, and as most of the students were already working in special education I inquired about laws regarding children with autism whose parents cannot legally stay in the United States. I was told that in such a case the parents could either decide to take the child with them or leave the child behind. I pushed further, asking specifically about countries without special education resources, and I was informed that if the parents choose to do so, they could leave their child as a ward of the state. When I insisted that it would be difficult for a parent to leave a child behind, my classmates quickly responded that many immigrants chose this option. Leaving a child behind seemed the normal thing to do, something expected of parents who do not have US citizenship. This option was also presented as though it was an easy choice; no one in my class considered how much it must have cost those parents to make such a decision.

This sentiment can be analyzed by looking at the literature on attitudes to immigrants and peoples from developing countries, particularly those from Africa and its diaspora. There is an "us vs. them" approach to interacting with peoples of immigrant background, especially those from postcolonial, third-world societies. Arguably, this approach has become more widespread since the September 11 attacks. Edward Said's monumental work *Orientalism* (1978) marked a historical point in academia for a discussion on otherness. The Orient referred to places in the Middle East as well as the countries of North Africa. Said asserts that the colonized people living in these areas were often described as "inferior, irrational, depraved and childlike" in many of the scholarly and literary works produced by Europeans (Sardar and Van Loon 1997, 107).

In terms of Africa and the Caribbean, the African "other" is seen predominantly in the media, and mainstream media promotes negative stereotypes of Africa. "Usually there is emphasis on the sensational, preference for catastrophes such as droughts, the use of simplistic notions of conflict causes, notably "tribalism," and a focus on non-Africans as victims or "helpers" (Palmberg 2001, 9). On the other hand, the Caribbean is seen as "paradise" and mainly as a tourist destination. Tourism is a major income generation in many of these islands, and the people are expected to conform to the stereotypes created by tourists. As Polly Pattulo (1996, 142) explains: "The Caribbean person, from the Amerindians whom Columbus met in that initial encounter to the twentieth-century taxi driver whom tourists meet at the airport, is expected to satisfy those images associated with paradise and Eden. The images are crude: of happy, carefree, fun loving men and women, colorful in behavior; whose life is one of daytime indolence beneath the palms and a night time of pleasure though music, dance and sex." Caribbean people are therefore not seen as subjects but as objects; they are seen as part of the packaged vacation and not as complex human selves. The immigration officer and my classmates saw my mother not as a mom trying to do what is best for her son but as a noncitizen, which equates to "not one of us."

RETURNING HOME

My mother was determined to find a solution for her son. She remained in Canada for a year searching for options but faced similar situations. Canadian immigration was more sympathetic than US immigration and they allowed her to stay in Canada for a longer period of time. However, she quickly found that without at least a landed immigrant status, there was very little she could do. My brother went to school during that time, but they were not eligible for health care or any social service benefits. After one year of living in Canada, she decided to go home to Antigua.

While much has been written about womanhood in the Caribbean, very little has been written about mothering and disability. Once home, my mother faced an uphill battle. Special-education resources are limited, particularly quality accessible services. There is a school on the island for children who have various visible disabilities—physical, mental, emotional. However, the objective of this school is not to educate; the objective is to babysit these children. Most of the teachers at this school have very little, if any, special-educational training. My mother was dismayed at the situation, especially because she knew that things could be different. She decided to send my brother to this school and then try as much as she could to practice with him the things he had learned in school while he was in the United States and Canada.[2] My mother has no formal educational training, but during her sojourn in the United States and Canada she had enrolled in several special-education classes and was very active in educating herself by watching videos on autism and other disabilities.

A reality that mothers with disabled children face is harsh criticism from others. This criticism is based on attitudes toward disability and also connected to ideals of respect and respectability that define Caribbean womanhood. Some people questioned her efficacy as a mother, implying that she did something wrong either during her pregnancy or immediately after giving birth. Others questioned her actions, suggesting that she did something she should not have done or participated in some sort of physical activity that was inappropriate for a mother carrying a baby. Her life was scrutinized—some of her fellow churchgoers questioned her faithfulness to the Lord. They were convinced that she had committed a grave sin, and that was why she had a son born with a disability. Some suggested that she develop better parenting skills; they advised that what my brother needed was discipline—that he needed to learn how to sit and be quiet. Even the way she is identified has changed. My mom has five children, but now she is only the mom of the "fooley" boy. Usually "mother" is an identifier: for example, that woman is John's mom. In the case of

2. I am by no means suggesting that US models of special education be imposed on the Antiguan educational system, nor do I suggest that education in the United States and Canada are ideal, as there are problems of low educational outcomes along race, social class, and gender lines.

my mother, she is identified as the mother of a son who is an "idiot" (i.e., fooley), demonstrating the negative labels and stigma attached to having a child with a disability.

In Antigua a person with a disability is often ridiculed. As I mentioned earlier, there are no public schools that include students with visible disabilities;[3] many teachers do not know how to work with students who have ability differences. The very first day that Malcom was enrolled in preschool, my mom got a call from the director only two hours after she had dropped him off at school. She was told that she needed to come and pick up her son because something was wrong with him—he was not like the kids at school. My mother was alarmed and upset. This event occurred before the diagnosis of autism, but it demonstrates the school's attitudes. Keep in mind that my brother's autism is very mild. He is a very friendly and social little boy. He loves interacting with people, and he is extremely close to my mother. My mother told us that when she was refused entry to the United States, she just sat down, unsure of what to do next; Malcom came up to her and threw his arms around her and kissed her—which affirmed to her that she needed to continue her fight for his sake.

It is important to analyze these experiences within their social context. Antigua is a former British colony and inherited many of the legacies of colonialism and slavery. In writing about disability and postcolonialism, Cindy Lacom (2002) cites Jean-Paul Sartre (1963, 22), who wrote in his preface to Fanon's *The Wretched of the Earth*, "the European has only been able to become a man through creating slaves and monsters." She then suggests that "the colonized are only able to 'become men,' to establish a national identity in the historical moment of decolonization, through the reification of a new category of *monsters*—the disabled, the deformed, the mad" (141). Evidence of the creation of "monsters" can be seen in the way some people with disabilities are treated. I was once told of a mother who locked her son in a shed outside of their home. This child was chained and food was carried out to him. The social worker who saw this child

3. Most students are not assessed for disabilities, hence it is only when the disability is noticeable that schools are not able to accommodate students.

asked the parents why the child was being treated in this manner, and she was told that the child was not human, so he could not be in the house. Some children with disabilities are abandoned by their family and left to roam the streets. On the streets they are subject to a lot of abuses—sexual, physical, and emotional—a serious problem that demands investigation.

Another colonial legacy is the use of the Bible in oppressing groups. A justification made for slavery was the argument that Africans are the descendants of Ham, and according to biblical prophecy his generation were to become slaves. In a similar way some Antiguans use the Bible to argue that disability is a result of sin. In the Old Testament, a priest could not make an offering to God if he was disabled in any way (Lev. 21:16–23), and in the New Testament, after encountering a blind man Jesus's disciples questioned, "Who sinned, this man or his parents, that he was born blind?" (John 9:2). This text is taken to mean that disability could be a result of sin even though Jesus responded that no one had sinned, neither the man nor his parents. The effects of colonization and slavery are far-reaching and affect the lives of those in postcolonial societies. It is within this environment that my mother works to create a bright future for my brother.

ACTIVISM

My mom returned to Antigua with a goal: to make sure that more attention is given to children with disabilities on the island. She began by researching existing organizations, finding only one on the island. She quickly concluded that this group was not very successful in influencing government policies and changing public opinion. Her next step was to meet with government officials. She recounts the story of mentioning special education and discovering that some of the officials had never heard that such programs were possible. At the same time she began looking at schools and finding parents who were facing similar conditions. She found that there was a private school for disabled children; however, this school catered to the children of expatriates. The school was expensive, and the average Antiguan could not afford the fees. This discovery led her back to the government-run school that houses all children with disabilities.

She was disappointed with what she saw there. Unlike the schools she saw in the United States and Canada, these schools have dramatically lower expectations for students. In Antigua, because most teachers lack training in this area they do not expect these students to be able to learn. Instead, this place is seen as a center where parents can bring their children while they are at work. My mother recognizes that there are a handful of teachers who are interested in working with disabled students and who are doing their best. However because of limited resources and lack of specialized training in special education, these teachers face many challenges.

In response to these discoveries, my mom and other parents facing similar challenges have formed a new organization particularly for parents and children with autism. The group is still in its infancy, and its members are still in the process of networking with international organizations and developing public awareness campaigns. They have been able to meet with government officials, but no real policy for special education has yet been implemented. Funding is a major issue. The group is planning several fund-raisers, with the objective of meeting some of their financial needs.

There are many amazing stories of Antiguan mothers caring for their children with disabilities. I know of another mother who goes to school with her child every day to help her in her high school. Her daughter is blind, and the school has no services to assist this child, so it has become the role of her mother to ensure that she has the help she needs to be successful. Not every mother can perform this role, particularly because there is a high percentage of single-parent households mostly headed by women. In fact, because most mothers work outside the home, this level of care and assistance is nearly impossible. I also have heard about another mother who carried her son on her back for years because at the time they could not afford a wheelchair.

Looking at disability and mothering through a postcolonial lens presents an interesting perspective for research. Postcolonial feminism investigates the lives of women in third-world and other postcolonial societies. While there is work in the area of postcolonial feminism and mothering, research is scarce in the area of disability and mothering in postcolonial societies, particularly Caribbean societies. The limited research in this area may lead one to conclude that these women are invisible or voiceless; on the contrary, these women are active. But as Molara Ogundipe-Leslie questions in reference to African women: "Are African women voiceless or do we fail to look for their voices where we may find them, in the sites and forms in which these voices are uttered? . . . We must look for African women's voices in women's spaces and modes such as ceremonies and work songs" (qtd. in Kolawole 1997, 9). We have to search for the voices of postcolonial mothers of children with disabilities and bring them from the margins to the center.

My preliminary research in this area suggests that mothers of children with disabilities are first of all postcolonial subjects. Part of the postcolonial identity involves migration in search of education, health care, and other services for the purpose of finding better opportunities for their families. However, once these families have migrated, they often face exclusion because of nationality, gender, and race. At home, exclusion is also an issue, particularly when gender and ability intersect. My mother's example demonstrates that it is possible to maneuver within the home environment, but this seems to be dependent on education, information, and socioeconomic status. In addition, having high expectations for children is essential. However, environment in the home country presents a catch-22 situation: change will one day come about, but change is slow, and for children with disabilities, early intervention is critical. My mom and mothers like her hope that when change does come it will not be too late for their children. As a mom myself, I yearn for the day when the hopes and dreams of all children will be realized. Just like my son, they deserve the very best.

21

Mothering, Disability, and Poverty

Straddling Borders, Shifting Boundaries,
and Everyday Resistance

SHAWN A. CASSIMAN

In this chapter I draw upon original research, in-depth interviews with disabled single mothers living in poverty, and detail their resistance to dominant social constructions of themselves as suspect because they are both disabled and welfare recipients. The interview data and corresponding analysis indicate that these women straddle many borders. They occupy policy borderlands, qualifying for disability benefits but requiring additional support for their children available through welfare. Welfare receipt carries with it a particular stigma of being bad or lazy mothers. They also occupy the borderlands of motherhood because of a stigma against mothering with disability. They resist these social constructions of themselves as "bad" mothers by demonstrating and arguing their commitment to their children. Their resistance strategies highlight how policy boundaries and the margins of motherhood are constructed and deconstructed through interactions with agency workers, medical professionals, and the general public. In the process of negotiating these interactions, these women construct themselves as both heroic resistors and victims of oppression. Their everyday resistance emphasizes the limited policy support for mothers in the United States following welfare reform, the impact and stigma associated with disability, and the selfless dedication demanded of all women who choose to mother in such an environment.

BORDERS OF MOTHERHOOD

Motherhood, like disability, is contested terrain. The increased attention to motherhood in recent decades is documented in Sharon Hays's (1998, 131–32) discussion of the social construction of mothering with attention to the "mommy wars," associated primarily with middle-class mothers in the United States. Competing ideologies of intensive mothering and "getting ahead" are played out as either "traditional" mothers devoted obsessively to home and family or as "supermoms" easily juggling careers and children. Although they may war over which is the appropriate or best way to mother, both types of mothers profess intensive mothering and selfless devotion to their children. Hochschild details the nature of mothering and marriage in *The Second Shift* (2003). She describes how "Supermoms," engaged in work or career, remain responsible for home and children, in essence working a second shift at home after completing the workday, highlighting, as does Hays, the contradictions associated with paid work and motherhood. Anne Crittenden (2001) describes in detail the economic sacrifices professional women make in choosing to mother in an environment focused upon the economic bottom line; many lose seniority if they take advantage of leave policies, which can also lead to lifetime wage "penalties" of more than one million dollars. Jane Juffer (2006) focuses her cultural critique upon the emergent "domestic intellectual," the lone or single mother resisting the patriarchal imperative of the nuclear family. Each of these texts details the conflicting social and cultural values of mothering and the inconsistencies encountered when women attempt to reconcile such values with the reality of paid work in a capitalist corporate culture.

There are some parallels between the literature on motherhood and the feminist literature on care, though the care literature offers a broader definition of care (i.e., beyond motherhood) and provides ample space for gender neutrality while still recognizing that the majority of care work is provided by women. Of particular interest to this project is that discussions of both motherhood and care draw attention to the financial implications of caring or mothering. Care work, and motherhood in particular, are devalued in a capitalist corporate culture (Mink 1998; Tronto 1994), and mothers are at a financial disadvantage in the paid work force upon returning to market work (Crittenden 2001).

If we shift our focus to the conservative or neoliberal discourses about welfare recipients, mothers living in poverty, mothers with impairments, or mothers of color, the character of these discourses becomes increasingly one of suspicion, loathing, and disgust, as pointed out by Hancock (2004), emphasizing the need for surveillance (Swift 1995; Roberts 2002) and rehabilitation (Reich 2008). Disability studies analyses argue that mothers with disabilities are not disabled by virtue of their impairments but by inadequate social-welfare policies and the built environment. However, even with resources, they remain subject to some of the same surveillance that led to the sterilization of many women with intellectual impairments in our recent past (Reich 2008). That is, disabled women who desire children are frequently considered "selfish" or unrealistic (Morris 1996). When they become parents, often in opposition to family members and friends' heartfelt advice, their parenting practices are subject to continual scrutiny and met with suspicion (Olkin 1999; Wates 1997).

Mothers living in poverty, particularly single mothers of color, have also endured the scrutiny of their mothering practices, and more recently their work habits, for much of their lives. They have been blamed for the outcomes of their children, the emasculation of black men, and for the breakdown of the American family (Lubiano 1992; Swift 1995). These women have also been especially targeted for forced sterilization and child removal (Roberts 2002) as a result of the denigration of their mothering practices, the attempt to "rehabilitate" their parenting practices (Reich 2008), and their inability or refusal to sacrifice their cultural modes to meet the norms associated with mainstream motherhood.

POLICY BORDERS

The passage of welfare reform legislation in 1996 had a profound impact upon mothers in poverty and mothers with disabilities, eliminating mothering as a category worthy of support while ignoring the gendered nature of disability policy. While there is a relatively large literature on the impact of welfare reform on single mothers living in poverty, the plight of mothers with disabilities in poverty following welfare reform remains largely unexamined (Parish, Magaña, and Cassiman 2008; Magaña, Parish, and Cassiman 2008; Cassiman 2008).

The *Personal Responsibility and Work Opportunity Reconciliation Act (PRWORA)* of 1996 evidenced a decided ideological policy shift from material support, however minimal, for single mother families to a focus upon "work first." In effect, the legislation eliminated mothering as a category deserving of support by the welfare state. Gwendolyn Mink (1998, 58) argues that welfare reform stripped women living in poverty of the rights of citizenship, as "they alone are not paid for their labor." She goes on to argue that without supportive welfare policy, women are forced, "to choose wages over children" (58). Welfare reform's imperative of market work over mothering or care work was, as Anna Marie Smith (2007, 77) argues, not only designed to encourage low-wage work among welfare claimants, but "also presses them to become childless low-wage workers." She describes this imperative as a form of neoeugenics, in which mothers living in poverty or welfare mothers are being forced to relinquish their children because of the overwhelming nature of their material deprivation or are having them removed from the home based on increased scrutiny by the child-welfare system and expanded definitions of "neglect." This assertion emerges in some of the statements made by women in the research project, who reveal the incredible pressures they are under in attempting to raise their children with minimal financial support—for instance, when Dolores suggests she could be like "some women" and let someone else raise her children.

Disability policies in the United States also possess a gender-based bias. Two programs provide the majority of benefits for people with disabilities in the United States—Social Security Disability Insurance (SSDI) and Supplemental Security Income (SSI). In order to secure the relatively generous benefits of SSDI, a claimant must have a strong work history. SSI requires no work experience, but also provides significantly lower levels of material support with a poverty rate among claimants of 41 percent (Martin and Davies 2004). Fifty-six percent of those receiving SSI benefits are women, while they constitute only 41 percent of those on the SSDI roles as of 1998 (SSA 2011). Women's care responsibilities often shape their employment patterns and histories (Lockhart 1989), perhaps explaining their overrepresentation among SSI claimants.

THE RESEARCH PROJECT

The research project informing this analysis consisted of in-depth interviews of fourteen disabled mothers from Madison and Milwaukee, Wisconsin, living in poverty. The women ranged in age from their early twenties to their mid-sixties. Approximately half of the women identified as African American and half Caucasian; one woman identified as Latina. The women experienced a variety of impairments, including cancer and its aftermath, lupus, and other such diseases, mental illness, intellectual disability, and orthopedic impairments. Many women reported more than one disabling condition. In all, fourteen in-person interviews were conducted.[1]

My analysis—grounded in conceptualizations of "everyday resistance" described by Scott (1985) and others (Cassiman 2008; Parish, Magaña, and Cassiman 2008; Denis 2003; Hollander 2002; McCormack 2004; Riessman 2000; Shorter-Gooden 2004)—focuses upon participants' resistance to the construction of themselves as "bad" mothers or "unfit" mothers. In conceptualizing resistance, I draw upon a typology developed by Hollander and Einwohner (2004). They describe core elements of resistance as action and opposition. Actions are conceptualized broadly and include talk as well as more physical sorts of actions. To classify an act as resistant, the actor must also be working in opposition to something: discourse, social constructions, policy, or physical restraint, for instance. Of central concern in developing the typology was determining what might be included as resistance. Hollander and Einwohner distinguish between the "everyday" resistance strategies described by Scott and more formally

---

1. Recruitment began by contacting participants for an earlier focus group study and continued with attempts to contact recipients of the Care Taker Supplement program (CTS), a program unique to Wisconsin. Of the almost five hundred contacts listed in the two-year-old dataset, I was able to reach only eighteen. In-depth interviews were semistructured. Twelve were conducted in participant homes and two in restaurants. Data consisted of interview transcripts, field notes, and observations.

organized and recognized forms of resistance such as social movements, which are more visible. This distinction is pertinent to my project because, as Scott argues, everyday resistance often goes unnoticed by the powerful and is often ordinary in nature. The following section includes analysis of the everyday resistance strategies evident in the interview transcripts of the mothers in this study.

SURVEILLANCE

In contrast to the stereotypes of mothers living in poverty and disabled mothers as "unfit," the participants in this study were highly invested in their children and their success, with many women detailing their involvement in their children's education and reporting their focus on "teaching children about the world." They were also acutely aware of the scrutiny they were under as mothers and the social constructions of unfit mothers. This scrutiny existed at multiple levels, in institutions of education and policy as well as in society more generally, and concerned not only their disability, poverty, or welfare receipt, but also their status as single or lone mothers. Their awareness of this scrutiny was reflected in the strategies they chose to contest or resist the negative constructions of poverty, disability, and single parenthood. This sense of visibility, of being under the "gaze" of others, was consistent in the interviews. When possible, some women removed themselves, a form of covert resistance, from situations that exposed them to the potential for scrutiny, whether the scrutiny was real or perceived. Robin, for example, describes a resistance strategy sometimes associated with covert resistance—withdrawal or hiding: "I just knew everybody was staring at me. I said, 'Bill, they stared at me when I went to the store,' and he said, 'There's no one staring at you.' I said, 'yes they are.' I didn't go out for a while."

Robin avoided going out in public unless it was very important to her son, such as school visits. She moved from Madison to a suburb because she thought her son would have a better education. She is in her late twenties and white. She has epilepsy and also deals with mental illness. Her first son was removed from her care when she attempted suicide following his birth. She is less reluctant to talk about her epilepsy, feeling it is more evident, but is more sensitive about her mental health. Her experience at the community pool suggests that this is a reasonable strategy:

> I had a seizure one time when I took my son to the pool and the lifeguards and EMTs didn't know what to do. They wouldn't let my son use the magnet, he knows how. [She had a surgically implanted device that is triggered by a special magnet. It often reduces the severity and length of her seizures]. I got so mad and frustrated. The EMT at the pool, said, *"How can you do this to your son?"* I couldn't believe he said that!

At other times, interviewees reported withdrawing as a tactic to prevent others from "seeing" the pain in their eyes. For example, Mary shared her desire to protect the viewer or observer from "her pain." It was evident that she was worried that the rawness, the depth, of her pain would leave her further vulnerable not only to pity or compassion, but also to further scrutiny.

Susan is a white woman in her early forties. She was diagnosed at the age of ten with rheumatoid arthritis. She has learned to navigate the benefit system and is acutely aware of her rights under the Americans with Disability Act (ADA), the only participant who expressed such knowledge. She has two children, a son in college and a teenage daughter soon to graduate from high school. She expressed great pride in her children and their accomplishments. She lives in Madison and is involved in disability-rights organizations and had insightful policy suggestions to offer. We interviewed over lunch in a quiet restaurant and talked for over two hours. Issues of visibility were a major concern for Susan. She made the point that those not obviously disabled are subject to a particular kind of scrutiny most often associated with welfare recipients: "What should a disabled person look like? If I'm not in a wheelchair or blind, people think I am faking—to get welfare. Ha!"

STIGMA

The women in this study were very forthcoming, seeming to welcome an opportunity to share their experiences and conceptualizations of their experiences with an interested listener. For the most part, they lived lives of isolation, with a few friends, church members and family their primary contacts other than medical professionals. Their relief at sharing their experiences sometimes led them to tears. The stigma associated with the poverty experience was a frequent topic of discussion and many times was tangled with the stigma of benefit receipt or the increase in status associated with market work.

Pam lives in a suburb outside of Madison and receives a rent subsidy. She is in her mid-thirties and identifies as Latina. She has one son in high school. He is very involved in band. She said that experiencing abuse at the hands of her husband for years has made her better able to bear the challenges life places in her path. Her main disability is her mental-health condition. Pam also details her awareness of the stigma associated with welfare: "It feels like people look down on the disabled—you know, the taxpayers versus the nontaxpayers. There's a lot of stigma, like you're under a magnifying glass."

Disability was also associated with perceptions of stigma. In fact, participants were highly aware of the stigma associated with particular impairments, such as mental illness. Susan shared her family's response, one familiar to many of the women: "As for parenthood, my parents didn't react well when I told them I was going to have my son. My father said, 'You don't have the physical ability to raise a child or the means!' He thought I had no business having a child, that I couldn't take care of one."

Single-mother status was also a concern of note in the interviews, with many women aware of inhabiting the margins or borders of motherhood, seeing their realities as juxtaposed against the "normal" married mother. Dolores represents the experience of many when she suggests that people judge single mothers harshly without an understanding of their situation: "What's she doin'? That kid don't have no daddy but I bet she gets welfare." Dolores's disabilities are primarily complications of obesity. She is African American, in her early forties, and lives in subsidized housing in Madison, having lived in the same house for seven years. Her house is warm and filled with family photos. It is also one of the most immaculate houses I have ever seen. She is acutely aware of the stereotypes of obese women and resisted the stereotype of lazy that is often associated with obesity or welfare receipt: "I always tried to dispel the stereotype of obese people. I didn't want people to think since I was obese I had a nasty house or I cooked instant food, or that I was nasty, I didn't groom myself. I wanted to dispel all of that because it's not true of *all* obese people."

She is also quick to demonstrate her "fitness" as mother by pointing out what a good job she is doing raising her children without a father: "I raised them to be gentlemen. They open the door for other people and they'll say, thank you, that's so rare nowadays. Every time we're in a restaurant people will come up and compliment on how well behaved they are."

It is evident that single mothering takes on a particular societal meaning when configured along class or racial lines. Unlike the "domestic intellectuals" described by Juffer (2006), fiercely resisting the patriarchal imperative of two-parent families, the women in this study argued and demonstrated their conceptualizations of themselves as "good" mothers, primarily by embracing the desire for a happy marriage in the future, and their sense of themselves as ideal mothers, fiercely dedicated to their children and placing their own needs after those of their children. They endured the scrutiny and stigma primarily in order to provide for their children by accessing benefit programs. As other scholars note (Reich 2008), they do not have the luxury of being able to opt out of the public benefit system, unlike their middle- and upper-class sisters.

RESISTANCE

I share Ruth Sidel's frustration with the societal discourse surrounding single mothers living in poverty. "It is ironic," she notes, "and particularly poignant that single mothers are being denigrated for what could be cited as their greatest strength: staying and caring for their children under almost all circumstances, frequently at great cost to themselves" (2006, 65). It is ironic, but understandable, as our understanding of such populations is informed by the denigrating discourse associated with single mothers living in poverty (Cassiman 2008; Hays 1998; Mink 1998), mothers of color (Ferguson 2001; Lubiano 1992; Roberts 2002; Swift 1995), and mothers with impairments (Reich 2008).

The women who participated in this project organized their resistance strategies in order to challenge the stigma and social constructions associated with their status as welfare recipients and single disabled mothers, and in order to resist their material realities. Much like the participants in McCormack's study (2004), they embraced the intensive mothering ideology in an effort to resist the stereotypes associated with "bad" or "unfit" mothers. McCormack draws attention to the difficulties women living in poverty encounter in the incorporation of such ideals, ideals that require time and financial commitments unrealistic in the current workfare environment. Although many of the participants in my study expressed a desire to "work" in an effort to avoid the stigma of benefit receipt and poverty, some were quite happy to claim their status as stay-at-home mothers and the effort it entails. Staying at home would not be an option for non-disabled mothers after welfare reform.

Their commitment to the ideal, intensive mother role was evident in their discussion of how they conceptualized caring and mothering, and in this way they straddled worlds of "fit" and "unfit" mothers. All of the women talked about their children as being the first priority and of themselves as "coming last in line" in terms of needs and desires. Many times they identified their children as their reason for living, for persevering in a life otherwise filled with pain and disappointment. They discussed their roles as teachers, protectors, and providers, teaching their children about the world and "how to be good people," protecting them from that same world, often in relation to dangerous neighborhoods, and providing for them financially, physically, and emotionally. In short, with a few exceptions, they described typical concerns of mothers. While the nature of their caring may reflect typical social values of mothering, the will to carry them out in such difficult and challenging circumstances requires persistent effort and therefore represents a remarkable commitment. In sharp contrast to discourses on "unfit" mothers, the women that I interviewed were fiercely protective of their children and invested both their limited material resources and their emotional resources in their children. They viewed their children as the utmost priority, putting themselves, their needs and desires on what one participant called "the back burner." Another described her experience as a single mother—"Mothers are like marines, the first in and the last out"—emphasizing the nature of mothering as an ongoing struggle to care for her children and the need to be ever vigilant. Their references to the child welfare system—as, for example, when some said they could have taken the "easy way out" and let someone else raise their children—are of particular interest to our discussion of "fit" and "unfit" mothers, showing that these women have a resistant view of the system's meanings of these terms.

CONCLUSION: ON THE BORDER, VICTIMS AND HEROES

These women, like many others, suffer from oppressions associated with gender, age, ability, class and race/ethnicity. However, to suggest that they are simply passive victims of oppression does them a grave disservice, while perpetuating the myth of women as weak and dependent (McCormack 2004). To draw attention to the strengths women evidence in the most oppressive of situations, scholars have recently begun to examine the evidence they uncover of resistance as a coping strategy (Parish, Magaña, and Cassiman 2008) and other "everyday" modes of resistance in which many marginalized women engage (Cassiman 2008; Denis 2003; Hollander 2002; McCormack 2004; Riessman 2000; Shorter-Gooden 2004).

In this study, I found that women organize their resistance strategies in order to defend against the stigma and scrutiny associated with their disabilities, single motherhood, and welfare receipt. Sometimes the resistance manifests itself as withdrawal in order to avoid perceptions of being under scrutiny, whether such perceptions are accurate or not. It is important to note that while withdrawal may be a legitimate resistance strategy and serve short-term goals of privacy, it may also mean that women are missing out on resources or support services available to more visible women. Conversely, withdrawal from scrutiny may mean that these women will be less likely to engage the services of child welfare professionals, an important consideration for single mothers on welfare. Visibility is of further concern because, as Susan reminded me, "What you don't see, you don't need to worry about."

While social movements and other organized types of struggles and modes of resistance receive much attention, as do their leaders, we are often ignorant of everyday sorts of resistance. Furthermore, focusing upon women and mothers as *either* victims *or* heroes serves to reinscribe the dualism associated with both liberal thought and positivist research methods. Rather, their position as heroic (Sidal 2006) resisters *and* an oppressed group marks them as both exceptional and average.

Their straddling of these two positions also demonstrates the connections that exist among all mothers. As I have argued elsewhere, relegating some mothers to the social margins serves to obscure similarities while emphasizing differences. However, we are all border dwellers. All mothers are subject to the whims of social and family policy. Swift (1995, 12) reminds us that by sending some mothers to the margins, "the common interests and problems shared by all mothers disappear." For instance, framing welfare as dependence obscures all people's dependencies and interdependence (Fineman 2004). Mink (1998, 19) argues that we should, "reconceive welfare as the income owed to persons who work inside the home caring for, nurturing, and protecting children—mothering." We might then call it something different, like child or care allowance. Segal (2007, 335) suggests that policy should be designed from an empathic position. She argues, "When we have social empathy, we are more likely to develop practices, services, programs, and policies that promote social justice." I have argued elsewhere for the inclusion of a trauma paradigm to aid in discussions of the impact of structural violence or poverty. Policy organized to prevent such trauma would go a long way in service to the women of this study and many others. It is clear that means-tested policy, designed to deal with poverty after the fact, does nothing to address the structural roots of the oppression of poverty and deprivation.

It is important to emphasize that the women in this study, while living extremely difficult lives, were in at least one respect very fortunate; they had the benefit of subsidized housing. I was able to contact them for recruitment because they were less likely to have moved than the majority of the women I attempted to contact from a two-year-old data set. Unfortunately, housing subsidies have been cut in recent federal budgets, meaning that many eligible families are on waiting lists for three years or more. To my knowledge, Wisconsin is the only state to have made specific policy provisions for parents with disabilities. Women in other states may experience even greater levels of hardship.

In addition we must remember that all mothers are subject to the scrutiny of their mothering practices. For some mothers—those living in poverty, welfare reliant, disabled, and mothers of color—the border dwellers, the scrutiny is increased and its impact potentially more devastating. That they choose to mother in a world made so hostile is a testament to their very real commitment to their children, and constitutes heroic effort. However, even a heroine's strength, endurance, and fortitude are finite. We must not allow our social policies to continue to place mothers at risk of losing their children or discourage them from their desire for children, or we, all women and mothers, risk shifting the borderlands until they become the mainland, with no safe haven for mothers and their children.

Afterword(s)

CYNTHIA LEWIECKI-WILSON

and JEN CELLIO

With a nod to Raymond Williams (1976), who collects and analyzes a vocabulary of culturally charged words, and Evelyn Fox Keller and Elisabeth Lloyd (1992), who assemble keywords of evolutionary biology, we have chosen to conclude this volume with a compendium of key words.

We have not compiled this list as a dictionary, index, or glossary in the traditional sense. Our goal is not to stabilize meanings, but instead to surface issues and tensions embedded in these terms and to unravel the perhaps too neat stitches between connections we have made so that other threads may become visible. For as we look back over the editing of this collection, we see a repetition of key concepts that could be arranged in a number of alternate ways or considered as complex subjects in themselves. We also recognize that by placing certain chapters together, and gathering these into thematic sections, we have privileged some ways of understanding the interplay of disability and mothering over other possibilities. In truth, the connections among these chapters and concepts are flexible, and they can be reassembled differently, creating new avenues for future inquiry. We hope this gathering of keywords may thus suggest to readers other ways of adapting concepts to their own disciplinary frameworks, other ways of understanding and using histories of past inquiry, and new areas for future investigation.

While disability and feminist mothering is the topic of this book, and feminist and disability studies inform our approaches, we the editors are also situated in writing and rhetoric. This disciplinary framework for interpreting and analyzing culture is grounded in language and tends to understand worlds first through words. Words have what Keller and Lloyd call traveling power (2); they can move beyond their situated moment and generalize worlds, and in this regard we wish to be careful. As we argued in the introduction, we do not want to forget embodied knowledge, situated experience, and complex histories and structures—that is, the complex contexts of words and concepts. On the one hand, then, the emphasis on the power of language to inform attitudes, to make meaning, to shape reality, to persuade, to move, and to inform has led us to compile key words as a way of reflecting on this volume. In doing so, we agree with Williams (1976, 15) that "certain uses" of language bind "together certain ways of seeing culture and society." And when readers reassemble these words, concepts, and chapters in different ways, they are beginning the process of re-seeing culture. On the other hand, as Keller and Lloyd note in their introduction (6), keywords are also repositories of historical scientific constructs at a particular moment. They also embed disciplinary perspectives. And they can provide "a rough map" of "some of the territory of dispute and change" (6). Although they can be reassembled, history, time, disciplinarity, and even entrenched debates limit their pliability and reconstructive possibilities, too. With those cautions in mind, we present this set of keywords and concepts with the hope that readers may use these as starting points for discussion and further inquiry.

Abelism: A term in disability studies somewhat parallel to racism, sexism, or homophobia, ableism expresses the preference for and social advantages of being nondisabled. Ableism is an ideology through which the nondisabled see themselves as able and normal and part of the mainstream, and thereby deserving of social arrangements that are organized to suit their needs. Ableism is also closely aligned with naturalist arguments that those who hold power do so because they have been endowed by nature with superior abilities. Writing of Cindy Sheehan's antiwar rhetorical strategies, Abby Dubisar notes that Sheehan often risks reinforcing ableism when Sheehan points to maimed, disabled veterans produced by war as a terrible tragedy. This is a rhetorical move that reinforces the dominant view of disability as monstrous. Julie Minich notes that Cherríe Moraga's play *Heroes and Saints* veers away from contesting ableism when Moraga seems to link body normativity with a reimagined Chicana nationalism. On the preference for fitness, see Jen Cellio's "'Healthy, Accomplished, and Attractive': Representations of 'Fitness' in Egg Donors"; on the presumed advantage and greater rights of being nondisabled, see Samantha Walsh's "'What Does It Matter?' A Meditation on the Social Positioning of Disability and Motherhood." See also *Fit, fitness*.

Access, accommodations: Perhaps no other elements of disability rights law are as crucial or revolutionary as are the concepts of insuring access through accommodations. The two necessarily go together. Access is the freedom to approach, enter, and use a resource, but to be actualized, access requires accommodations for the individual or group; otherwise, it just remains an abstraction. Ramps, automatic doors, bathroom rails are obvious accommodations that promote access for people with physical disabilities, but just as important are other kinds of accommodations and broader definitions of access. Are health care, educational resources, and a curriculum accessible to a wide range of people, for instance? See Whitney Jones-Garcia on her attempts to access mental-health supports for her mother, Denise Hughes-Tafen on her mother's struggles to access an appropriate education for her autistic son, and Rachel Robertson on the need for a standard curriculum to accommodate the particular learning needs and talents of her son. Access and accommodations are disability concepts that can be productively applied across other categories of exclusion.

Activism, allies: In disability studies, as in feminism, activism has often been placed in opposition to academic study, and mothers have rarely been considered activists. In addition to the obvious examples in this collection of activists—not only the pieces collected in part 4, but also the day-to-day activist parenting as exemplified by Heather Kuttai's diary on breastfeeding or Rachel Robertson's narrative of parenting her son—how can alliances among subjugated groups create networks of activism? In what ways are allies enmeshed in "nested" relations of care with activists (see discussion of Eva Feder Kittay in the introduction)? How can the concept of interdependency and the action of allies expand and empower activism?

Care, dependency: In the last thirty years, a feminist ethic of care (Noddings 1984; Kittay 1999) has been proposed as well as contested, particularly on the grounds that it risks essentializing and reinscribing patriarchal gender roles in which women are relegated to the private sphere and are expected to care for others, especially to provide bodily care for others. For these reasons we are likewise wary of a feminist ethic of care. Yet theorizing care—what its role in the social order is, who gives care and how it is dispensed, what its relation is to justice—is a fundamental issue in disability studies. In our introduction, we cite Eva Kittay's work on care, especially her theory of nested relations of obligation to care for those giving care. Kittay's philosophy grows out of social contract theory and is grounded in the embodied experiences of mothering a child with disability. As we note in the introduction, we prefer the term *interdependency* to dependency relations (the term she uses), for its rhetorical efficacy in conveying that all humans, not just some, live in relation to and dependence upon myriad others, and that all humans, not just women, are already enmeshed in relations of caring. Many contributors to this volume write about the complexities and relations of care: Kristin Lindgren and Suzanne Bost on the need of disabled mothers for support in mothering; Corinne Manning and Marilyn Dolmage on institutions of care; Shawn Cassiman and Heather Kuttai on the beneficial effect of caring for others, even when poor or in pain; Elizabeth Metcalf for a cataloging of her mother's care. See also *Interdependency.*

Citizenship, civil rights: Disability theorists Tobin Siebers (2008, 18–20) and Paul Longmore and Lauri Umansky (2001, 1), among others, consider disability a minority-group identity, citing the ADA as a model of a civil rights law that brings people with disabilities from "the margins of society into the mainstream" of a multicultural society. There are notable tensions, however, with this view. Most obviously, disability is not a single identity in the same way that a racial category is. Further, identities are multiple and complicating—as related, for example, in Hughes-Tafen's narrative of her mother's noncitizen border troubles. While her disabled son, born in the United States, had a right to a public education, this right could not be easily secured because his mother was a noncitizen. And multicultural politics itself has troubles, as discussed in Lewiecki-Wilson's "Uneasy Subjects." Multicultural identity politics can be a means through which neoliberalism sustains itself. And neoliberal policies—such as those described by Cassiman in "Mothering, Disability, and Poverty"—are not disability friendly. While extolling disability rights as a cause for national pride, neoliberal policies on the local and national level reduce supports for the disabled.

Political citizenship in the second half of the twentieth century took visible form through group actions like strikes and marches. Group demonstrations like the ADAPT bus action of 1978, Gallaudet's 1988 "Deaf President Now Action" (Disability History Timeline 2002), and 1990's Capitol Hill Crawl, led up to the passage of the ADA. However, in the twenty-first century, biopolitics and "biological citizenship" (Rose 2007, 6)—discussed briefly by Cellio in "Healthy, Accomplished, and Attractive" and Lewiecki-Wilson in "Uneasy Subjects"—grounded in an ethic of the individual's healthy body, may be replacing older notions of group politics and political citizenship. In both neoliberal and biological models of citizenship, the disabled are seen as a burden, not self-reliant enough, and subject to "regulating rationalities" (Rose 2007, 95). Which models of citizenship and rights will prevail in national debates about health care, social supports, and work policies? How will people with disabilities fare in an age of "biological citizenship" when biological self-sufficiency may be a warrant for political rights?

Embodiment: The concept of embodiment, explored in many chapters of this volume, contains many tensions: moment-to-moment bodily experiences and their role in creating knowledge; the historical and cultural construction of bodies and ideal bodies; the devaluing of bodily experience; the body in pain; regimens and demands for fit bodies; the relation of a body to its environment. Some authors, such as Heather Kuttai and Samantha Walsh, construct bodily narratives, sharing their experiences as physical and social beings in their environments. Similarly, Felicity Board-man offers firsthand accounts of embodiment in the lives of women living with SMA. Other authors present bodies and embodiment as a space for inquiry into social mores and norms: see Terri Beth Miller's discussion of the deviant body and Abby Wilkerson's on the stigma attached to dif-ference and the possibilities for using bodily adornment to resist what Lennard Davis (1995) has called the hegemony of normalcy. We could cite many other examples from this volume. As our title suggests, the phe-nomenology of experience and the historical and cultural construction of bodies mutually constitute one another, meet, and overlap in the liminal spaces of situated embodiment.

Fit, fitness: Although the first uses of these words predate the nineteenth century by some three hundred years, fit and fitness come down to us laden with the nineteenth century's legacy of Social Darwinism's "survival of the fittest." That legacy also includes the history of eugenics, a social and polit-ical movement that sought to improve a nation's population through birth control, sterilization of the "unfit," and barriers to immigrations for certain ethnic and racial groups. The disabled, as well as the poor and immigrants, were the primary objects of these policies of exclusion and came to repre-sent the "unfit." Apart from its more historical eugenic and Social Darwin-istic uses, the notion of being "fit" for motherhood and parenting retains both social and biological connotations that leave women with disabilities, with fertility complications, or with markers for genetic diseases open to judgment and criticism. For example, a common response to women who cannot conceive or bear children "naturally" is that they are not "fit" to be mothers. In her essay on egg donor websites, Jen Cellio explores the ana-logical relationship between so-called "fit" donors and the "unfit" women who seek their assistance. Likewise, as Samantha Walsh, Terri Beth Miller, and Felicity Boardman note, women with disabilities are often presumed to be incapable of mothering or selfish/delusional for trying. The fact that "fitness" today is mostly associated with personal health does not obviate these former meanings, but demonstrates the ways in which sociopolitical concepts have morphed into personal, bioethical imperatives.

Identity: Disability cannot really be said to be an identity because there are so many different kinds of disability, because many disabilities are experienced as fluctuating and not steady states, and because other kinds of identity (sexual, racial, ethnic, class, immigrant, or citizen, for example) might intersect with and complicate its effects or override the disability, determining in sharper ways how one is treated and what barriers one faces. Yet disabled people can and do come together and claim a disability identity for political purposes. Cumulatively, the essays in this book suggest that disability identity is one of many overlapping identities, and that it emerges from a confluence of embodied experiences and social constructs. See also *Subjectivity.*

Institutions, institutionalization: The role of institutions in disability studies and mothering is fraught—both as a historical subject and as a current debate. On one hand, institutions for those who were then called criminally insane or feeble-minded (Trent 1994) could be cruel and cold. Treatments ranged from ineffective to untested to barbaric and torturous; inhabitants were often held against their will with no hope for release. Often cited as "a last resort," individuals who could not cope with or meet the needs of a loved one might find themselves with little choice apart from an institution. On the other hand, such institutions could be viewed as "safe places" where a loved one might possibly receive the care he or she truly needed. Unlike a jail, an institution might contain certified physicians and knowledgeable staff, offering the hope of treatment or comfort. Unlike the home, an institution could provide constant companionship and monitoring, attention family members could not or would not provide.

Our complicated relationship with institutions and institutionalization continues, and many of the same concerns emerge in essays contained in this volume. For Whitney Jones-Garcia, the institution presents a paradox: her mother requires full-time assistance and care, yet her mother's refusal to enter willingly, coupled with recent accounts of neglect at nearby hospitals and care facilities, leaves Jones-Garcia questioning her own judgment. Abby Wilkerson's account of her daughter's treatment at a modern facility casts doubt on the quality of care individuals receive.

For Marilyn Dolmage, a brother's institutionalization and the surrounding secrecy prompted her life of activism and her decision to care for her son Matt at home. Corinne Manning's historical study of Kew Cottages in Australia reveals the intricate relationships and hazy distinctions between caretakers and residents.

Interdependency: The *Oxford English Dictionary* cites the first uses of this word in the 1830s—with the general meaning of mutual dependence. Later in the nineteenth century its meaning seems associated with evolution—that all living things are interdependent. It is our belief that the pairing of disability and mothering highlights this universal condition of mutual relationality and interdependence.

Writing about education and community support for the disabled, Condeluci (1995, 90) sees interdependence as a new paradigm that "defines the problem of disability not from what is wrong with the person but from the context of limited supports." In this new paradigm, educators and community service providers help in the building of relationships that extend opportunities for participation. Yet interdependence carries a quite different meaning in political science and international relations. Derived from liberal cooperation theory, interdependence is the term for a belief in global, international cooperation, based on shared capitalist interests, beyond the nation-state (Sterling-Folker 2002). In our use of the word, we emphasize mutual responsibility for care and acknowledgment of mutual dependency, which is markedly different from the neoliberal capitalist sense of cooperation by autonomous nations to enhance mutual interests. Is it possible to reclaim this word from capitalist theories of international relations? Is there really a difference between the terms dependency relations and interdependency, as both are used in liberal social contract theory? See also *Care, dependency.*

Medicalization: In disability studies, medicalization refers to the historical fact that by the eighteenth century disability came under the purview of medicine—became something to be diagnosed, treated, and preferably cured. Medicalized, the disabled body (for the person recedes from view) became objectified, classified, and isolated, often in specialized institutions. In the twenty-first century disabilities are still predominantly viewed as medical conditions, to be cured or contained, and it is not surprising that a number of contributors write of wishing to resist diagnosis (Rodas) or to escape the clutches of medical control (Wilkerson). Yet medical treatment also offers help to the disabled, as a number of other contributors detail. Whether surgery (Kuttai), mental health services (Jones-Garcia), or rehabilitation (Maybee), people with disability and their families seek to access medical resources as well as to critique the ways they are delivered. Between these poles—of being dominated and objectified by medicine and being aided by it—there is a space for those working in disability studies to build more disability-centered theories of bioculture and biopolitics.

Mothering: We chose the form of a verbal—not a noun (person, place, or thing)—to suggest the practices and activities involved with caring for others, activities that are not necessarily limited by genes, gender, or generation. While all the pieces in this volume are related to mothering, see Whitney Jones-Garcia, "My Mother's Mental Illness," for an example of a daughter mothering her mother; Kristin Lindgren, "Reconceiving Motherhood," on the need for caretaking for birth mothers; Linnéa Franits on generational narratives of mothering; and Corinne Manning, "From Surrender to Activism: The Transformation of Disability and Mothering at Kew Cottages, Australia," for examples of mothering by adult disabled women in institutional settings. Mothering can thus be thought of as an action and a form of activism in relation to others, not an identity.

Nation, nationalism: The movement for disability rights extends across the globe and is not limited to one or a few countries. The United Nations Convention on the Rights of Persons with Disabilities (2008) promotes the right of the disabled to be treated as autonomous civil subjects possessing human dignity, not as objects of charity, medical treatment, or protective custody. That said, it is still difficult for people with disability around the globe to secure these rights. Serious impediments are caused by poverty, civil unrest or war, a nation's intent to remain independent from outside influence, immigration laws, geographical isolation, and more. Even when disabled people live inside a country granting them rights, they may face problems crossing national borders. Transnational migrants with disability fare even worse. Historically, immigration laws in the United States barred people with disability, especially mental disability, from entering the country in the belief they would become a public burden or weaken the national stock. People from particular ethnic groups were excluded or their numbers restricted; those with various illnesses and homosexuals were also denied entry. Although most of these restrictions were removed with the Immigration Act of 1990, their legacy lives on in common beliefs associating national vigor and patriotism with normatively sexed and raced, able bodies. Contributors to this volume analyze these contradictions of nation for the disabled. Julie Minich explores the intersection of nation, race, sexuality, and disability in "You Gotta Make Aztlán Any Way You Can." Denise Cordella Hughes-Tafen traces the many border crossings of her mother and brother, in their search to secure his right to an appropriate education in "Intersecting the Postcolonial Mother and Disability," while Abby Dubisar analyzes the how disability metaphor is precariously used in antiwar rhetoric of Cindy Sheehan.

Normativity: Since the 1990s, scholars in disability studies (Garland-Thomson 1997, L. Davis 1995) have been interrogating the history and dominance of the norm. As Lennard Davis writes (1995, 24), "the 'problem' is not the person with disabilities; the problem is the way that normalcy is constructed to create the 'problem' of the disabled person." Just as whiteness has a history and functions as an unexamined center around which "race" as difference revolves and comes into view, so the concept of the norm has a history and functions similarly. Invisible and unexamined assumptions about the "normal" body make the disabled body visible as different, deficient, or deviant. Sally Chivers and Nicole Markotić (2010) call the nonnormative body the "the problem body" and argue that, projected onto the flat surface of film, disabled bodies allow the audience to inhabit a range of fantasy positions in relation to it. As we write in the introduction, the fantasy is, of course, that nondisabled people feel as though they inhabit whole, able, and "normal" bodies and are securely separate from "them," the disabled, and all the deviant others marked off as "not me." How forcefully a society draws a boundary line, cordoning off disability, is seen in a number of pieces in this volume, especially in part 1 on the practices and normative values in reproductive technologies. What may be more surprising, however, is how frequently embodied experiences of disability lead people to reject normative assumptions, to think afresh and independently, to go against the grain, whether in taking risks or in refusing to be made to fit into the social role of the "problem" body. Examples are Felicity Boardman's "Negotiating Discourses of Maternal Responsibility, Disability, and Reprogenetics: The Role of Experiential Knowledge"; Terri Beth Miller's "Stalking Grendel's Mother: Biomedicine and the Disciplining of the Deviant Body"; and Abby Wilkerson's "Refusing Diagnosis: Mother-Daughter Agency in Confronting Psychiatric Rhetoric."

Passing, queer studies, race studies: The concept of passing, first developed in critical race studies, has been fruitfully applied to disability. Brenda Jo Brueggemann (1997), a hard of hearing disability scholar, has written about her coming out and rites of passage amid hearing and Deaf worlds. Tobin Siebers (2008) has used the term *masquerade* to describe the strategy of sometimes appearing more disabled than at other times for particular purposes. In this volume, Julia Miele Rodas meditates on the benefits and drawbacks of coming out as disabled. "Coming out" is another borrowed concept, this time from queer studies. Such borrowings demonstrate the productivity of alliances across identity studies areas (see McRuer 2006), but moreover suggest the overlaps, complexity, and fluidity of identity itself.

Subjectivity, subjectification, vulnerable subjects: Many disability scholars follow Judith Butler (1999a and 1999b) in considering identities multiple, performative, and fluid subject positions we are called to take up. Often they don't quite fit, or we don't fit the expected roles, and in that sense we are subjected to them as well as subjectified by them. Samantha Walsh writes about her unease with the social positioning of motherhood for a disabled woman. Julie Maybee analyzes the ways that her positions, as feminist, white, and married to an African American, and then as mother of a disabled daughter, pull her between a number of conflicting positions. Suzanne Bost details two writers, Nancy Mairs and Cherríe Moraga, who eschew the more typical autonomy of American identity and instead embrace vulnerable subjectivity and interdependence. See also *identity*.

References

Index

References

Abel, Emily K., and Carole Browner. 1998. "Selective Compliance with Biomedical Authority and the Uses of Experiential Knowledge." In *Pragmatic Women and Body Politics,* edited by Margaret Lock and Patricia Kaufert, 310–26. Cambridge: Cambridge Univ. Press.

Agamben, Gorgio. 1998. *Homer Sacer: Sovereignty, Power, and Bare Life.* Translated by D. Heller-Roazan. Stanford: Stanford Univ. Press.

Albrecht, Gary, Ray Fitzpatrick, and Susan Scrimshaw, eds. 2003. *Handbook of Social Studies in Health and Medicine.* Thousand Oaks: Sage.

Alonso, Harriet Hyman. 1993. *Peace as a Woman's Issue: A History of the United States Movement for World Peace and Women's Rights.* Syracuse: Syracuse Univ. Press.

Americans with Disability Act of 1990, as Amended (ADA). 2009. Department of Justice. http://www.ada.gov/pubs/ada.htm.

Aristotle. 1991. *On Rhetoric: A Theory of Civil Discourse.* Translated by George A. Kennedy. New York: Oxford Univ. Press.

Asch, Adrienne. 1999. "Prenatal Diagnosis and Selective Abortion: A Challenge to Practice and Policy." *American Journal of Public Health* 89, no. 11:1649–57.

———. 2000. "Why I Haven't Changed My Mind about Prenatal Diagnosis: Reflections and Refinements." In *Prenatal Testing and Disability Rights,* edited by Erik Parens and Adrienne Asch, 234–60. Washington, DC: Georgetown Univ. Press.

———. 2001. "Disability, Bioethics, and Human Rights." In *Handbook of Disability Studies,* edited by Gary L. Albrecht, Katherine D. Seelman, and Michael Bury, 297–326. Thousand Oaks: Sage.

———. 2004. "Critical Race Theory, Feminism, and Disability: Reflections on Social Justice and Personal Identity." In *Gendering Disability,* edited by Bonnie G. Smith and Beth Hutchison, 9–44. New Brunswick, NJ: Rutgers Univ. Press.

Ashe, Bertram D. 1995. "'Why Don't He Like My Hair?' Constructing African-American Standards of Beauty in Toni Morrison's *Song of Solomon* and Zora

317

Neale Hurston's *Their Eyes Were Watching God.*" *African American Review* 29, no. 4:579–92.

Asperger, Hans. 1991. "'Autistic Psychopathy' in Childhood." In *Autism and Asperger Syndrome,* edited by Uta Frith, 37–92. New York: Cambridge Univ. Press.

Aston, Maxine. 2003. *Aspergers in Love: Couple Relationships and Family Affairs.* London: Jessica Kingsley.

Atkinson, Dorothy. 2004. "Research and Empowerment: Involving People with Learning Difficulties in Oral and Life History Research." *Disability and Society* 19, no. 7:691–702.

Atkinson, Dorothy, Mark Jackson, and Jan Walmsley. 1997a. *Forgotten Lives: Exploring the History of Learning Disability.* Kidderminster, UK: BILD Publications.

———. 1997b. *Research and Empowerment: Involving People with Learning Difficulties in Oral and Life History Research.* Kidderminster, UK: BILD Publications.

Atkinson, Dorothy, et al. 2000. *Good Times, Bad Times: Women with Learning Difficulties Telling Their Stories.* Kidderminster, UK: BILD Publications.

Atkinson, Dorothy, et al. 2005. *Witnesses to Change: Families, Learning Difficulties and History.* Kidderminster, UK: BILD Publications.

Atkinson, Rebecca. 2008. "My Baby, Right or Wrong." *The Guardian,* 10 Mar., sec. G2, 16.

Barnes, Colin, and Geoff Mercer. 2003. *Disability.* Cambridge: Polity.

Barrow, Christine. 1996. *Family in the Caribbean: Themes and Perspectives.* Kingston, Jam.: Ian Randle.

Bazerman, Charles. 1988. *Shaping Written Knowledge: The Genre and Activity of the Experimental Article in Science.* Madison: Univ. of Wisconsin Press.

"Becoming an Egg Donor." 2008. *New York State Department of Health.* http://www.health.state.ny.us/publications/1127/.

Bell, Rudolph M., and Virginia Yans, eds. 2008. *Women on Their Own: Interdisciplinary Perspectives on Being Single.* New Brunswick, NJ: Rutgers Univ. Press.

Benjamin, Medea, and Jodie Evans, eds. 2005. *Stop the Next War Now: Effective Responses to Violence and Terrorism.* Maui: Inner Ocean.

Bérubé, Michael. 1996. *Life as We Know It: A Father, a Family, and an Exceptional Child.* NY: Pantheon.

Biklen, Douglas, et al. 2005. *Autism and the Myth of the Person Alone.* New York: New York Univ. Press.

Birke, Lynda. 2000. *Feminism and the Biological Body.* New Brunswick, NJ: Rutgers Univ. Press.

Body of War. 2007. Produced and directed by Ellen Spiro and Phil Donahue. Docurama Films.

Bogdan, Robert, and Steven Taylor. 1976. "The Judged, Not the Judges: An Insider's View of Mental Retardation." *American Psychologist* 31:47–52.

———. 1982. *Inside Out: The Social Meaning of Retardation.* Toronto: Univ. of Toronto Press.

Bonner, Lynn. 2008. "Report Rips N.C. Hospital Staff: Man Died After Being Ignored for 22 Hours." *Chicago Tribune Online*, 20 Aug., http://articles.chicagotribune.com/2008-08-20/news/0808190609_1_hospital-staff-nurses-investigators-report.

Born on the Fourth of July. 1989. Directed by Oliver Stone. Ixtlan Productions.

Boston Women's Health Course Collective. [1973] 1992. *The New Our Bodies, Ourselves: A Book By and For Women.* New York: Simon and Schuster.

Bould, Sally. 1993. "Familial Caretaking: A Middle-Range Definition of Family in the Context of Social Policy." *Journal of Family Issues* 14, no. 1:133–51.

Bowler, Emma. 2006. "How Will I Cope with a 'Normal' Baby?" *The Guardian*, 11 Dec., sec. G2, 16.

Bowman, James E. 1977. "Genetic Screening and Public Policy." *Phylon* 38, no. 2:117–42.

Boyd, Susan. 2004. *From Witches to Crack Moms: Women, Drug Law, and Policy.* Durham: Carolina Academic Press.

Brady, Wilfrid. 1962. "The Mental Health Act." *Australian Children Limited* 1:345.

Brigham, Lindsay, et al. 2000. *Crossing Boundaries: Change and Continuity in the History of Learning Disability.* Kidderminster, UK: BILD Publications.

Brownworth, Victoria A. 1999. "Introduction." In *Restricted Access: Lesbians on Disability*, edited by Victoria A. Brownworth and Susan Raffo, xi–xxii.

Brownworth, Victoria A., and Susan Raffo, eds. 1999. *Restricted Access: Lesbians on Disability.* Seattle: Seal Press.

Brueggemann, Brenda Jo. 1997. "On (Almost) Passing." *College English* 59, no. 6:647–60.

———. 1999. *Lend Me Your Ear: Rhetorical Constructions of Deafness.* Washington: Gallaudet Univ. Press.

Bryan, Alison, Teresa Blankmeyer-Burke, and Steven Emery. 2006. "Human Fertilisation and Embryology Bill: Genetic Selection and the Deaf Community." Slideshare, http://www.slideshare.net/grumpyoldeafies/human-fertilisation-and-embryology-bill-genetic-selection-the-deaf-community-presentation.

Buck v. Bell, 274 U.S. 200. 1927. *United States Reports: Decisions of the United States Supreme Court.* http://ftp.resource.org/courts.gov/c/US/274/274.US .200.292.html.

Burke, Kenneth. 1966. *Language as Symbolic Action: Essays on Life, Literature and Method.* Berkeley: Univ. of California Press.

Butler, Judith. 1999a. *Bodies That Matter: On the Discursive Limits of "Sex."* New York: Routledge.

———. 1999b. *Gender Trouble: Feminism and the Subversion of Identity.* New York: Routledge.

Cassiman, Shawn A. 2006. "Of Witches, Welfare Queens, and the Disaster Named Poverty: The Search for a Counter-Narrative." *Journal of Poverty* 10:51–66.

———. 2008. *Everyday Resistance among Poor Disabled Single Mothers.* PhD diss., Univ. of Wisconsin. Ann Arbor, MI.

Castelnuovo, Shirley, and Sharon Guthrie. 1998. *Feminism and the Female Body: Liberating the Amazon Within.* Boulder: Lynne Rienner.

Charo, R. Alta, and Karen H. Rothenberg. 1994. "'The Good Mother': The Limits of Reproductive Accountability and Genetic Choice." In *Women and Prenatal Testing: Facing the Challenges of Genetic Technology,* edited by Karen H. Rothenberg and Elizabeth J. Thomson, 105–30. Columbus: Ohio State Univ. Press.

Chivers, Sally, and Nicole Markotić. 2010. *The Problem Body: Projecting Disability on Film.* Columbus: Ohio State Univ. Press.

Clare, Eli. 1999. *Exile and Pride: Disability, Queerness, and Liberation.* Cambridge, MA: South End Press.

Clark, Camille (Autism Diva Blogspot). 2006. "Conferences, Culture, Communication, Ages, Aegis and Diagnosis." 22 Aug., http://autismdiva.blogspot.com/ .../conferences-culture-communication-ages.html.

Cocks, Errol, et al., eds. 1996. *Under Blue Skies: The Social Construction of Intellectual Disability in Western Australia.* Perth: Centre for Disability Research and Development, Faculty of Health and Human Sciences, Edith Cowan Univ.

Coleborne, Catharine, and Dolly MacKinnon, eds. 2003. *Madness in Australia: Histories, Heritage and the Asylum.* St. Lucia: Univ. of Queensland Press.

Collins, Patricia Hill. 1990. *Black Feminist Thought: Knowledge, Consciousness, and the Politics of Empowerment.* New York: Routledge.

———. 1998. *Fighting Words: Black Women and the Search for Justice.* Minneapolis: Univ. of Minnesota Press.

Coming Home. 1978. Directed by Hal Ashby. Jerome Hellman, United Artists Productions.

Condeluci, Al. 1995. *Interdependence.* 2nd ed. Winter Park, FL: GR Press, Inc.

"Convention on the Rights of Persons with Disabilities." 2008. United Nations Enable: Rights and Dignity of Persons with Disabilities. http://www.un.org/disabilities/default.asp?id=150.

"Couple 'Choose' to Have Deaf Baby." 2002. *BBC News,* 8 Apr., http://news.bbc.co.uk/2/hi/health/1916462.stm.

Couser, G. Thomas. 2008. "From Conflicting Paradigms: The Rhetorics of Disability Memoir." In *Disability and the Teaching of Writing,* edited by Cynthia Lewiecki-Wilson and Brenda Brueggemann, 190–97. New York: St. Martin's Press.

Crittenden, Ann. 2001. *The Price of Motherhood: Why the Most Important Job in the World Is Still the Least Valued.* New York: Metropolitan Books.

Crowley, Sharon. 2006. *Toward a Civil Discourse: Rhetoric and Fundamentalism.* Pittsburgh: Univ. of Pittsburgh Press.

Cudd, Ann. 1994. "Oppression by Choice." *Journal of Social Philosophy* 25:22–44.

Curra, John. 2000. *The Relativity of Deviance.* Thousand Oaks: Sage.

Dalley, Gillian. 1996. *Ideologies of Caring.* New York: Macmillan.

Davis, Lennard J. 1995. *Enforcing Normalcy: Disability, Deafness, and the Body.* New York: Verso.

———. 2006. "The End of Identity Politics and the Beginning of Dismodernism: On Disability as an Unstable Category." In *The Disability Studies Reader,* 2nd ed., 231–42. New York: Routledge.

Dax, Eric. 1961. *Asylum to Community: The Development of the Mental Hygiene Service in Victoria, Australia.* Melbourne: F. W. Cheshire.

Dekker, Martijn. 2006. "On Our Own Terms: Emerging Autistic Culture." Original URL unavailable; article archived at http://www.aspiesforfreedom.com/archive/index.php/thread-315.html.

Deleuze, Giles. 2005. *Pure Immanence: Essays on a Life.* Translated by A. Boyman. New York: Zone Books.

Denis, Ann B. 2003. "Globalization, Women, and (In)Equity in the South: Constraint and Resistance in Barbados." *International Sociology* 18:491–512.

Diagnostic and Statistical Manual of Mental Disorders (DSM-IV). 1994. 4th ed. Arlington: American Psychiatric Association.

Disability History Timeline. 2002. http://isc.temple.edu/neighbor/ds/disabilityrightstimeline.htm.

Dolmage, Jay. 2005. "Between the Valley and the Field." *Prose Studies* 27, no. 1:108–19.

Dolmage, Jay, and Cynthia Lewiecki-Wilson. 2010. "Refiguring Rhetorica: Linking Feminist Rhetoric and Disability Studies." In *Rhetorica in Motion: Researching Feminist Rhetorical Methods and Methodologies,* edited by Eileen Schell and Kelly Rawson, 36–60. Pittsburgh: Univ. of Pittsburgh Press.

Dowling, Monica, and Linda Dolan. 2001. "Families with Children with Disabilities—Inequalities and the Social Model." *Disability and Society* 6, no. 1: 21–35.

Dragonas, Thalia. 2001. "Whose Fault Is It? Shame and Guilt for the Genetic Defect." In *Before Birth: Understanding Prenatal Screening,* edited by Elizabeth Ettorre, 127–42. Aldershot, UK: Ashgate.

Dubowitz, Victor. 1995. "Disorders of the Lower Motor Neuron: The Spinal Muscular Atrophies." In *Muscle Disorders in Childhood,* 2nd ed. London: Saunders.

Duggan, Lisa. 2003. *The Twilight of Equality?: Neoliberalism, Cultural Politics, and the Attack on Democracy.* Boston: Beacon Press.

Echols, Alice. 1992. "'Women Power' and Women's Liberation: Exploring the Relationship Between the Antiwar Movement and the Women's Liberation Movement." In *Give Peace a Chance: Exploring the Vietnam Antiwar Movement,* edited by Melvin Small and William D. Hoover, 171–81. Syracuse: Syracuse Univ. Press, 1992.

Education for All Handicapped Children Act. 1970. Amended 1974. http://edocket.access.gpo.gov/cfr_2005/janqtr/7cfr15b.3.htm.

Edwards, Steven D. 2004. "Disability, Identity, and the 'Expressivist Objection.'" *Journal of Medical Ethics* 30:418–20.

"Egg Donation for Recipient Parents." 2008. *The Egg Donor Program.* http://www.eggdonation.com/.

Egg Donation, Inc. Online. 2008. Egg Donation, Inc. https://eggdonor.com/.

Elman, Julie Passanante. 2008. "Medicalizing Edutainment: Enforcing Disability in the Teen Body, 1970–2000." PhD diss., George Washington Univ., Washington, DC.

Equal Rights Amendment (ERA). n.d. Alice Paul Institute and the National Council of Women's Organizations. http://www.equalrightsamendment.org/.

Esquibel, Catrióna Rueda. 2006. *With Her Machete in Her Hand: Reading Chicana Lesbians.* Austin: Univ. of Texas Press.

Estabrook, Arthur H. 1916. "The Jukes in 1915." Carnegie Institution of Washington, Disability History Museum, http://www.disabilitymuseum.org/lib/docs/759.htm.

Etchegary, Holly, et al. 2008. "The Influence of Experiential Knowledge on Prenatal Screening and Testing Decisions." *Genetic Testing* 12, no. 1:115–24.

Fahnestock, Jeanne. 2002. *Rhetorical Figures in Science.* Oxford: Oxford Univ. Press.

Fanon, Frantz. 1963. *Wretched of the Earth.* Translated by Constance Farrington. New York: Grove.

Fausto-Sterling, Anne. 2005. "The Bare Bones of Sex: Part 1—Sex and Gender." *Signs: Journal of Women in Culture and Society* 30, no. 2:1491–1527.

Ferguson, Philip M. 2001. "Mapping the Family: Disability Studies and the Exploration of Parental Responses to Disability." In *Handbook of Social Studies in Health and Medicine,* edited by Gary L. Albrecht, Katherine D. Seelman, and Michael Bury, 373–95. Thousand Oaks: Sage.

Ferner, Mike. 2006. *Inside the Red Zone: A Veteran for Peace Reports from Iraq.* Westport: Praeger.

Fineman, Martha Albertson. 2004. *The Autonomy Myth: A Theory of Dependency.* New York: New Press.

Finger, Anne. 1990. *Past Due: A Story of Disability, Pregnancy, and Birth.* Seattle: Seal Press.

Fletcher, Agnes. 2002. "Making It Better? Disability and Genetic Choice." In *Designer Babies: Where Should We Draw the Line?,* edited by Ellie Lee. London: Hodder and Stoughton.

Flohr, Fritz. "Against Psychiatry." *Gay Shame,* http://www.gayshamesf.org/against psychiatry.html.

Forest Gump. 1994. Directed by Robert Zemeckis. Paramount Pictures.

Foucault, Michel. [1975] 1999. *Abnormal: Lectures at the College de France, 1974–1975.* Translated by Graham Burchell. New York: Picador.

———. 1977. *Discipline and Punish.* Translated by Alan Sheridan. New York: Vintage.

———. 2003. "The Birth of Biopolitics." *Michel Foucault: Ethics, Subjectivity and Truth.* Edited by Paul Rabinow. New York: New Press.

———. 2006. *Ethics: Subjectivity and Truth. Essential Works of Foucault, 1954–1984.* Vol. 1. Translated and edited by Paul Rabinow. New York: New Press.

Frank, Arthur. 2004. "Asking the Right Question about Pain: Narrative and Phronesis." *Literature and Medicine* 23, no. 2: 209–26.

Fraser, Nancy, and Linda Gordon. 1994. "A Genealogy of Dependency: Tracing a Keyword of the U.S. Welfare State." *Signs* 19, no. 2:309–36.

Fregoso, Rosa Linda. 2003. *MeXicana Encounters: The Making of Social Identities on the Borderlands.* Berkeley: Univ. of California Press.

Galleymore, Susan. 2004. MotherSpeak. 14 Jan., http://www.motherspeak.org/.

———. 2009. *Long Time Passing: Mothers Speak about War and Terror.* London: Pluto.

Garland-Thomson, Rosemarie. 1997. *Extraordinary Bodies: Figuring Physical Disability in American Culture and Literature*. New York: Columbia Univ. Press.

———. 2006. "Integrating Disability, Transforming Feminist Theory." In *The Disability Studies Reader*. 2nd ed., edited by Lennard Davis, 257–73. New York: Routledge.

Garrison, Michelle M., et al. 2004. "Mental Illness Hospitalizations of Youth in Washington State." *Archives of Pediatrics and Adolescent Medicine* 158, no. 8:781–85.

Gates, Henry Louis, Jr. 1994. "In the Kitchen." In *Colored People: A Memoir*, 40–49. New York: Knopf.

"Gene Testing." 2008. Human Genome Project Information. http://www.ornl.gov/sci/techresources/Human_Genome/medicine/genetest.shtml.

Gentner, Dedre, and Michael Jeziorski. 1979. "The Shift from Metaphor to Analogy in Western Science." In *Metaphor and Thought*. 2nd ed., edited by Andrew Ortony, 447–80. Cambridge: Cambridge Univ. Press.

Gerber, David A., ed. 2000. *Disabled Veterans in History*. Ann Arbor: Univ. of Michigan Press.

Glaser, Barney G., and Anselm L. Strauss. 1967. *The Discovery of Grounded Theory: Strategies For Qualitative Research*. New York: Aldine de Gruyter.

Glenn, Cheryl. 1997. *Rhetoric Retold: Regendering the Tradition from Antiquity Through the Renaissance*. Carbondale: Southern Illinois Univ. Press.

Goddard, Henry. [1912] 1925. *The Kallikak Family: A Study of the Heredity of Feeblemindedness*. New York: Macmillan.

Godwin, Louise, and Catherine Wade. 2007. *Kew Cottages Parents' Association: The First Fifty Years*. Melbourne: Kew Cottages Parents' Association.

Goffman, Erving. [1963] 1986. *Stigma: Notes on the Management of Spoiled Identity*. New York: Simon and Schuster.

Goggin, Gerard, and Christopher Newell. 2005. *Disability in Australia: Exposing a Social Apartheid*. Sydney: Univ. of New South Wales Press.

Gonzales, Rodolfo (Corky). 1997. "I Am Joaquín." *Latin American Studies*, http://www.latinamericanstudies.org/latinos/joaquin.htm.

Goode, David. 1994. *A World Without Words: The Social Construction of Children Born Deaf and Blind*. Philadelphia: Temple Univ. Press.

Gordon, Meg, Linda Rosenman, and Monica Cuskelly. 2007. "Constrained Labour: Maternal Employment When Children Have Disabilities." *Journal of Applied Research in Intellectual Disabilities* 20, no. 3:236–46.

Gottlieb, Eli. 1998. *The Boy Who Went Away*. New York: St. Martin's.

Graves, Heather Brodie. 1998. "Marbles, Dimples, Rubber Sheets, and Quantum Wells: The Role of Analogy in the Rhetoric of Science." *Rhetoric Society Quarterly* 28, no. 1:25–48.

Green, Sara Eleanor. 2007. "'We're Tired, Not Sad': Benefits and Burdens of Mothering a Child with Disability." *Social Science and Medicine* 64, no. 1:150–63.

Greenspan, Stanley I., and Serena Wieder. 2006. *Engaging Autism: Using the Floortime Approach to Help Children Relate, Communicate, and Think*. Cambridge: Da Capo Press.

Groce, Nora Ellen, and Jonathan Marks. 2000. "The Great Ape Project and Disability Rights: Ominous Undercurrents of Eugenics in Actions." *American Anthropologist* 102, no. 4:818–22.

Gross, Alan. 1990. *The Rhetoric of Science*. Cambridge, MA: Harvard Univ. Press.

Hacker, Andrew. 1995. *Two Nations: Black and White, Separate, Hostile, Unequal*. New York: Ballantine.

Haddon, Mark. 2004. *The Curious Incident of the Dog in the Night-Time*. New York: Doubleday.

Hallowell, Nina. 1999. "Doing the Right Thing: Genetic Risk and Responsibility." *Sociology of Health and Illness* 21, no. 5:597–621.

Hancock, Ange-Marie. 2004. *The Politics of Disgust: The Public Identity of the Welfare Queen*. New York: New York Univ. Press.

Haraway, Donna. [1990] 1999. *Primate Visions: Gender, Race, and Nature in the World of Modern Science*. New York: Routledge.

———. 1997. *Modest_Witness@Second_Millennium. FemaleMan©_Meets_OncoMouse: Feminism and Technoscience*. New York: Routledge.

Hayles, N. Katherine. 1999. *How We Became Posthuman: Virtual Bodies in Cybernetics, Literature, and Informatics*. Chicago: Univ. of Chicago Press.

Hays, Sharon. 1998. *The Cultural Contradictions of Motherhood*. New Haven: Yale Univ. Press.

Hayward, Anna. 2001. "'Alien' Parenting: Experiences of a Mother with Asperger's Syndrome." *Disability Pregnancy and Parenthood International* 34:3–5.

Hochschild, Arlie. 2003. *The Second Shift*. New York: Penguin.

Hollander, Jocelyn A. 2002. "Resisting Vulnerability: The Social Reconstruction of Gender in Interaction." *Social Problems* 49:474–96.

Hollander, Jocelyn A., and Rachel L. Einwohner. 2004. "Conceptualizing Resistance." *Sociological Forum* 19, no. 4:533–54.

Holmes, Steven. 1991. "Radio Talk about TV Anchor's Disability Stirs Ire in Los Angeles." *New York Times,* http://www.nytimes.com/1991/08/23/news/radio-talk-about-tv-anchor-s-disability-stirs-ire-in-los-angeles.html.

hooks, bell. 1989. "Black Is a Woman's Color." *Callaloo* 39:382–88.

Hoopmann, Kathy. 2006. *All Cats Have Asperger Syndrome.* London: Jessica Kingsley.

Howlin, Patricia, Simon Baron-Cohen, and Julie Hadwin. 1999. *Teaching Children with Autism to Mind-Read: A Practical Guide for Teachers and Parents.* Chichester, UK: Wiley.

Hubbard, Ruth. 2006. "Abortion and Disability: Who Should and Who Should Not Inhabit the World." In *The Disability Studies Reader,* 2nd ed., edited by Lennard Davis, 93–103. New York: Routledge.

Hudson-Weems, Clenora. 1993. *Africana Womanism: Reclaiming Ourselves.* Troy, MI: Bedford.

Huet, Marie-Helene. 1993. *Monstrous Imagination.* Cambridge, MA: Harvard Univ. Press.

Hyde Amendment. 1976. Patricia R. HARRIS, Secretary of Health and Human Services, Appellant,v. Cora McRAE et al. 448 U.S. 297. United States Reports: Decisions of the United States Supreme Court, http://ftp.resource.org/courts.gov/c/US/448/448.US.297.79-1268.html.

Immigration Act of 1990. U.S. Citizenship and Immigration Services. http://www.uscis.gov/portal/site/uscis/menuitem.5af9bb95919f35e66f614176543f6d1a/?vgnextoid=84ff95c4f635f010VgnVCM1000000ecd190aRCRD&vgnextchannel=b328194d3e88d010VgnVCM10000048f3d6a1RCRD.

Individuals with Disabilities Education Act (IDEA). 1990. http://www.ojjdp.gov/pubs/walls/appen-f.html.

Jacobs-Huey, Lanita. 2006. *From the Kitchen to the Parlor: Language and Becoming in African American Women's Hair Care.* Oxford: Oxford Univ. Press.

Jacobson, Denise Sherer. 1999. *The Question of David: A Disabled Mother's Journey Through Adoption, Family, and Life.* Berkeley: Creative Arts.

Johnson, Kelley, and Rannveig Traustadóttir, eds. 2005. *Deinstitutionalization and People with Intellectual Disabilities: In and Out of Institutions.* London: Jessica Kingsley.

Jones, Maxwell. 1953. *The Therapeutic Community: A New Treatment Method in Psychiatry.* New York: Basic.

Judge, Cliff, and Fran van Brummelen. 2002. *Kew Cottages: The World of Dolly Stainer.* Melbourne: Spectrum.

Juffer, Jane. 2006. *Single Mother: The Emergence of the Domestic Intellectual.* New York: New York Univ. Press.

Kallianes, Virginia, and Phyllis Rubenfeld. 1997. "Disabled Women and Reproductive Rights." *Disability and Society* 12, no. 2:203–21.

Kanner, Leo. [1943] 1985. "Autistic Disturbances of Affective Contact." *Nervous Child* 2 (1943): 217–50. In *Classic Readings in Autism,* edited by Anne M. Donnellan, 11–52. New York: Teacher's College.

Keller, Evelyn Fox, and Elisabeth A. Lloyd, eds. 1992. *Keywords in Evolutionary Biology.* Cambridge, MA: Harvard Univ. Press.

Kenen, Regina. 1994. "The Human Genome Project: Creator of the Potentially Sick, Potentially Vulnerable, and Potentially Stigmatized?" In *Life and Death under High Technology Medicine,* edited by Ian Robinson, 49–64. Manchester, UK: Manchester Univ. Press.

Kent, Deborah. 2000. "Somewhere a Mockingbird." In *Prenatal Testing and Disability Rights,* edited by Erik Parens and Adrienne Asch, 57–63. Washington, DC: Georgetown Univ. Press.

King, Deborah K. 1988. "Multiple Jeopardy, Multiple Consciousness: The Context of a Black Feminist Ideology." *Signs* 14, no. 1:42–72.

Kittay, Eva Feder. 1999. *Love's Labor: Essays on Women, Equality, and Dependency.* New York: Routledge.

Kittler, Friedrich A. 1990. *Discourse Networks, 1800/1900.* Translated by Michael Metteer, with Chris Cullens. Stanford, CA: Stanford Univ. Press.

Kleege, Georgiana. 1999. *Sight Unseen.* New Haven: Yale Univ. Press.

Knighton, Ryan. 2006. *Cockeyed: A Memoir.* New York: Public Affairs.

Knipfel, Jim. 1999. *Slackjaw: A Memoir.* New York: Berkeley Books.

Kolawole, Mary Ebun Modupe. 1997. *Womanism and African Consciousness.* Trenton: African World Press.

Kozol, Jonathan. 1991. *Savage Inequalities: Children in America's Schools.* New York: Crown.

Kristeva, Julia. 1986. "Stabat Mater." In *The Kristeva Reader,* edited by Toril Moi, 160–86. NY: Columbia Univ. Press.

Kudlick, Catherine. 2008. "Modernity's Miss-Fits: Blind Girls and Marriage in France and America, 1820–1920." In *Women on Their Own: Interdisciplinary Perspectives on Being Single,* edited by Rudolph M. Bell and Virginia Yans, 201–18. New Brunswick, NJ: Rutgers Univ. Press.

Kuusisto, Stephen. 1998. *Planet of the Blind: A Memoir.* New York: Delta.

Lacom, Cindy. 2002. "Revising the Subject: Disability as 'Third Dimension' in *Clear Light of Day and You Have Come Back.*" *NWSA Journal* 14, no. 3:138–54.

Landsman, Gail. 1998. "Reconstructing Motherhood in the Age of Perfect Babies." *Signs* 24, no. 1:69–99.

———. 1999. "Does God Give Special Kids to Special Parents? Personhood and the Child with Disabilities as Gift and as Giver." In *Transformative Motherhood: On Giving and Getting in a Consumer Culture,* edited by Linda L. Layne, 133–65. New York: New York Univ. Press.

Leiter, Valerie, et al. 2004. "The Consequences of Caring: Impacts of Mothering a Child with Special Needs." *Journal of Family Issues* 25, no. 3:379–403.

Lewiecki-Wilson, Cynthia. 2011. "Ableist Rhetorics, Nevertheless: Disability and Animal Rights in the Work of Peter Singer and Martha Nussbaum." *JAC: Rhetoric, Writing, Culture, Politics* 31, nos. 1–2:711–41.

Lewiecki-Wilson, Cynthia, and Brenda Jo Brueggemann, eds. 2008. *Disability and the Teaching of Writing: A Critical Sourcebook.* Boston: Bedford/St. Martin's.

Lewis, Suzan, Carolyn Kagan, and Patricia Heaton. 2000. "Dual-Earner Parents with Disabled Children: Family Patterns for Working and Caring. *Journal of Family Issues* 21:1031–60.

Linton, Simi. 1998. *Claiming Disability: Knowledge and Identity.* New York: New York Univ. Press.

———. 2008. "From Reassigning Meaning." In *Disability and the Teaching of Writing: A Critical Sourcebook,* edited by Lewiecki-Wilson and Brenda Brueggemann, 174–81. Boston: Bedford/St. Martin's.

Lippman, Abby. 1991. "Prenatal Genetic Testing and Screening: Constructing Needs and Reinforcing Inequities." *American Journal of Law and Medicine* 17, no. 1–2:15–50.

Lloyd, Arthur. 1987. *Payment by Results: Kew Cottages First 100 Years 1887–1987.* Melbourne: Kew Cottages and St. Nicholas Parents' Association.

Lockhart, Charles. 1989. *Gaining Ground: Tailoring Social Programs to American Values.* Berkeley: Univ. of California Press.

Lombardo, Paul. 2011. "Eugenic Sterilization Laws." Image Archive of the American Eugenics Movement, http://www.eugenicsarchive.org/eugenics/list2.pl.

Longmore, Paul, and Lauri Umanski, eds. 2001. *The New Disability History: American Perspectives.* New York: New York Univ. Press.

López Austin, Alfredo. 1988. *The Human Body and Ideology: Concepts of the Ancient Nahuas.* Translated by Thelma Ortiz de Montellano and Bernard Ortiz de Montellano. Salt Lake City: Univ. of Utah Press.

Lorde, Audre. 1995. "Breast Cancer: Power Versus Prosthesis." In *Feminism and Philosophy: Essential Readings in Theory, Reinterpretation, and Application,* edited by Nancy Tuana and Rosemary Tong, 420–29. Boulder: Westview.

Lubiano, Wahneema. 1992. "Black Ladies, Welfare Queens, and State Minstrels: Ideological War by Narrative Means." In *Race-ing Justice, Engendering Power: Essays on Anita Hill, Clarence Thomas, and the Construction of Social Reality,* edited by Toni Morrison, 323–63. New York: Pantheon.

Lyall, Sarah. 2005. "In Trafalgar Square, Much Ado about Statuary." *New York Times,* 10 Oct., http://www.nytimes.com/2005/10/10/arts/design/10traf.html?_r=1.

Magaña, Sandra, Susan L. Parish, and Shawn A. Cassiman. 2008. "Policy Lessons from Low-Income Mothers with Disabilities. *Journal of Women Politics and Policy* 29:181–206.

Mairs, Nancy. 1993. *Ordinary Time: Cycles in Marriage, Faith, and Renewal.* Boston: Beacon.

———. 1996. *Waist-High in the World: A Life among the Non-Disabled.* Boston: Beacon Press.

———. 2002. "Sex and Death and the Crippled Body: A Meditation." In *Disability Studies: Enabling the Humanities,* edited by Sharon Synder, Brenda Jo Brueggemann, and Rosemarie Garland-Thompson, 156–70. New York: MLA.

Manning, Corinne. 2008. *Bye-Bye Charlie: Stories from the Vanishing World of Kew Cottages.* Sydney: Univ. of New South Wales Press.

Marcus, Neil. 1996. *Storm Reading.* Adapted for the stage by Rod Lathim, Neil Marcus, and Roger Marcus. Storm Reading Video Production.

Martin, Teran, and Paul S. Davies. 2004. "Changes in the Economic and Demographic Characteristics of SSI and DI Beneficiaries Between 1984 and 1999." *Social Security Bulletin* 65, no. 2, http://www.ssa.gov/policy/docs/ssb/v65n2/index.html.

Marzuli, John. 2008. "Hospital Video Shows No One Helped Dying Woman." *New York Daily News,* 30 June, http://www.nydailynews.com/ny_local/brooklyn/2008/06/30/2008-06-30_hospital_video_shows_no_one_helped_dying.html.

Mayes, Susan Dickerson, Susan L. Calhoun, and Dana L. Crites. 2001. "Does DSM-IV Asperger's Disorder Exist?" *Journal of Abnormal Child Psychology* 29, no. 3: 263–71, http://www.springerlink.com/content/l15514241h4p3602/.

McClintock, Anne, Aamir Mufti, and Ella Shohat, eds. 1997. *Dangerous Liaisons: Gender, Nation, and Postcolonial Perspectives.* Minneapolis: Univ. of Minnesota Press.

McCormack, Karen. 2004. "Resisting the Welfare Mother: The Power of Welfare Discourse and Tactics of Resistance. *Critical Sociology* 30:355–83.

McKeever, Patricia, and Karen-Lee Miller. 2004. "Mothering Children Who Have Disabilities: A Bourdieusian Interpretation of Maternal Practices." *Social Science and Medicine* 59, no. 6:1177–91.

McRuer, Robert. 2006. *Crip Theory: Cultural Signs of Queerness and Disability.* New York: New York Univ. Press.

Mental Health Act of 1959. Australia. http://www.pathwaysvictoria.info/biogs/ E000629b.htm.

Michalko, Rod. 2002. *The Difference That Disability Makes.* Philadelphia: Temple Univ. Press.

Miller, Carolyn. 1992. "Kairos in the Rhetoric of Science." In *A Rhetoric of Doing: Essays on Written Discourse in Honor of James L. Kinneavy,* edited by Roger Cherry et al., 310–37. Carbondale: Southern Illinois Univ. Press.

Mink, Gwendolyn. 1998. *Welfare's End.* Rev. ed. Ithaca, NY: Cornell Univ. Press.

Mitchell, David T. 2002. "Narrative Prosthesis and the Materiality of Metaphor." In *Disability Studies: Enabling the Humanities,* edited by Sharon L. Snyder, Brenda Jo Brueggemann, and Rosemarie Garland-Thomson, 15–30. New York: MLA.

Mohammed, Patricia, ed. 1998. "Toward Indigenous Feminist Theorizing in the Caribbean." *Feminist Review* 59:6–33.

Mohanty, Chandra, Ann Russo, and Lourdes Torres. 1991. *Third World Women and the Politics of Feminism.* Bloomington: Indiana Univ. Press.

Momsen, Janet. "The Double Paradox." 2001. In *Gendered Realities Essays in Caribbean Feminist Thought,* edited by Patricia Mohammed, 22–44. Kingston, Jam.: Univ. of the West Indies Press.

Montgomery, Cal. 2001. "Critic of the Dawn." *Ragged Edge Online,* http://www .ragged-edge-mag.com/0501/0501cov.htm.

Moraga, Cherríe. [1983] 2001. *Loving in the War Years: lo que nunca pasó por sus labios.* Boston: South End Press.

———. 1994. *Heroes and Saints and Other Plays.* Albuquerque: West End Press.

———. 1997. *Waiting in the Wings: Portrait of a Queer Motherhood.* Ithaca: Firebrand.

———. 2001. *The Hungry Woman and Heart of the Earth.* Albuquerque: West End Press.

———. 2002. *Watsonville: Some Place Not Here / Circle in the Dirt: El Pueblo de East Palo Alto.* Albuquerque: West End Press.

———. 2003. "A Xicanadyke Codex of Changing Consciousness." In *Sing, Whisper, Shout, Pray! Feminist Visions for a Just World,* edited by M. Jacqui Alexander, et al., 91–102. Canada: Edgework.

Morris, David B. 2001. "Narrative, Ethics, and Pain: Thinking with Stories." *Narrative* 9, no. 1:55–77.

Morris, Jenny. 1991. *Pride Against Prejudice: Transforming Attitudes to Disability.* London: Women's Press.

———. 1996. *Encounters with Strangers: Feminism and Disability.* London: Women's Press.

Morrison, Toni, ed. 1992. *Race-ing Justice, Engendering Power: Essays on Anita Hill, Clarence Thomas, and the Construction of Social Reality.* New York: Pantheon.

Murkoff, Heidi, and Mazel, Sharon. 2008. *What to Expect When You're Expecting.* 4th ed. New York: Workman Pub. Co.

Murphy, Robert F. 1987. *The Body Silent.* New York: Henry Holt.

National Exchange for Egg Donation and Surrogacy (NEEDS). 2007. http://www.fertilityneeds.com/ForAspiringParents/Default.asp.

Nelson, Amy. 2004. "Declaration from the Autism Community That They Are a Minority Group." 18 Nov., http://amynelsonblog.blogspot.com/search?q=Declaration+from+the+autism+community.

Nelson, Hilde Lindemann, ed. 1997. *Stories and Their Limits: Narrative Approaches to Ethics.* New York: Routledge.

Noddings, Nel. 1984. *Caring: A Feminine Approach to Ethics and Moral Education.* Berkeley: Univ. of California Press.

O'Brien, Ruth. 2005. *Bodies in Revolt: Gender, Disability, and a Workplace Ethic of Care.* New York: Routledge.

Okin, Susan Moller. 1989. *Justice, Gender, and the Family.* New York: Basic.

Olkin, Rhoda. 1999. *What Psychotherapists Should Know about Disability.* New York: Guilford.

O'Neill, Brendan. 2007. "Statue of Limitations." *The Guardian,* 17 May, http://www.guardian.co.uk/commentisfree/2007/may/17/statueoflimitations.

O'Neill, Jasmine. 1999. *Through the Eyes of Aliens: A Book about Autistic People.* London: Jessica Kingsley.

Padden, Carol. 1996. "From the Cultural to the Bi-cultural: The Modern Deaf Community." In *Cultural and Language Diversity and the Deaf Experience,* edited by Illa Parasini, 79–98. Cambridge: Cambridge Univ. Press.

Palmberg, Mai, ed. 2001. *Encountering Images in the Meetings Between Africa and Europe.* Uppsala, Swed.: Nordic Africa.

Parish, Susan L., Sandra Magaña, and Shawn A. Cassiman. 2008. "It's Just That Much Harder: Multi-Layered Hardship Experiences of Low-Income Mothers with Disabilities." *Affilia* 23:51–65.

Pattulo, Polly. 1996. *Last Resorts: The Cost of Tourism in the Caribbean.* London: Cassell.

Perks, Robert, and Alistair Thomson, eds. 2006. *The Oral History Reader.* 2nd ed. London: Routledge.

Personal Responsibility and Work Opportunity Reconciliation Act (PRWORA). 1996. U.S. Department of Health and Human Services HHS. http://www .hhs.gov/ocr/civilrights/resources/specialtopics/tanf/crlawsandwelfare reformoverview.html.

Pitt, David. 1999. *For the Love of the Children: My Life and Medical Career.* Melbourne: Pitt Publishing.

Planned Parenthood of Southeastern Pa. v. Casey, 505 U.S. 833. 1992. United States Reports: Decisions of the United States Supreme Court. http://ftp.resource .org/courts.gov/c/US/505/505.US.833.91-902.91-744.html.

Prelli, Lawrence J. 1989. *A Rhetoric of Science: Inventing Scientific Discourse.* Columbia: Univ. South Carolina Press.

Press, Nancy, et al. 1998. "Provisional Normalcy and 'Perfect Babies': Pregnant Women's Attitudes Toward Disability in the Context of Prenatal Testing." In *Reproducing Reproduction: Kinship, Power, and Technological Innovation,* edited by Sarah Franklin and Helena Ragoné, 46–65. Philadelphia: Univ. of Pennsylvania Press.

Price, Janet, and Margrit Shildrick. 2002. "Bodies Together: Touch, Ethics, and Disability." In *Disability/Postmodernity: Embodying Disability Theory,* edited by Mairian Corker and Tom Shakespeare, 62–75. London: Continuum.

Price, Margaret. 2011. *Mad at School: Rhetorics of Mental Disabilty and Academic Life.* Ann Arbor: Univ. of Michigan Press.

Prince-Hughes, Dawn. 2004. *Songs of the Gorilla Nation: My Journey Through Autism.* New York: Three Rivers.

Purdy, Laura. 1996. "Reproductive Risk: Can Having Children Be Immoral?" *Reproducing Persons: Issues in Feminist Bioethics.* Ithaca, NY: Cornell Univ. Press.

Quinn, Marc. 2005. *Alison Lapper Pregnant.* The Fourth Plinth. *The Guardian,* http:// www.guardian.co.uk/arts/gallery/2007/nov/07/1.

Rainman. 1988. Directed by Barry Levinson. United Artists.

Rapley, Mark. 2004. *The Social Construction of Intellectual Disability.* Cambridge: Cambridge Univ. Press.

Rapp, Rayna. 1988. "Chromosomes and Communication: The Discourse of Genetic Counseling." *Medical Anthropology Quarterly* 2, no. 2:143–57.

———. 1998. "Refusing Prenatal Diagnosis: The Meanings of Bioscience in a Multicultural World." *Anthropological Approaches in Science and Technology Studies.* Special issue, *Science, Technology, and Human Values* 23, no. 1:45–70.

Rapp, Rayna, and Faye Ginsburg. 2001. "Enabling Disability: Rewriting Kinship, Reimagining Citizenship." *Public Culture* 13, no. 3:533–56.

raúlrsalinas. 1999. *Un Trip Through the Mind Jail y Otras Excursions.* Houston: Arte Público Press.

Read, Janet. 2000. *Disability, the Family and Society: Listening to Mothers.* Buckingham, UK: Open Univ. Press.

Rehabilitation Act. 1973. http://www.dotcr.ost.dot.gov/documents/ycr/REHAB ACT.HTM.

Reich, Jennifer A. 2008. "The Child Welfare System and State Intervention in Families: From Historical Patterns to Future Questions." *Sociology Compass* 2, no. 3:888–909.

Riessman, Catherine K. 2000. "Stigma and Everyday Resistance Practices: Childless Women in South India." *Gender and Society* 14:111–35.

Ripley, Amanda. 2005. "A Mother and the President." *Time* 166, no. 8 (22 Aug.): 23–25.

Roberts, Dorothy. 2002. *Shattered Bonds: The Color of Child Welfare.* New York: Basic.

Rodas, Julia Miele. 2003. "The Satellite Syndrome: Disability in Victorian Literature and Culture." PhD diss., Graduate Center of the City University of New York.

———. 2007. "Misappropriations: Hugh Stuart Boyd and the Blindness of Elizabeth Barrett/Browning." *Victorian Review* 33, no. 2:103–18.

Roe v. Wade, 410 U.S. 113. 1973. United States Reports: Decisions of the United States Supreme Court. http://ftp.resource.org/courts.gov/c/US/410/410.US.113 .70-18.html.

Rogers, Chrissie. 2007. "Disabling a Family? Emotional Dilemmas Experienced in Becoming a Parent of a Child with Learning Disabilities." *British Journal of Special Education* 34, no. 3:136–43.

Rogers, Lois. 1999. "Having Disabled Babies Will Be a 'Sin,' Says Scientist." *Times* (London), 4 July, 28–29.

Rose, Nikolas. 2007. *The Politics of Life Itself: Biomedicine, Power, and Subjectivity in the Twenty-First Century.* Princeton: Princeton Univ. Press.

Rothman, Barbara Katz. 1992. "Not All That Glitters Is Gold." *Hastings Center Report* 22, no. 4 (July–Aug.): S11–S15.

Rowley, Michelle. 2001. "Reconceptualizing Voice: The Role of Matrifociality in Shaping Theories and Caribbean Voices." In *Gendered Realities Essays in Caribbean Feminist Thought*, edited by Patricia Mohammed, 22–44. Kingston, Jamaica: Univ. of the West Indies Press.

Ruddick, Sara. 1995. *Maternal Thinking: Toward a Politics of Peace*. New York: Random House.

———. 1998. "'Woman of Peace': A Feminist Construction." In *The Women and War Reader*, edited by Lois Ann Lorentzen and Jennifer Turpin, 213–26. New York: New York Univ. Press.

Russell, Marta. 1998. *Beyond Ramps: Disability at the End of the Social Contract*. Monroe, ME: Common Courage.

Ryan, Sara, and Katherine Runswick-Cole. 2008. "Repositioning Mothers: Mothers, Disabled Children, and Disability Studies." *Disability and Society* 23, no. 3:199–210.

Sacks, Oliver. 1990. "The Autist Artist" and "The Twins." In *The Man Who Mistook His Wife for a Hat and Other Clinical Tales*, 95–233. New York: Harper.

———. 1995. *An Anthropologist on Mars*. New York: Knopf.

Said, Edward. W. 1978. *Orientalism*. New York: Pantheon Books.

Sandoval, Chela. 2000. *Methodology of the Oppressed*. Minneapolis: Univ. of Minnesota Press.

Sardar, Ziauddin, and Borin Van Loon. 1997. *Introducing Cultural Studies*. New York: Totem.

Sartre, Jean Paul. 1963. Preface to *The Wretched of the Earth*, by Frantz Fanon, 7–31. New York: Grove Press.

Savarese, Ralph. 2007. *Reasonable People: A Memoir of Autism and Adoption*. New York: Other Press.

Saxton, Marsha. 1984. "Born and Unborn: The Implications of Reproductive Technologies for People with Disabilities." In *Test-Tube Women: What Future For Motherhood?*, edited by Rita Arditti, Renate Duelli-Klein, and Shelley Minden, 298–312. London: Pandora Press.

———. 1999. "Disabled Women's View of Selective Abortion: An Issue for All Women." *Journal of the American Medical Women's Association* 54:26–28.

———. 2006. "Disability Rights and Selective Abortion." In *The Disability Studies Reader*, 2nd ed., edited by Lennard Davis, 105–16. New York: Routledge.

Scarry, Elaine. 1985. *The Body in Pain: The Making and Unmaking of the World*. New York: Oxford Univ. Press.

Schopler, Eric, et al. 1999. "Asperger Syndrome or High-Functioning Autism?" *Contemporary Psychology.* 44, no. 4:280.

Scott, James C. 1985. *Weapons of the Weak: Everyday Forms of Peasant Resistance.* New Haven: Yale Univ. Press.

Scully, Jackie Leach. 2002. "A Postmodern Disorder: Moral Encounters with Molecular Models of Disability." In *Disability/Postmodernity: Embodying Disability Theory,* edited by Mairian Corker and Tom Shakespeare, 48–61. London: Continuum.

Segal, Elizabeth. 2007. "Social Empathy: A Tool to Address the Contradiction of Working But Still Poor." *Families in Society: Journal of Contemporary Social Services.* 88:333–37.

Segal, Judy Z. 2005. *Health and the Rhetoric of Medicine.* Carbondale: Southern Illinois Univ. Press.

Shah, Anup. 2010. "Women's Rights." Global Issues: Social, Political, Economic, and Environmental Issues that Affect Us All, http://www.globalissues.org/article/166/womens-rights.

Shakespeare, Tom, Kath Gillespie-Sells, and Dominic Davies. 1996. *The Sexual Politics of Disability: Untold Desires.* London: Cassell.

Sheehan, Cindy. 2005. *Not One More Mother's Child.* Kihei, HI: Koa Books.

———. 2006a. *Dear President Bush.* San Francisco: City Lights Books.

———. 2006b. *Peace Mom: A Mother's Journey Through Heartache to Activism.* New York: Atria Books.

———. 2007. "Good Riddance Attention Whore." *Daily Kos,* May 28, http://www.dailykos.com/story/2007/5/28/12530/1525.

Sherry, Mark. 2004. "Overlaps and Contradictions Between Queer Theory and Disability Studies." *Disability and Society* 19, no. 7:769–83.

Shildrick, Margrit. 2002. *Embodying the Monster: Encounters with the Vulnerable Self.* London: Sage.

Shipler, David K. 1998. *A Country of Strangers: Blacks and Whites in America.* New York: Vintage.

Shorter-Gooden, Kumea. 2004. "Multiple Resistance Strategies: How African American Women Cope with Racism and Sexism." *Journal of Black Psychology* 30, no. 3:406–25.

Sidal, Ruth. 2006. *Unsung Heroes: Single Mothers and the American Dream.* Berkeley: Univ. of California Press.

Siebers, Tobin. 2001. "Disability in Theory: From Social Constructionism to Realism of the Body." *American Literary History* 13, no. 4:737–54.

———. 2003. "What Can Disability Studies Learn from the Culture Wars?" *Cultural Critique* 55: 182–214.

———. 2008. *Disability Theory*. Ann Arbor: Univ. of Michigan Press.

Silberman, Steve. 2001. "The Geek Syndrome." *Wired,* http://www.wired.com/wired/archive/9.12/aspergers_pr.html.

Silvers, Anita. 2006. "Rights Redux: Dislodging Discrimination Dead-ends in Identity Impasse." Robert T. Harris Lecture. Miami Univ., Oxford, OH. 17 Nov.

Silvers, Anita, and Leslie Pickering Francis. 2005. "Justice Through Trust: Disability and the 'Outlier Problem' in Social Contract Theory." *Ethics* 116 (Oct.): 40–76.

Sinclair, Jim. 1993. "Don't Mourn for Us." Autism Network International, http://www.autreat.com/dont_mourn.html.

———. 1999. "Why I Dislike Person First Language." http://replay.web.archive.org/20090210190652/http://web.syr.edu/~jisincla/person_first.htm.

———. n.d. "Jim Sinclair's Web Site." http://jisincla.mysite.syr.edu/.

Skinner, Debra, et al. 1999. "Narrating Self and Disability: Latino Mothers' Construction of Identities vis-à-vis Their Child with Special Needs." *Exceptional Children* 65, no. 4:481–94.

Smiley, Susan, dir. 2006. *Out of the Shadow*. Vine Street Pictures.

Smith, Anna Marie. 2007. *Welfare Reform and Sexual Regulation*. Cambridge: Cambridge Univ. Press.

Smith, Barbara Hernnstein. 2006. *Scandalous Knowledge: Science, Truth, and the Human*. Durham: Duke Univ. Press.

Smith, Raymond T. 1996. *The Matrifocal Family: Power, Pluralism and Politics*. New York: Routledge.

Social Security Administration (SSA). 2011. "Working While Disabled—How We Can Help." Social Security Online, http://www.socialsecurity.gov/pubs/10095.html.

Soto, Sandra K. 2005. "Cherríe Moraga's Going Brown: 'Reading Like a Queer.'" *GLQ* 11, no. 2:237–63.

Steinberg, Deborah L. 1996. "Languages of Risk: Genetic Encryptions of the Female Body." *Women: A Cultural Review* 7:259–70.

Stepan, Nancy Leys. 1986. "Race and Gender: The Role of Analogy in Science." *Isis* 77, no. 2:261–77.

Sterling-Folker, Jennifer. 2002. *Theories of International Cooperation and the Primacy of Anarchy*. Albany: SUNY Press.

Swerdlow, Amy. 1993. *Women Strike for Peace: Traditional Motherhood and Radical Politics in the 1960s*. Chicago: Univ. of Chicago Press.

Swift, Karen J. 1995. *Manufacturing "Bad Mothers": A Critical Perspective on Child Neglect.* Toronto: Univ. of Toronto Press.

Tammet, Daniel. 2007. *Born on a Blue Day: Inside the Extraordinary Mind of an Autistic Savant.* New York: Free Press.

Thomas, Carol. 2004. "How Is Disability Understood?: An Examination of Sociological Approaches." *Disability and Society* 19, no. 6:569–83.

Titchkosky, Tanya. 2003. *Disability, Self, and Society.* Toronto: Univ. of Toronto Press.

———. 2007. *Reading and Writing Disability Differently: The Textured Life of Embodiment.* Toronto: Univ. of Toronto Press.

Tobe, Keiko. 2007. *With the Light: Raising an Autistic Child.* Translated by Satsuki Yamashita. Originally published in Japanese as *Hikari To Tomoni.* New York: Yen Press.

Todd, Stuart, and Julia Shearn. 1996. "Struggles with Time: The Careers of Parents with Adult Sons and Daughters with Learning Disabilities. *Disability and Society* 11, no. 3:379–401.

Tremain, Shelley. 2001. "On the Government of Disability." *Social Theory and Practice* 27, no. 4:617–36.

———. 2002. "On the Subject of Impairment." In *Disability/Postmodernity: Embodying Disability Theory,* edited by Mairian Corker and Tom Shakespeare, 32–47. London: Continuum.

———, ed. 2005. *Foucault and the Government of Disability.* Ann Arbor: Univ. of Michigan Press.

———. 2006a. "On the Government of Disability: Foucault, Power, and the Subject of Impairment." In *The Disability Studies Reader,* 2nd ed., edited by Lennard Davis, 185–96.

———. 2006b. "Reproductive Freedom, Self-Regulation, and the Government of Impairment in Utero." *Hypatia* 21, no. 1:35–53.

Trent, James W. 1994. *Inventing the Feeble Mind: A History of Mental Retardation in the United States.* Berkeley: Univ. of California Press.

Tribe, Laurence H. 2008. *The Invisible Constitution.* Oxford: Oxford Univ. Press.

Tronto, Joan C. 1994. *Moral Boundaries: A Political Argument for an Ethic of Care.* New York: Routledge.

UNESCO. 2001. "UNESCO Universal Declaration on Cultural Diversity." United Nations Educational, Scientific and Cultural Organization, http://portal.unesco.org/en/ev.php-URL_ID=13179&URL_DO=DO_TOPIC&URL_SECTION=201.html.

United Nations Convention on the Rights of Persons with Disabilities. 2008. United Nations Enable. http://www.un.org/disabilities/.

UPIAS and Disability Alliance. 1976. Fundamental Principles of Disability : Being a Summary of the Discussion Held on 22nd November, 1975 and Containing Commentaries from Each Organisation. London: The Union and The Disability Alliance.

Valdez, Luis. 2005. *Mummified Deer and Other Plays*. Houston: Arte Público Press.

Vidali, Amy. 2010. "Seeing What We Know: Disability and Theories of Metaphor." *Journal of Literary and Cultural Disability Studies* 4, no. 1:33–54.

Viges, Hart. 2006. Foreword to *Dear President Bush*, by Cindy Sheehan, xxiii–xxx. San Francisco: City Lights Books.

Walker, Alice. 1983. *In Search of Our Mother's Gardens*. San Diego: Harcourt.

Walker, Bree. 2004. Interview with Larry King. *Larry King Live*. CNN. 19 Dec.

Walker, Dan, et al. 1976. "Abortion: For Whose Sake?" *The Hastings Center Report* 6, no. 4:4–33.

Walmsley, Jan. 2006. "Life History Interviews with People with Learning Disabilities." In *The Oral History Reader*, 2nd ed., edited by Robert Perks and Alistair Thomson, 126–39. London: Routledge.

Walmsley, Jan, and Kelly Johnson. 2003. *Inclusive Research with People with Learning Disabilities: Past, Present, and Futures*. London: Jessica Kingsley.

Wates, Michele. 1997. *Disabled Parents: Dispelling the Myths*. Cambridge: National Childbirth Trust.

Waxman, Barbara F. 1993. "The Politics of Eugenics." *Disability Rag* 14, no. 3 (May/June): 6–7.

Weithorn, Lois A. 1988. "Mental Hospitalization of Troublesome Youth: An Analysis of Skyrocketing Admission Rates." *Stanford Law Review* 40, no. 3:773–838.

Wendell, Susan. 1996. *The Rejected Body: Feminist Philosophical Reflections on Disability*. New York: Routledge.

———. 2006. "Toward a Feminist Theory of Disability." In *The Disability Studies Reader*, 2nd ed., edited by Lennard Davis, 243–56. New York: Routledge.

White, Lucie E. 1991. "Subordination, Rhetorical Survival Skills and Sunday Shoes: Notes on the Hearing of Mrs. G." In *Feminist Legal Theory: Readings in Law and Gender*, edited by Katharine T. Bartlett and Rosanne Kennedy, 404–28. Boulder: Westview Press.

Wilkerson, Abby. 2002. "Disability, Sex Radicalism, and Political Agency." *NWSA Journal* 14, no. 3:33–57.

Index